The
Freelance
Photographer's
Market
Handbook
1994

The Freelance Photographer's Market Handbook 1994

Edited by John Tracy & Stewart Gibson
Listings Coordinator: James Clancy

BFP BOOKS London

All information was believed correct at the time of going to press. However, market information is subject to change, and readers are advised to check with the publication concerned before preparing a contribution. Members of the Bureau of Freelance Photographers are kept in touch with changes in the marketplace through *Market Newsletter*. Every care has been taken in the compilation of this book, but the publisher can assume no responsibility for any errors or omissions, or any effects arising therefrom.

British Library Cataloguing in Publication Data:

A catalogue record for this book is available from the British Library

ISBN 0-907297-31-5

Tenth Edition

Published for the Bureau of Freelance Photographers by BFP Books, Focus House, 497 Green Lanes, London N13 4BP. Typesetting and page layout by BFP Books. Text set in New Century Schoolbook. Printed in Great Britain by BPCC Wheatons Ltd, Exeter.

CONTENTS

PREFACE

The 1994 edition of *The Freelance Photographer's Market Handbook* offers a number of significant improvements and refinements over previous editions, though perhaps not ones that are apparent at first glance.

Most importantly, typesetting and layout has for the first time been carried out entirely in-house by the BFP's own staff. Users of the *Handbook* should therefore find that this year's edition is more accurate than ever before. As well as cutting out several links in the chain where minor errors can creep in, the tighter production schedule means that we now have much greater leeway for the inclusion of last minute amendments, new entries and deletions. With production (apart from final printing) now fully under the control of the BFP's own research team, we have been able to update the information daily to ensure that this edition is by far the most up-to-date and accurate yet published.

Apart from this, long-time users of the *Handbook* should notice a number of other small but significant improvements.

For example, a number of magazine listings now also include the name of a picture editor or art editor as well as the overall editor. In the past this was less important, because only the very top titles employed a person to deal with photographers in this capacity. But nowadays even smaller publications are beginning to employ a specific person for the job, largely because of the much greater emphasis on pictures and graphics in this highly visual age.

Similarly, in the picture agency section, it is now the person or persons responsible for primary contact with photographers that are named, rather than the agency's chief executive.

We hope that users will also appreciate an improved, clearer typeface.

The past year of continuing recession has taken its toll in the magazine world, as the list of deleted titles will show, but generally the magazine market has remained in remarkably good health. The card and calendar section continues to shrink though, reflecting the fact that these publishers increasingly prefer to use picture agencies for most of their needs. The agency section itself has expanded to feature just over 70 entries.

As usual every previous entry has been scrupulously checked and thoroughly updated to reflect current market conditions. At the same time, the complete resetting of the text has given us the opportunity to try to "clean up" some of the inevitable inconsistencies that have crept in over recent editions, and to achieve a greater uniformity of style in the entries to aid quick reference.

Another small sign of the times is the new section for "Computer Software" in the Services and Supplies listings. For the growing number of freelances who have access to a personal computer, the various filing and labelling systems now on the market can provide a real boost to speed and efficiency.

We hope that users will appreciate the improvements in this edition, and be assured that we are continually striving to make the *Market Handbook* a yardstick for reference books of its kind.

ABOUT THE BFP

Founded in 1965, the Bureau of Freelance Photographers is today the major body for the freelance photographer. It has a worldwide membership, comprising not only full-time freelances, but also amateur and semi-professional photographers. Being primarily a service organisation, membership of the Bureau is open to anyone with an interest in freelance photography.

The major service offered to members is the *Market Newsletter,* a confidential monthly report on the state of the freelance market. A well-researched and highly authoritative publication, the *Newsletter* keeps freelances in touch with the market for freelance pictures. It gives full information on the type of pictures currently being sought by a wide range of publications and other outlets. It gives details of new magazines and their editorial requirements, and generally reports on what is happening in the publishing world and how this is likely to affect the freelance photographer.

The *Newsletter* is considered essential reading for the freelance and aspiring freelance photographer, and because it pinpoints changes in the marketplace as they occur, it also acts as a useful supplement to the *Handbook.* The *Handbook* itself is an integral part of BFP membership services; members paying the full annual fee automatically receive a copy every year as it is published.

Other services provided to members for the modest annual subscription include:
● Advisory Service. Individual advice on all aspects of freelancing is available to members.
● Fee Recovery Service. The Bureau tries to protect its members' interests in every way it can. In particular, it is often able to assist individual members in recovering unpaid reproduction fees.
● Exclusive items and special offers. The Bureau regularly offers books and other items to members, usually at discount prices. It originated

Editorial Submission Forms for use by members, and is also able to supply Model Release Forms. In addition, under the Photographic Services & Supplies section of this *Handbook* can be found a number of companies providing special discounts to BFP members on production of a current membership card.

For further details and an application form, write to Bureau of Freelance Photographers, Focus House, 497 Green Lanes, London N13 4BP, or telephone 081-882 3315.

HOW TO USE THIS BOOK

Anyone with the ability to use a camera correctly has the potential to make money from their pictures. Taking saleable photographs isn't difficult; the difficulty lies in finding the market. It isn't enough for you, the photographer in search of a sale, to find what you think *might* be a suitable market; rather you must find *exactly* the right magazine, publisher, agency or whatever for your particular type of work. Many a sale is lost when work which is, in itself, technically perfect fails to fulfil the total requirements of the buyer.

The Freelance Photographer's Market Handbook has been designed to help resolve these difficulties. It puts you in touch with major markets for your work, telling you exactly what each is looking for, together with hints and tips on how to sell to them and, wherever possible, an idea of the rates they pay.

The *Handbook* covers five big markets for your pictures: magazines (by far the largest), newspapers, book publishers, picture agencies, and card and calendar companies. There are three ways of using the book, depending on the way you need or wish to work:

1. If you are out to sell to magazines and you can offer coverage on a theme particularly applicable to a certain type of publication (i.e. gardening, angling, sport) turn to the magazine section and look for the subject. The magazines are listed under 38 categories, each of which has a broad heading covering specific magazines. The categories are in alphabetical order, as are the magazines within those categories. You need only read through them to discover which is best for your type of work.

2. If you have a set of pictures that fall into a specific photographic category (i.e. landscapes, children, glamour, etc.), turn to the subject index on page 21. Look up your chosen subject and there you will find a list of all the

magazines interested in that particular type of picture. You have only then to look up each one mentioned in the appropriate section for precise details of their requirements. (If in doubt as to where to find a particular magazine consult the general index at the back of the book.) There is a separate subject index for agencies on page 180, showing you which agents specialise in what subjects.

3. If you are looking for the requirements of a specific magazine, book publisher, agency, card or calendar publisher, whose name is already known to you, simply refer to the general index at the back of the book.

Some points to remember

With this wealth of information open to you, and with those three options for finding the right market, there is no reason why you shouldn't immediately start earning good cash from your camera. But before you rush off to put your pictures in the post, here are some points worth bearing in mind and which will help you to more successful sales:

1. The golden rule of freelancing: don't send people pictures they don't want. Read the requirements listed in the various parts of this directory and obey them. When, for instance, a Scottish magazine says they want pictures of all things Scottish with the exception of kilts and haggis, you can be sure they are over-stocked with these subjects. They are not going to make an exception just for you, however good you think your pictures might be.

2. If you are working in colour, and unless the listing states otherwise, always supply transparencies rather than prints. Unless otherwise stated, it can be assumed that any size of transparency, from 35mm up, can be accepted.

3. When submitting pictures, make sure they are accompanied by detailed captions. And don't forget to put your own name and address on each photograph.

4. If you have an idea for a picture or feature for a particular publication, don't be afraid to telephone first to discuss what you have in mind. Nearly every editor or picture buyer approached when the *Handbook* was being compiled said they would be delighted to hear from potential freelances in advance, rather than have inappropriate pictures or words landing on their desks.

5. If seeking commissions, always begin by making an appointment with the appropriate person in order to show your portfolio and/or cuttings. Do not turn up at a busy editor's office unannounced and expect to be met with open arms.

6. Never send anything to a market on spec without a stamped addressed envelope for its return.

APPROACHING THE MARKET

You've chosen your market, taken the pictures and written the captions. Full of hope and expectation, you put your work in the post. A week later, it comes back with a formal rejection slip. Why? Where did you go wrong?

You have only to look through the pages of this book to see that there are a lot of markets open to the freelance photographer, yet the sad fact remains that a great many of those who try their hand at editorial freelancing fail the first few times, and many never succeed at all. That isn't meant to be as discouraging as it might sound. On the contrary, because so many freelances fail, *you*, with the inside knowledge gleaned from these pages, stand a better chance of success than most. What's more you can gain from the experience of others.

So let's take a look at some of the areas where the inexperienced freelance goes wrong. Knowing the common mistakes, you can avoid them and consequently stand the best chance of success with your own work.

The first big mistake made by the novice is in the actual format of pictures supplied. The easiest type of photograph to take and produce today is the colour print. Unfortunately, colour prints are difficult to sell. Enprints, such as those produced by commercial processing houses, never sell – except in the most exceptional of circumstances. Most buyers in today's market require black and white prints and/or colour slides.

Look at your intended market to see just how much colour they use as opposed to black and white. If the colour pages are in a minority compared with the mono pages, then do your best to restrict your submission to black and white prints. If your market uses mostly colour, then send transparencies.

The quality of your work must be first class. Colour slides should be perfectly exposed, or ever around one-third to half a stop under-exposed, to give strong, saturated colours. Most publishers and agencies generally insist that you submit originals; however, in some cases, really good "reproduction-quality" dupes may be acceptable.

Mono prints should have a sharp bite of contrast, coupled with a good range of tones all the way from white through to black. The surface of the paper on which your prints are presented matters too. It is difficult for printers to make good reproductions from prints on matt or lustre surfaces, so stick to glossy.

Never send flat, grey mono prints or over-exposed, washed-out colour slides.

For some markets, the size of your transparencies is important. Most today accept 35mm, but some – such as calendars and greetings cards – often demand larger formats: 6x6cm as a minimum and even 5x4in for preference. If your chosen market stipulates a medium or larger format, don't send 35mm.

So much for picture format, but what of the actual subject of your pictures? Here again, a lot of fundamental mistakes are made. The oldest rule in the freelancing book is this: don't take pictures, then look for markets; find a market first and then shoot your pictures specifically with that market in mind.

Every would-be freelance knows that rule; yet the many who ignore it is frankly staggering. Remember that rule and act accordingly. First find your market, analyse it to see the sort of pictures it uses, then go all out to take *exactly* the right type of picture.

Editors see a lot of pictures every day, and the vast majority are totally unsuited to their market. Of those that are suited, many are still rejected because, despite being the right *type* of pictures, the subjects are still uninspiring. They are subjects the editor has seen over and over again; and the type that the magazine will already have on file. So once again, the work gets rejected.

Remember this and learn from it. Most of the pictures that fall on an editor's desk are pretty ordinary. If you want to make yours sell, you have to show them something different. It might be a fairly straightforward view of an unusual subject, or it might be a more common subject, seen and photographed from a new angle. Either way, it will be different.

So when you set out to take your pictures, really look at your subject and, even before you press the shutter, ask yourself, why an I taking this picture? Why will an editor want to buy it? What's so different or unusual about it? How can I make a few changes here and now to give it a better chance of success?

Good, traditional picture composition also plays a part in a picture's chances. Many would-be freelances submit pictures of people in which the principal subject is far too small and surrounded by a wealth of unwanted, distracting detail. So make a point, whenever you shoot, of moving in close and really filling the viewfinder with your subject.

Many potentially saleable landscapes are ruined by a flat perspective. So watch out for, and try to include, foreground interest in such pictures.

People at work on a craft or a hobby can be good sellers, but a good many pictures depicting such subjects are shot candidly without the necessary thought needed to really show the subject to its best. Always pose pictures like these before you take them.

Finally, a word about presentation. It's true that a good picture can often find a sale, no matter how badly it is presented; but it is equally true that bad presentation can just as easily influence an editor or picture buyer and so ruin your chances of success. So why make things difficult for yourself?

When you send prints, make sure they are stiffly-packed between thick cardboard or in special cardboard envelopes. Present slides in plastic filing wallets and make them easy to view with the minimum of fuss. If you are sending words – either captions to pictures or a full-blown articles – always type them, rather than writing them by hand. Type on one side of the paper only and leave a double space between lines with good margins on each side. Send your submission with a brief letter, not with pages of explanations about the work. The sale will stand or fall by your pictures and/or words, never by the excuses you offer as to why certain pictures might not be too good. If they're not good enough, they won't sell.

Give your editor what he or she wants. Give them originality and sparkle, and present the whole package in the best way you can. Learn the rules and you'll be on your way to a good many picture sales.

But don't think that anyone is going to break those rules just for you. If your pictures don't measure up to what is required, there will always be another envelope right behind full of pictures that do. And there are no prizes for guessing which submission is going to make the sale.

MAGAZINES

The British magazine market is vast. Anyone who doubts that has only to look at the racks of periodicals in any major newsagent. And this is only the tip of the iceberg, the largest section of the consumer press. Beneath the surface there is the trade press, controlled circulation magazines and many smaller publications that are never seen on general sale. At the last count more than 8,000 magazines were being published on a regular basis in Britain.

In this section you will find detailed listings of magazines which are looking for freelances. Some pay a lot, others are less generous, but all have one thing in common – they are here because they need freelance contributions on a regular basis and they are willing to pay for them.

When you come to start looking at these listings in detail, you might be surprised by the number of magazines of which you have never heard. Don't let that put you off. What the newcomer to freelancing often fails to realise is that there are as many, if not more, trade magazines as there are consumer publications, and very few of these are ever seen on general sale.

Trade magazines, as the term implies, are aimed at people whose business is making money from the particular subject concerned. As such, their requirements are usually totally different to their consumer counterparts.

As an example, consider boating. A consumer magazine on that subject will be aimed at the boat owner or enthusiast and could contain features on boats and the way they are handled. A trade magazine on the same subject is likely to be more interested in articles about the profits being made by the boating industry and pictures of shop displays of boating accessories.

Trade magazines do not necessarily have a separate section to themselves. If the subject is a common one, such as the example above in which there are both trade and consumer publications, they have been listed for your convenience under a common heading. Despite that, however, there *is* a section specifically for trade. This contains trade magazines that have no consumer counterparts, as well as magazines whose subject is actually trade itself and trading in general.

As you go through these listings, therefore, it is important for you to realise that there is a very real difference between the two sides of the subject, but it is a difference which is explained under each publication's requirements. So don't ignore trade magazines of whose existence you were not previously aware. Very often such a magazine will have just as big a market for your pictures and the fees will be just as much, and in some cases more, than those offered by the consumer press.

It is often a good idea for the freelance to aim at some of the more obscure publications listed here. Simply because they are a little obscure, they may not have been noticed by other freelances and, as such, your sales potential will be higher.

Another factor that will become apparent as you look through this section of the *Handbook* is the degree to which black and white illustrations are still needed as well as colour. It's wise, then, to remember this when you are shooting pictures for publication. If possible, shoot both colour and mono for those markets that require both.

When you are looking through the entries, don't stop at the section on illustrations. Read what the magazine needs in the way of text too. A publication that might appear to have a very small market for individual pictures often has a larger potential for illustrated articles, and all you need to do to make a sale is add a few words.

You will also find that many publications talk about needing mainly commissioned work. Don't be misled by this. The commissions are given to freelances and, although this means they won't consider you work on spec, they could well be interested in giving you a commission if you can prove you are worth it. That's where previous experience comes in. When trying for commissions, you should always have examples of previously published work to show an editor.

Many of the larger magazines employ a specific editor to deal with picture submissions and with photographers. They may go under various titles – picture editor, art editor, art director – but this is the person directly responsible for picture selection and for commissioning photographers for specific jobs. This, therefore, is the person you should approach when sending pictures or seeking photographic assignments. When sending written material though, illustrated or not, your approach is best made direct to the editor.

The magazine market is one of the largest available to the freelance. You might not receive as large a fee per picture as you would from, say, the calendar market, or for certain sales that might be made on your behalf by an agency, but what this field does offer is a *steady* income.

There are so many magazines, covering so many different subjects, that freelances who have their wits about them would be hard put *not* to find one to which their own style and interests can be adapted. Make yourself known to a few chosen magazine editors, let them see that you can turn out good quality work on the right subject, at the right time, and there is no reason why this market shouldn't make you a good, regular income, either part time or full time.

New Listings, Changes & Deletions

The following is designed to alert readers to possible new markets as well as to important changes that have taken place since the last edition of the *Handbook*. 'New Listings' includes magazines that have been launches since the last edition appeared as well as established titles that appear in the *Handbook* for the first time. 'Title Changes' lists publications that have changed their names (previous titles in brackets). 'Deletions' lists publications that appeared in the previous edition but are omitted from this one. Publications under this heading have not necessarily ceased publication – they may have been deleted because they no longer offer a worthwhile market for the contributor.

To find the page number for any magazine, refer to the main Index at the back of the book.

New Listings

American Car World
Bedrooms & Bathrooms: The Magazine
Boating Business
The Boatman
Camping Magazine
Camping & Caravanning
Car Week
Caravan Plus
Check It Out!
Cycle Sport
Everywoman
Financial Pulse
Fore!
Future Music
Gardens Illustrated
The Golfer
Good Woodworking
Harrington Kilbride Publishing

Here's How
Homes & Gardens
House Beautiful
Improve Your Sea Fishing
Non-League Football
OK! Magazine
Outdoor
Perfect Home
Performance Cyclist
Personal Water Craft News
Police Review
Practice Nurse
Practice Nursing
Sainsbury's The Magazine
The Skier
Sports Quarterly
Stillwater Trout Angler
Waterski Illustrated Magazine
Woodcarving
Your Garden

Title Changes

AEA Times (AT/AEA Times)
Carer's World (Practical Caring)
Clocks (Antique Clocks)
Glass Age & Window Construction (Glass Age)

Gloucestershire & Avon Life (Gloucestershire Life)
Horse Review (Hurlingham Polo & Horse Review)
Jet Skier & P. W. Magazine (Jet Skier)
Runner's World (Running Magazine)

Top Race & Rally (Rally Car)
VQ (The Vegetarian)

Widescreen International (International
 Widescreen)

Deletions

Air Report
Aquarium
Athletics Today
Bicycle Magazine
Blinds & Shutters
Cambridgeshire Life
Car Classics
Caravan Answers
Classic Car Weekly
Coin News
Custom Cycle
Fashion & Craft
Gridiron
Home Improvements Guides
Huna London
IMLS Gazette
International Broadcast Engineer
Japanese Classics
Kent Life
Lady Golfer
Magic Carpet
Making Music
Medal News
Milk Producer
Modern Africa
Motocross Rider
Motorhome Magazine
New Builder

Northern Woman
On Board Windsurfing Magazine
Openmind
Opera Now
Pensions & Employee Benefits
Photo Plus
Plastics & Rubber International
Port of London Magazine
Practical Classics & Car Restorer
Railway Express
The Rambler
Replay
Retirement Homes & Finance
Rock Power
Saleroom & Auction Monthly
Scotland's What's On Magazine
Skateboard
Southern Life Magazine
Television Week
Tempo
Thames User
Tobacco
Traditional Homes
Video Home Entertainment
Vogue Patterns
Woodworking International
World Magazine
World Sports Cars

Subject Index

Only magazines are included in this index, but it should be noted that many of these subjects are also required by Agencies (pp.176-199), Card & Calendar publishers (pp. 172-175) and Book publishers (pp.159-171). A separate Subject Index for agencies appears in the Agency section.

To find the page number for any magazine, refer to the main Index at the back of the book.

Aeroplanes

Aeroplane Monthly
Air International
Airforces Monthly
Aviation News
British Airways News
Commuter World
Flight International
Flight Safety Bulletin
Flyer
Military Firefighter
Pilot
Popular Flying

Agricultural Scenes

Crops
Dairy Farmer
Dairy Industries International
Farmers Weekly
Harrington Kilbride Publishing Group
The Jewish Vegetarian
The Landworker
Pig Farming
Poultry World
VQ

Architecture & Buildings

Architecture Today
Build It
Building Today
Country Homes and Interiors
FX
Glass Age & Window Construction
House Builder
House & Garden
New Civil Engineer
Period Living
Professional Interiors

RIBA Journal
World of Interiors

Army and Navy

Air International
Defence
Defence Helicopter World
The Legion
Navy International

Arts and Crafts

The Clockmaker
Good Woodworking
Here's How
The Lady
Popular Crafts
Woodcarving
Woodturning
Woodworker

Boating & Yachting

Action Holidays
Boat International
The Boatman
Canal & Riverboat
Classic Boat
International Boat Industry
Jet Skier & P. W. Magazine
Motor Boat and Yachting
Motorboats Monthly
Personal Water Craft News
RYA News
Regatta
Sportsboat & Waterski International
Waterways World
Yachting Monthly
Yachting World
Yachts and Yachting

Business Scenes

Accountancy Age
Africa Economic Digest
CA Magazine
Commerce Magazine
Computer Weekly
The Director
The Economist
Export Times
FX
Journal
MEED
Management Accounting
Marketing
Practical PC

Celebrities

Bella
Big!
Check It Out!
Company
Expression
Hello!
Look-In
Mizz
More!
19
OK! Magazine
Options
Radio Times
Saga
The Stage & Television Today
TV Times
Titbits Magazine
Woman
Woman & Home
Woman's Journal
Woman's Own

Children

Amateur Photographer
The Brownie
Guide Patrol
Guiding
Harrington Kilbride Publishing Group
Junior Education
Mother & Baby
Nursery World

Parents
Photo Answers
Practical Photography
Right Start
Safety Education
Scouting

Cinema & Television

Big!
Broadcast Hardware International
International Broadcasting
Look-In
Radio Times
The Stage and Television Today
TV Times
What Satellite
What Video

Domestic and Farm Animals

Amateur Photographer
Animal Life
Animal World
Bird Keeper
Cage and Aviary Birds
Cats
Dairy Farmer
Dairy Industries International
Dogs Today
Horse and Pony
Horse and Rider
The Jewish Vegetarian
Kennel Gazette
Pig Farming
Photo Answers
Pony
Poultry World
Practical Photography
Riding
VQ
Vegetarian Living

Domestic Environment

Bedrooms & Bathrooms: The Magazine
Best
Country Homes & Interiors
Do It Yourself Magazine
Elle Decoration
First Choice

Good Housekeeping
Here's How
Home Cooking
Homes & Gardens
House Beautiful
House & Garden
Jewish Chronicle
Mrs Beeton Traditional Housekeeping Today
Options
Perfect Home
Practical Householder
Prima
Woman Alive
Woman and Home
Woman's Journal
World of Interiors

Fashion

Bella
Best
Chat
Company
Cosmopolitan
Drapers Record
Elle
Esquire
Essentials
Fashion Extras
Fashion Weekly
France
GQ
Good Housekeeping
Harpers & Queen
Hello
Jewish Chronicle
The Lady
MG
Marie Claire
Men's Wear
More
Ms London Weekly
19
Prima
Sainsbury's The Magazine
She
Sky Magazine
Woman
Woman's Journal
Woman's Own
Woman's Realm

Glamour

Amateur Photographer
Club International
Fiesta
Knave
Mayfair
Men Only
Penthouse
Practical Photography
Superbike
Titbits Magazine

Horticulture

Amateur Gardening
BBC Gardeners' World
Country Homes & Interiors
First Choice
The Garden
Garden Answers
Garden News
Garden Trade News International
The Gardener
Gardens Illustrated
Good Housekeeping
Horticulture Week
House & Garden
Practical Gardening
Sainsbury's The Magazine
Your Garden

Humour

Amateur Photographer
Bella
Best
Auto Express
Car Week
Chat
The Christian Herald
Driving Magazine
Horse and Pony
Look-In
Mizz
Titbits Magazine
Woman Alive

Industrial Scenes

Chemistry & Industry

Containerisation International
The Director
Education in Chemistry
Eurofruit Magazine
Food Industry News
Harrington Kilbride Publishing Group
Industrial Diamond Review
Ink and Print
MEED
Management Accounting
Post Magazine: The Insurance Weekly
Roustabout
Sign World
Tin International
Urethanes Technology
Works Management

Landscapes

Amateur Photographer
Angling Times
BBC Holidays
Bird Watching
Camping Magazine
Caravan Business
Catholic Gazette
The Christian Herald
Coarse Angler
Coarse Fisherman
Cotswold Life
Country
Country Homes & Interiors
Country Life
Country Walking
The Countryman
Devon & Cornish Life
Dorset Life – The Dorset Magazine
Essex Countryside
Gloucestershire & Avon Life
The Great Outdoors
Hertfordshire Countryside
The Lady
Lakescene
Lancashire Life
Lincolnshire Life
Manx Life
Motor Caravan World
Outdoor
Photo Answers
Practical Caravan
Practical Gamefishing

Practical Photography
RYA News
Rambling Today
Scots Independent
The Scots Magazine
Somerset and Avon Life
The Somerset Magazine
Sussex Life
This England
Trout Fisherman
Trout & Salmon
Waterways World
Woman Alive

Motor Vehicles

American Car World
Auto Express
Autocar & Motor
The Automobile
Car Choice
Car Numbers Magazine
Car Week
Cars & Car Conversions
Classic Amercian
Classic & Sportscar
Company Car
Driving Magazine
Fleet News
Formula 1 News
4 x 4 Magazine
International Off Roader
Land Rover Owner
Motor Trader
Motoring & Leisure
911 & Porsche World
Off Road & Four Wheel Drive
Performance Ford
Popular Classics
Rally Car Magazine
Street Machine
Top Race & Rally
Truck
VW Motoring

Motorcycling

Back Street Heroes
British Bike Magazine
Classic Bike
The Classic Motor Cycle

Heavy Duty
Motorcycle International
Scootering
Superbike

Performing Arts

Dance and Dancers
English Dance and Song
Radio Times
The Stage and Television Today
TV Times

Pop Stars & Musicians

Big!
Blues and Soul
Echoes
Future Music
Just Seventeen
Kerrang!
Keyboard Player
Look-In
MG
Melody Maker
New Musical Express
Q
RAW
Rhythm
Riff Raff
Rock CD
Sky Magazine
Smash Hits
Vox

Railways

International Railway Journal
Model Railways
Rail
Railnews
Scale Model Trains
Steam Classic
Steam Railway
Steam Railway News

Shipping

Containerisation International
Marine Engineers Review

Sport

Air Gunner
Amateur Photographer
Bike
Boat International
Boxing Monthly
Cars & Car Conversions
Country
Cricket World
The Cricketer International
Cycle Sport
Cycling Plus
Darts World
Esquire
Fighters – The Martial Arts Magazine
First Down
Fore!
Formula 1 News
France
GQ
Golf Monthly
Golf World
The Golfer
Harrington Kilbride Publishing Group
Horse Review
Martial Arts Illustrated
Martial Arts Today
Match
Motorboats Monthly
Mountain Biking UK
90 Minutes
Non-League Football
On The Line
Performance Cyclist
Photo Answers
Pot Black Magazine
Practical Photography
Racing Pigeon Pictorial
Rally Sport
Rangers News
Regatta
Rugby Leaguer
Rugby News
Rugby World & Post
Scotland's Runner
Sea Angler
Shoot!
Shooting Gazette
Shooting Times & Country Magazine
Ski Survey

The Skier
Snooker Scene
Snowboard UK
Sports Boat and Waterski International
Sports Quarterly
Swimming Times
Target Gun
Tennis World
Today's Golfer
Today's Runner
Top Race & Rally
Waterski Illustrated Magazine
Watford
Windsurf Magazine
Wisden Cricket Monthly
Yachts and Yachting

Technology

Chemistry In Britain
Chemistry & Industry
Clean Air & Environmental Protection
Design Engineering
ETI
Electrical Times
Electronics World and Wireless World
The Engineer
Gas World
International Railway Journal
Manufacturing Chemist
Natural Gas
New Scientist
Process Engineering
Professional Engineering

Travel

Action Holidays
Africa Economic Digest
Africa Health
Amateur Photographer
BBC Holidays
British Airways News
Business Traveller
Coach & Bus Week

The Diplomat And Lady Diplomat
The Director
Executive Travel
Expression
Far East Health
First Choice
France
Good Housekeeping
Harrington Kilbride Publishing Group
International Tax-Free Trader
The Lady
The Middle East
Motor Caravan World
Motoring & Leisure
Options
Parents
Photo Answers
Practical Caravan
Practical Photography
Saga
The Traveller
Woman and Home
Woman's Realm
Yours

Wildlife

Amateur Photographer
Animal Life
Animal World
Bird Life
Bird Watching
Birds
Birds Illustrated
Birdwatch
Country
The Countryman
Green Magazine
The Lady
Natural World
Photo Answers
The Scottish Sporting Gazette
Shooting Times and Country Magazine
Wild Cat
Wildfowl & Wetlands

Angling

ANGLER'S MAIL
IPC Magazines Ltd, King's Reach Tower, Stamford Street, London SE1 9LS. Tel: 071-261 5883.
Editor: Roy Westwood.
Weekly publication with news and features for followers of coarse, sea and game fishing in the UK.
Illustrations: Colour only. Topical news pictures of successful anglers with their catches. Captions should give full details concerning weight and circumstances of capture. Covers: colour pictures of anglers with exceptional specimen fish or catches.
Text: Features on coarse, sea and game fishing topics only. Up to 800 words.
Overall freelance potential: Minimal for non-angling freelances. Regular freelance sources are known specialists in the field.
Editor's tips: Most pictures and text seen from non-anglers are not acceptable because of lack of knowledge and experience on the part of the contributor.
Fees: By agreement.

ANGLING TIMES
EMAP Pursuit Publishing Ltd, Bretton Court, Bretton, Peterborough PE3 8DZ. Tel: 0733 266222.
Editor: Keith Higginbottom.
Weekly newspaper format publication covering all ranges of angling, i.e. coarse, sea and game. Includes news, features and general instruction.
Illustrations: General angling subjects – catches, action and scenics.
Text: Features on all aspects of the hobby. Up to 800 words.
Overall freelance potential: Very good. High percentage used each week.
Fees: By agreement.

COARSE ANGLER
NFA Publications Ltd, 12 Appletongate, Newark, Notts NG24 1JY. Tel: 0246 410601.
Editor: Jim Baxter.
Monthly magazine for the British coarse angling community with special reference to members of the National Federation of Anglers.
Illustrations: B&W and colour. Pictures solely relating coarse fishing. Covers: colour pictures of picturesque coarse fishing scenes and locations or close-ups of anglers with spectacular catches – medium format only.
Text: Articles on any aspect of coarse fish or fishing. 1,000–1,250 words.
Overall freelance potential: Around 50 per cent of each issue is contributed by freelances.
Fees: Text, from £25; B&W pictures, from £7.50 according to size; covers, £25.

COARSE FISHERMAN
Metrocrest Ltd, 67 Tyrrell Street, Leicester LE3 5SB. Tel: 0533 511277.
Editor: Simon Roff.
Monthly magazine covering all aspects of coarse fishing.
Illustrations: B&W and colour. Pictures of anglers in action or displaying riverside or lakeside scenes where such angling takes place. Covers: colour pictures of anglers displaying particularly fine catches.
Text: Articles of 1,000–2,000 words, accompanied by B&W or colour pictures. On any coarse fishing topic, but most usually first person accounts of angling experiences.
Overall freelance potential: Excellent scope for angling specialists.
Fees: B&W pictures from a minimum of £5 upwards. £10 upwards for colour, £25 per 1,000 words for text.

FLY-FISHING & FLY-TYING

Gamefishing Publications Ltd, The Lodge, Meridian House, Orton Southgate, Peterborough PE2 0XU. Tel: 0733 371937.

Editor: Mark Bowler.

Bi-monthly magazine for the stillwater fly-fisherman and fly-tyer. Concentrating on the smaller still-water trout fisheries.

Illustrations: B&W and colour. Shots of anglers in action, scenics of stillwater locations, flies and fly-tying, and appropriate insect pictures.

Text: Illustrated articles on all aspects of stillwater game fishing.

Overall freelance potential: Fairly good.

Editor's tips: Good pictures of stillwater locations are sometimes hard to achieve; make an effort to avoid bland, uninteresting results.

Fees: B&W from £12–£29; colour from £24–£58; Covers £45. Text £48 per 1,000 words.

IMPROVE YOUR COARSE FISHING

EMAP Pursuit Publishing Ltd, Bretton Court, Bretton, Peterborough PE3 8DZ. Tel: 0733 266222.

Acting Editor: Kevin Wilmot.

Monthly "hints and tips" style magazine for coarse fishing enthusiasts.

Illustrations: B&W and colour. Photographs depicting all aspects of coarse fishing.

Text: Ideas for features from experienced angling writers always considered. Length variable.

Overall freelance potential: Small; much of the editorial content is produced in-house.

Editor's tips: Always query the editor before submitting.

Fees: By negotiation.

IMPROVE YOUR SEA FISHING

Harmsworth Active, 10 Sheet Street, Windsor, Berks SL4 1BG. Tel: 0753 856061.

Editor: Chris Pearce.

Monthly magazine for sea anglers.

Illustrations: Mainly colour. Good stock shots depicting any aspect of sea fishing.

Text: Illustrated instructional articles. Length around 1,200 words.

Overall freelance potential: Fair.

Fees: By negotiation.

PRACTICAL GAMEFISHING

EMAP Pursuit Publishing Ltd. Editorial: 118 Manor Way, Deeping St James, Peterborough PE6 8PY. Tel: 0733 264666.

Editor: John Wilshaw.

Monthly covering all aspects of gamefishing including bait fishing.

Illustrations: B&W and colour. Scenic shots incorporating anglers, angling action, location pictures (rivers, streams, lakes) and appropriate insect photography.

Text: Firmly practical "how to" and "where to" type articles from contributors with expert knowledge of the subject. Length around 1,200 words.

Overall freelance potential: Excellent, the magazine is very heavily illustrated.

Fees: By negotiation.

SALMON, TROUT & SEA-TROUT

Gamefishing Publications Ltd, The Lodge, Meridian House, Orton Southgate, Peterborough PE2 0XU. Tel: 0733 51235.

Editor: David Goodchild.

Monthly magazine covering all aspects of game fishing, at home and abroad.

Illustrations: B&W and colour. Pictures of fishermen in action, general angling scenes, and close-ups

of flies and tackle. Covers: attractive scenic shots, in colour, featuring an angler.
Text: Articles on all aspects of game fishing.
Overall freelance potential: Good.
Fees: By negotiation.

SEA ANGLER
EMAP Pursuit Publishing Ltd, Bretton Court, Bretton, Peterborough PE3 8DZ. Tel: 0733 264666.
Editor: Mel Russ.
Monthly magazine dealing with the sport of sea angling from both boat and beach.
Illustrations: Colour. All aspects of the sport of sea fishing. Covers: colour, same subjects.
Text: Instructional features, fishing expeditions, match articles, etc. 1,000 words.
Overall freelance potential: 70 per cent of published material comes from freelance sources.
Fees: By negotiation.

STILLWATER TROUT ANGLER
IPC Magazines Ltd, King's Reach Tower, Stamford Stret, London SE1 9LS. Tel: 071-261 5829.
Editor: Roy Westwood.
Monthly magazine for trout fishing enthusiasts.
Illustrations: Colour only. Mostly commissioned to a specific brief, but very high quality general shots of trout fishing action, fisheries, etc. will be considered.
Text: Only for established contributors.
Overall freelance potential: Small.
Editor's tips: Quality is the ultimate criterion.
Fees: By negotiation, according to quality.

TROUT FISHERMAN
EMAP Pursuit Publishing Ltd, Bretton Court, Bretton, Peterborough PE3 8DZ. Tel: 0733 264666.
Editor: Chris Dawn.
Monthly magazine for the trout fishing enthusiast.
Illustrations: Colour. Photographs depicting any aspect of angling for trout – outstanding catches, angling locations, techniques, flies and equipment.
Text: Illustrated articles on all aspects of trout fishing, around 1,500 words.
Overall freelance potential: Excellent scope for top quality material.
Editor's tips: Too much angling photography is dull and uninteresting; an original and lively approach would be welcome.
Fees: On a rising scale according to size of reproduction or length of text.

TROUT AND SALMON
EMAP Pursuit Publishing Ltd, Bretton Court, Bretton Centre, Peterborough PE3 8DZ. Tel: 0733 264666.
Editor: Sandy Leventon.
Monthly magazine for game fishermen.
Illustrations: Colour only. Photographs of trout or salmon waters, preferably with an angler included in the picture. Close-up and action shots to illustrate particular techniques. Captioned news pictures showing anglers with outstanding catches. Covers: good colour pictures of game fishing waters, always with an angler present.
Text: Instructional illustrated articles on all aspects of game fishing.
Overall freelance potential: Excellent for those who can produce the right sort of material.
Fees: Pictures inside according to use. Cover shots, £60. Text according to length.

Animals and Wildlife

ANIMAL LIFE

Royal Society for the Prevention of Cruelty to Animals, Causeway, Horsham, West Sussex RH12 1HG. Tel: 0403 64181.

Editor: Michaela Miller.

Official journal of the RSPCA, published four times a year.

Illustrations: B&W and colour. Pictures relating to animal welfare and conservation, featuring both domestic and wild animals – always looking for the unusual. Topical pictures concerning RSPCA activities and interests, with accurate captions.

Text: Everything written in-house.

Overall freelance potential: Moderate.

Editor's tips: We prefer pictures that show real contact between animals and people. Not interested in "cutesy" pictures.

Fees: B&W pictures £15; colour £20–£30, dependent on size. Covers, £80.

ANIMAL WORLD

Royal Society for the Prevention of Cruelty to Animals, Causeway, Horsham, West Sussex RH12 1HG. Tel: 0403 64181.

Editor: Michaela Miller.

Junior Membership publication of the RSPCA, published six times a year.

Illustrations: Mainly colour. Pictures relating to animal welfare and conservation, featuring both domestic and wild animals. Send catalogue first.

Text: All written in-house.

Overall freelance potential: Fair.

Editor's tips: Eye contact is essential.

Fees: Colour £20–£30; covers, £80.

BIRD LIFE

Royal Society for the Protection of Birds, The Lodge, Sandy, Bedfordshire SG19 2DL. Tel: 0767 680551.

Editor: Samantha Ward-Dutton.

Alternate-monthly magazine for members of the RSPB Young Ornithologists' Club.

Illustrations: Colour (Kodachrome 64 preferred). Good stock shots, preferably with a conservation angle; news pictures of YOC groups and individual achievements. Covers: colour close-ups of wild birds in their native habitat.

Text: Short illustrated articles on wildlife and conservation, written with children aged 8–13 in mind. Length around 600 words. Use of unsolicited material rare.

Overall freelance potential: Good.

Fees: £80 per 1,000 words for text; photographs according to use.

BIRD WATCHING

EMAP Pursuit Publishing Ltd, Bretton Court, Bretton, Peterborough PE3 8DZ. Tel: 0733 264666.

Editor: Dave Cromack.

Monthly magazine devoted to birdwatching and ornithology.

Illustrations: B&W and colour. Top quality photographs of birds in the wild, both in the UK and overseas. Also, landscape shots of British bird watching sites. Potential contributors are asked to always send a list of subjects available in the first instance.

Text: Illustrated features on all aspects of birds and birdwatching.

Overall freelance potential: Excellent scope for wildlife specialists.

Fees: By negotiation.

BIRDS
Royal Society for the Protection of Birds, The Lodge, Sandy, Beds SG19 2DL. Tel: 0767 680551.
Editor: Rob Hume.
Quarterly magazine for RSPB members. Covers ornithology and general conservation issues.
Illustrations: Colour only. Photo features on particular birds, groups of birds or bird behaviour; interesting habitat shots (throughout Europe); imaginative shots of people enjoying birdwatching and the countryside. No captive birds or domestic birds.
Text: Illustrated articles on all aspects of birds in the wild, including conservation. Length 1,000–1,500 words.
Overall freelance potential: Fair.
Fees: Photographs from £40 to £120; £120 per 1,000 words for text.

BIRDS ILLUSTRATED
EMAP Pursuit Publishing Ltd, Bretton Court, Bretton, Peterborough PE3 8DZ. Tel: 0733 264666.
Editor: Dave Cromack.
Heavily-illustrated quarterly for birdwatchers.
Illustrations: Mostly colour. Top quality photography of birds worldwide. Often focuses on the work of individual photographers.
Text: In-depth illustrated features on all aspects of birds and birdwatching.
Overall freelance potential: Excellent.
Editor's tips: The magazine maintains a seasonal bias, so submit relevant material at the appropriate time of year, i.e. spring/summer material in early winter.
Fees: By negotiation.

BIRDWATCH
Solo Publishing Ltd, 215 Bow House Business Centre, 153-159 Bow Road, London E3 2SE. Tel: 081-983 1855.
Editor: Dominic Mitchell.
Monthly magazine for all birdwatchers. Includes a strong emphasis on the photographic side of the hobby.
Illustrations: B&W and colour. Good photographs of British and European birds in their natural habitat. Those with collections of such material should send lists of subjects available, to picture editor Steve Young.
Text: Well-illustrated features on birdwatching topics, including practical articles on bird photography. 1,000–1,200 words, but send a synopsis first.
Overall freelance potential: Very good.
Fees: According to use.

CATS
Our Dogs Publishing Co. Ltd, 5 James Leigh Street, Manchester M1 6EX. Tel: 061-236 0577.
Editor: Brian Doyle.
Weekly publication aimed at the serious cat breeder and exhibitor and all cat lovers.
Illustrations: B&W only. Newsy photographs of interest to serious cat lovers. All pictures must be accompanied by informative captions.
Text: Limited scope for knowledgeable features of show reports.
Overall freelance potential: Limited to the coverage of serious cat matters.
Editor's tips: If the subject concerns cats, take a chance and submit it.
Fees: By negotiation.

DOGS TODAY
Pet Subjects Ltd, 6 Station Parade, Sunningdale, Berkshire SL5 0EP. Tel: 0344 875442.
Editor: Beverley Cuddy.
Bi-monthly magazine for the pet dog lover.

Illustrations: Mainly colour. News pictures, shots showing dogs in action or in specific situations, exciting or amusing photo sequences, and pictures of celebrities with their dogs. No simple dog portraits unless displaying a strong element of humour or sentiment. Almost full colour; only news pages and "Tail Ending" page remain mono.
Text: General illustrated features about dogs. Should be positive and have a "human interest" feel.
Overall freelance potential: Excellent for the right material.
Fees: According to use.

KENNEL GAZETTE
The Kennel Club, 1–5 Clarges Street, London W1Y 8AB. Tel: 071-493 6651.
Editor: C. L. S. Colborn.
Monthly publication for pedigree dog owners and exhibitors, the official journal of the Kennel Club.
Illustrations: B&W and colour. Pictures of pedigree dogs, with and without people; dog shows; working dogs. Covers: colour or B&W pictures of pedigree dogs.
Text: Articles on breeding, veterinary subjects, judging, grooming, police dogs, field trials, obedience classes etc. 500–2,000 words.
Overall freelance potential: For specialist material only.
Editor's tips: The readership is specialist. Submissions should reflect this. Pictures must illustrate relevant editorial unless they represent possible covers.
Fees: Inside: mono, £10; colour, £25. Covers, £40. Features by agreement.

NATURAL WORLD
RSNC The Wildlife Trust Partnership, 20 Upper Ground, London SE1 9PF. Tel: 071-928 2111.
Editor: Linda Bennett.
The magazine of RSNC The Wildlife Trusts Partnership, concerned with all aspects of wildlife and the countryside in the UK. Published three times per year.
Illustrations: Colour; in particular, mammals, amphibians, insects, flowers and trees. Subjects must be wild; no pets or zoo animals.
Text: Short photo-features on wildlife or conservation topics particularly connected with local Wildlife Trusts. Around 500 words.
Overall freelance potential: Limited.
Fees: £30 minimum for colour.

PET PRODUCT MARKETING
EMAP Pursuit Publishing Ltd, Bretton Court, Bretton, Peterborough PE3 8DZ. Tel: 0733 264666.
Editor: Peter Maskell.
Monthly trade journal for pet product retailers, wholesalers, manufacturers and importers. Controlled circulation.
Illustrations: Mainly B&W. Subjects connected with pet products and the pet trade. Some colour. Covers: colour of suitable subjects.
Text: Features on pets and pet products with specific relevance to the pet trade. 1,000 words.
Overall freelance potential: Limited.
Fees: £45 per 1,000 words. Pictures on merit.

VETERINARY PRACTICE
A. E. Morgan Publications Ltd, Stanley House, 9 West Street, Epsom, Surrey KT18 7RL. Tel: 0372 741411.
Editor: Chris Cattrall.
Twice-monthly newspaper for veterinary surgeons in general practice.
Illustrations: Pictures of veterinary surgeons engaged in activities either connected with or outside their professional work.

Text: Features particularly concerned with veterinary practice. 800–1,500 words.
Overall freelance potential: Small.
Fees: By agreement.

WILD CAT
Cat Survival Trust, The Centre, Codicote Road, Welwyn, Hertfordshire AL6 9TU. Tel: 043871 6873 or 6478.
Editor: Terry Moore.
Published twice per year for members, patrons and friends of the Cat Survival Trust, as well as zoological institutions, museums and libraries in many countries.
Illustrations: B&W only. Pictures of wild cats, especially less common species. Pictures taken in the wild or overseas zoos or private collections are particularly welcome. No domestic pets. Covers: B&W pictures of same.
Text: Articles on any aspect of wild cats, e.g. biology, management, breeding, conservation, etc. 1,000–2,000 words.
Overall freelance potential: Small but expanding.
Fees: Nominal, due to the publishers being a charity.

WILDFOWL & WETLANDS
The Wildfowl & Wetlands Trust, Slimbridge, Gloucester GL2 7BT. Tel: 0453 890333.
Editor: Tim Davis.
Twice-yearly magazine of The Wildfowl & Wetlands Trust.
Illustrations: B&W and colour. Pictures of water birds in their natural habitat, plus pictures of the wetland environment and other forms of wetland wildlife.
Text: Illustrated articles of a serious nature, concerning groups of waterfowl or particular species, or on threats to or conservation of wetland habitats. Travelogues considered as long as they concentrate on the relevant subject matter.
Overall freelance potential: Good scope limited only by the frequency of the publication.
Fees: On the low side as the publisher is a charity, but open to negotiation.

Arts and Entertainment

CLUB MIRROR
Quantum Publishing Ltd, 29/31 Lower Coombe Street, Croydon, CR9 1LX. Tel: 081-681 2099.
Editor: Lewis Eckett.
Monthly publication for officials, committee members and stewards of registered clubs throughout the UK; proprietary club owners and managers; and discotheque owners and managers.
Illustrations: B&W and colour. Interior pictures of new clubs, new club openings, interesting general pictures of club activities.
Text: Articles on new club openings, new clubs planned, news stories on clubs, special features on successful clubs. Also features on the club trade, i.e. catering services etc. 100–2,000 words.
Overall freelance potential: Good; 40 per cent from freelance sources.
Fees: By arrangement.

DANCE AND DANCERS
Dance & Dancers Ltd, 214 Panther House, 38 Mount Pleasant, London WC1X 0AP. Tel: 071-837 2711.
Editor: John Percival.
Monthly magazine covering dance and ballet. Includes reviews, features and information on the subject.
Illustrations: B&W only inside. Pictures of current dance performances, occasionally archive and historical material. Covers: colour pictures of current performances or personalities to tie in with a major

feature. Must be up to date.

Text: Reviews of current performances. General features on dance. Profiles of dancers. 500–2,000 words.

Overall freelance potential: Over 50 per cent is freelance, but mostly from regular contributors.

Editor's tips: Very specialist interest, using ballet/contemporary/ethnic dance only. No mime, pop dance or ballet school interest. Always check before submitting.

Fees: Text, £40 per 1,000 words; photographs negotiable.

ENGLISH DANCE AND SONG

English Folk Dance and Song Society, 2 Regents Park Road, London NW1 7AY. Tel: 071-485 2206.

Editor: Dave Arthur.

Published four times per year for traditional music, dance and song enthusiasts.

Illustrations: B&W only. Pictures of folk singers and musicians, dancers, instruments and traditional customs. Covers: B&W pictures of same.

Text: Features on subjects detailed above. 1,000–2,000 words.

Overall freelance potential: Most material bought from photographers who are also enthusiasts.

Fees: Variable.

INTERNATIONAL BROADCASTING

EMAP Business Publishing Ltd, 33-39 Bowling Green Lane, London EC1R 0DA. Tel: 071-837 1212.

Editor: Paul Marks.

Published 10 times per year, for professionals in the television broadcasting industry.

Illustrations: B&W and colour. Photographs of TV broadcast hardware, studios, sets, etc.

Text: Features on TV broadcast production. 600–1,500 words.

Overall freelance potential: Good.

Editor's tips: Always call with ideas.

Fees: By arrangement.

LEISURE WEEK

Centaur Communications, St Giles House, 50 Poland Street, London W1V 4AX. Tel: 071-494 0300.

Editor: Roberta Cohen.

Trade news weekly covering the whole leisure industry, from pubs and clubs to museums and theatres.

Illustrations: B&W and colour. News pictures covering happenings in any branch of the leisure industry.

Text: News stories and short features on leisure industry developments, profiles of individual operations etc.

Overall freelance potential: Quite good for those with access to specific leisure fields.

Fees: £100 per 1,000 words for text; photographs according to use.

RADIO TIMES

BBC Enterprises, Woodlands, 80 Wood Lane, London W12 0TT. Tel: 081-576 2000.

Editor: Nicholas Brett. **Art Editor**: Tim Walmsley.

Weekly magazine containing news and details of BBC radio and television programmes. Now includes ITV and Channel 4.

Illustrations: B&W and colour. Pictures concerned with broadcasting events, invariably by commission.

Text: Commissioned features on BBC personalities or programmes of current interest. 1,000 words.

Overall freelance potential: Fair for commissioned work.

Fees: Various.

THE STAGE AND TELEVISION TODAY

The Stage Newspaper Ltd, 47 Bermondsey Street, London SE1 3XT. Tel: 071-403 1818.

Editor: Jeremy Jehu.
Weekly newspaper for professionals engaged in arts and entertainment.
Illustrations: B&W only. News pictures. Pictures of current productions. Personality pictures for file.
Text: Features on the theatre and light entertainment. 1,000 words.
Overall freelance potential: Better for writers than for photographers.
Fees: By agreement.

TV TIMES
Independent Television Publications Ltd, King's Reach Tower, Stamford Street, London SE1 9LS. Tel: 071-261 5000.
Editor: *To be appointed*. **Art Editor**: Terry Brown.
Weekly magazine containing listings and features on ITV, BBC, Channel 4, Satellite television and radio programmes.
Illustrations: B&W and colour. Usually commissioned or requested from specialist sources. Covers: quality colour portraits or groups specific to current programme content.
Text: Articles on personalities and programmes.
Overall freelance potential: Between 50 and 75 per cent each week is freelance, but mostly from recognised contributors.
Fees: Negotiable.

WHAT SATELLITE TV
WV Publications, 57–59 Rochester Place, London NW1 9JU. Tel: 071-485 0011.
Editor: Geoff Bains.
Monthly magazine for satellite TV system buyers and users. Contains tests on receivers and dishes, general features, programme listings and reviews and the latest satellite news.
Illustrations: B&W and colour. Systems in situ, family/people shots in use. Covers: colour pictures of similar.
Text: Technical topics, plus programme reviews and personality pieces. 500–1,200 words.
Overall freelance potential: Around 50 per cent from such sources.
Fees: By agreement.

Aviation

AEROPLANE MONTHLY
Specialist Group, King's Reach Tower, Stamford Street, London SE1 9LS. Tel: 071-261 5849.
Editor: Richard Riding.
Monthly aviation history magazine, specialising in the period 1909–1960. Occasional features on modern aviation.
Illustrations: B&W and colour. Photographs for use in their own right or for stock. Main interests: veteran or vintage aircraft, including those in museums; preserved airworthy aircraft; unusual pictures of modern aircraft. Action shots preferred in the case of colour material, e.g. air-to-air, ground-to-air, or air-to-ground. Covers: high quality air-to-air shots of vintage or veteran aircraft. 6x6cm minimum.
Text: Short news stories concerning preserved aircraft, new additions to museums and collections, etc. Not more than 300 words.
Overall freelance potential: Most contributions are from freelance sources, but specialised knowledge and skills are often necessary.
Editor's tips: The magazine is always in the market for sharp, good quality colour transparencies of preserved aircraft in the air.
Fees: Colour photographs: full page £80; centre spread £100; covers £90. B&W from £10 upwards.

AIR INTERNATIONAL
Key Publishing Ltd, PO Box 100, Stamford, Lincolnshire PE9 1XQ. Tel: 0780 55131.
Editor: Malcolm English.
Monthly general aviation magazine with emphasis on modern military aircraft and the civil aviation industry. Includes some historical topics. Aimed at both enthusiasts and industry professionals.
Illustrations: B&W and colour. Topical single pictures or picture stories on aviation subjects world-wide.
Text: Illustrated features on topics as above, from writers with in-depth knowledge of the subject. Length variable.
Overall freelance potential: Very good for suitable material.
Editor's tips: Remember that the magazine is read by professionals and is not just for enthusiasts.
Fees: Colour based on full-page rate of £75, pro rata downwards for smaller reproductions. Covers, up to £120 for full-bleed sole reproduction. B&W from £10. Text £50 per 1,000 words.

AIRFORCES MONTHLY
Key Publishing Ltd, PO Box 100, Stamford, Lincolnshire PE9 1XQ. Tel: 0780 55131.
Editor: David Oliver.
Monthly magazine concerned with modern military aircraft.
Illustrations: B&W and colour. Interesting up-to-date pictures of military aircraft from any country.
Text: Knowledgeable articles concerning current military aviation. No historical matter.
Overall freelance potential: Good for contributors with the necessary knowledge and access.
Fees: £25 minimum for colour; £10 minimum for black and white. Covers: £120. Text: by negotiation.

AVIATION NEWS
Alan W Hall (Publications) Ltd, Douglas House, Simpson Road, Bletchley, Milton Keynes MK1 1BA. Tel: 0908 37759.
Editor: Alan W. Hall.
Fortnightly magazine covering aviation in general, past and present. Aimed at both the industry and the enthusiast.
Illustrations: B&W and colour. Photographs of all types of aircraft, both civil and military. Captioned news pictures of particular interest, but no space exploration or aircraft engineering matters.
Text: News items about current aviation matters. Historical contributions concerning older aircraft.
Overall freelance potential: About 45 per cent is contributed by freelances.
Fees: On a rising scale according to size of reproduction or length of text.

BRITISH AIRWAYS NEWS
British Airways plc, PO Box 10, Heathrow Airport, Hounslow, Middlesex TW6 2JA. Tel: 081-759 5511.
Editor: Jane Johnston.
Weekly newspaper of British Airways.
Illustrations: B&W and colour. Captioned news pictures relating to aviation or allied fields, such as travel and tourism.
Text: Only by commission.
Overall freelance potential: Limited.
Fees: By negotiation.

COMMUTER WORLD
Shephard Press Ltd, 111 High Street, Burnham, Buckinghamshire SL1 7JZ. Tel: 0628 604311.
Editor: Ian Harbison.
Alternate-monthly publication dealing with civil air travel of the commuter and regional type. Aimed at industry, business, and users.
Illustrations: B&W and colour. Photographs of commuter, executive and air taxi aeroplanes. News pictures concerning the aeroplane industry and airline business in the commuter/regional field. Covers: colour photographs relating to commuter/regional airline operation.

Text: Knowledgeable articles on any aspect of the commuter airline business. 1,500–2,500 words.
Overall freelance potential: Good.
Fees: By negotiation.

FLIGHT INTERNATIONAL
Reed Business Publishing Ltd, Quadrant House, The Quadrant, Sutton, Surrey SM2 5AS. Tel: 081-652 3882.
Editor: Allan Winn.
Weekly aviation magazine with world-wide circulation, aimed at aerospace professionals in all sectors of the industry.
Illustrations: B&W and colour. Weekly requirement for news pictures of aviation-related events. Feature illustrations on all aspects of aerospace, from airliners to satellites. Covers: colour pictures of aircraft – civil and military, light and business. 35mm minimum, medium format preferred.
Text: Features by prior arrangement. Over 750 words.
Overall freelance potential: Approximately 10 per cent of news and 5 per cent of features comes from outside sources.
Editor's tips: News copy must be submitted on spec. Feature ideas must be submitted to the Deputy Editor, owing to the technical nature of the subject. Pictures should be as new as possible or have a news relevance.
Fees: B&W, £19.61; colour, £48.56 up to 30 sq.in., £56.79 to £92.10 30–60 sq. in.; £223.30 for cover. News reports, minimum £7.07 per 100 words; commissioned features by negotiation.

FLIGHT SAFETY BULLETIN
General Aviation Safety Committee, Church House, 33 Church Street, Henley-on-Thames, Oxfordshire RG9 1SE. Tel: 0491 574476.
Editor: John Ward.
Quarterly publication aimed at promoting the development of general aviation in the UK along safe lines through encouraging competence among GA pilots and operators, by publishing articles and information on flight safety matters.
Illustrations: B&W only. Anything consistent with the aims of the journal. Pictures which show photographic evidence of a particular story are welcomed.
Text: Features on safety and accident investigations.
Overall freelance potential: Limited.
Editor's tips: Contact the editor and discuss proposals before taking any action.
Fees: Depends on the relevance of the subject.

FLYER
Insider Publications Ltd, PO Box 3016, London SW13 0XF. Tel: 081-878 0270.
Editor: David Hewson.
Monthly magazine for private pilots.
Illustrations: Mostly colour. Attractive and striking photographs of light aircraft of the type commonly used by the private pilot. Details of material available should be sent first, rather than speculative submissions.
Text: News items and illustrated articles from those with proper knowledge of the subject.
Overall freelance potential: Limited – mainly written by established contributors.
Editor's tips: All contributors should have a genuine understanding of the flying scene.
Fees: By negotiation.

HELICOPTER WORLD
Shepherd Press Ltd, 111 High Street, Burnham, Buckinghamshire SL1 7JZ. Tel: 0628 604311.
Editor: Frank Colucci.
Quarterly publication concerning civil and commercial helicopters. Aimed at both users and the helicopter industry.

Illustrations: B&W and colour. Photographs of all types of civil helicopters and related matters. Covers: good colour pictures, which should be exclusive and of upright format.
Text: Knowledgeable articles on any aspect of civil helicopter applications, and manufacture. 1,500–2,500 words.
Overall freelance potential: Good.
Fees: By negotiation.

PILOT
Pilot Publishing Co. Ltd, The Clock House, 28 Old Town, Clapham, London SW4 0LB. Tel: 071-498 2506.
Editor: James Gilbert.
Monthly publication for the general aviation (i.e. business and private flying) pilot.
Illustrations: Mostly colour. Pictures on topics associated with this field of flying. Covers: high quality colour.
Text: Features, preferably illustrated, on general aviation. 2,000–4,000 words.
Overall freelance potential: Excellent. Virtually all of the editorial matter in the magazine is contributed by freelances.
Editor's tips: Read a copy of the magazine before submitting and study style, content, subject and coverage.
Fees: £150–£800 for features. B&W and colour pictures, £25.00 each; covers, £200.

POPULAR FLYING
Popular Flying Association. Editorial address: Norfolk House, 196 Old Bedford Road, Luton, Bedfordshire LU2 7HW. Tel: 0582 37023.
Editor: Peter Underhill.
Bi-monthly for home builders of small (one/two seater) aircraft.
Illustrations: B&W and colour. Pictures of vintage and home-built aircraft. Covers: colour air-to-air shots only, minimum size 6x6cm (pin-sharp 35mm may be considered).
Text: Features of any length on anything concerning home-built vintage and classic aircraft in the UK.
Overall freelance potential: Good.
Editor's tips: The editor is always interested to receive articles/photographs on homebuilt or classic and vintage recreational and sporting aircraft for consideration, provided they are accompanied by a s.a.e. if their return is required.
Fees: By negotiation.

Boating and Watersport

BOARDS
Yachting Press Ltd, 196 Eastern Esplanade, Southend-on-Sea, Essex SS1 3AB. Tel: 0702 582245.
Editor: Jeremy Evans.
Monthly magazine devoted to boardsailing and windsurfing.
Illustrations: B&W and colour. Good clear action shots of boardsailing or windsurfing; pictures of attractive girls in a boardsailing context; and any other visually striking material relating to the sport. Covers: good colour action shots are always needed.
Text: Articles and features on all aspects of the sport.
Overall freelance potential: Very good for high quality material.
Editor's tips: Action shots must be clean, clear and crisp.
Fees: By negotiation.

BOAT INTERNATIONAL
Edisea Ltd, Ward House, 5–7 Kingston Hill, Kingston-Upon-Thames, Surrey KT2 7PW. Tel: 081-547 2662.
Editor: Jason Holtom.
Monthly glossy magazine featuring the very top level of boating activity.
Illustrations: Almost exclusively colour. Top quality photographs of top quality boating, from world class yacht racing to luxury motor cruising. 35mm acceptable for action shots, but larger formats preferred for static subjects.
Text: Mostly staff produced or commissioned from top writers in the field.
Overall freelance potential: Excellent for the best in boating photography.
Editor's tips: Only the very best quality is of interest.
Fees: By negotiation.

BOATING BUSINESS
Rushton Marine Press, Woodside, Burnhams Road, Little Bookham, Nr Leatherhead, Surrey KT23 3BA. Tel: 0372 453316.
Editor: Lizzie Wright.
Montly magazine for the marine trade.
Illustrations: B&W only. News pictures relating to the marine trade, especially company and overseas news. Some scope for commissioned work.
Text: Features on marine trade topics; always consult the editor first.
Overall freelance potential: Limited.
Fees: Photographs from £10; text £80 per 1,000 words.

THE BOATMAN
Waterside Publications Ltd, PO Box 1992, Falmouth, Cornwall TR11 3RU. Tel: 0326 375757.
Editor: Jenny Bennett.
Alternate-monthly magazine covering traditional boats of all types, from small recreational craft to large working boats. Emphasis on boat-building design and craftsmanship.
Illustrations: Mainly colour. Pictures of especially interesting boats considered, but most photography required to illustrate specific construction and restoration projects.
Text: Well-illustrated articles on suitable topics. Always submit a synopsis and sample pictures in the first instance.
Overall freelance potential: Good for those who have knowledge of the subject.
Editor's tips: Study at least one issue before considering a submission.
Fees: According to material and use.

CANAL & RIVERBOAT
A. E. Morgan Publications Ltd, Stanley House, 9 West Street, Epsom, Surrey KT18 7RL. Tel: 0372 741411.
Editor: Norman Alborough.
Monthly publication aimed at inland waterway enthusiasts and canal holidaymakers.
Illustrations: B&W and colour. Pictures of all inland waterway subjects. Covers: colour pictures with an original approach.
Text: Illustrated articles on canals, rivers, boats and allied subjects.
Overall freelance potential: Good for material with an original approach.
Fees: By negotiation.

CLASSIC BOAT
Boating Publications Ltd, Link House, Dingwall Avenue, Croydon CR9 2TA. Tel: 081-686 2599.
Editor: Robin Gates.
Monthly magazine for the serious enthusiast interested in traditional or traditional-style boats. The emphasis is on wooden sailing boats from any period up to the 1960s, but also covers traditional wood-

en power boats, steam vessels, and modern reproductions of classic styles.

Illustrations: B&W and colour. Pictures to accompany features and articles. Single general interest pictures with 100 word captions giving full subject details.

Text: Well-illustrated articles covering particular types of boat, combining well-researched historical background with hard practical advice about restoration and maintenance. Some scope for humorous pieces, but no general cruising articles.

Overall freelance potential: Good for those with specialist knowledge.

Editor's tips: Always send a detailed synopsis in the first instance. Contributors notes available.

Fees: By negotiation.

INTERNATIONAL BOAT INDUSTRY

Boating Publications Ltd, Link House, Dingwall Avenue, Croydon CR9 2TA. Tel: 081-686 2599.

Editor: Robert Greenwood.

Alternate-monthly business publication dealing with the marine leisure industry worldwide.

Illustrations: B&W and colour. Pictures of boat building and moulding, chandlery shops, showrooms, and new boats and equipment. Also, marinas.

Text: News items about the boat industry are always of interest.

Overall freelance potential: Good for those in touch with the boat trade.

Editor's tips: This is strictly a trade magazine – simple pictures of cruising or racing are not required.

Fees: Linear scale – £100 per page down.

JET SKIER & P.W. MAGAZINE

Cambridge Style Ltd, 45 Grafton Street, Cambridge CB1 1DS. Tel: 0223 460490.

Editor: Chris Boiling.

Monthly magazine devoted to small, powered water craft and related sports activity. Features Jet Skis, Wetbikes and other personal watercraft.

Illustrations: B&W and colour. Spectacular action shots and pictures of unusual individual craft and uses. Events coverage usually by commission.

Text: Some scope for illustrated articles from those with good knowledge of the subject. Submit ideas only in the first instance.

Overall freelance potential: Good.

Fees: By negotiation.

MOTOR BOAT & YACHTING

Specialist Group, IPC Magazines, King's Reach Tower, Stamford Street, London SE1 9LS. Tel: 071-261 5333.

Editor: Alan Harper. **Art Editor**: Peter Allen.

Monthly magazine for owners and users of motor cruisers and motor sailers.

Illustrations: B&W and colour. Pictures of motor cruisers at sea, harbour scenes, workboats. Covers: colour pictures, mostly of motor boats at sea. Also good harbour scenes, showing exceptional composition and/or lighting.

Text: Features on interesting, unusual or historic motor boats; first-person motor boat cruising accounts; technical motor boating topics; inland waterways topics. 1,500–2,500 words.

Overall freelance potential: Around 60 per cent of features and 40 per cent of pictures are contributed.

Fees: Good; on a rising scale according to the size of reproduction or length of article. Covers, £150.

MOTORBOATS MONTHLY

Boating Publications Ltd, Link House, Dingwall Avenue, Croydon CR9 2TA. Tel: 081-686 2599.

Editor: Kim Hollamby.

Monthly magazine for all motorboating enthusiasts, but mainly aimed at owners of boats of up to 60 feet. Covers all aspects, from top level international powerboat racing to inland waterway cruising.

Illustrations: Colour. News pictures, motor boat action, and shots of cruising locations, both in UK and overseas.
Text: Illustrated articles on any motorboat-related topic, UK and worldwide.
Overall freelance potential: Good.
Fees: On a rising scale according to size of reproduction or length of text.

PERSONAL WATER CRAFT NEWS

Seven Kings Publications Ltd, Garden Hall House, Wellesley Road, Sutton, Surrey SM2 5UF. Tel: 081-661 1626.
Editor: Neil Asten.
Alternate-monthly magazine covering all aspects of personal water craft, aimed at both enthusiasts and those in the trade. Includes trade news as well as competitive and leisure use.
Illustrations: Mainly colour. Good photographs of personal water craft in use, plus coverage of competitions and other events. Covers: especially good action shots; must be upright compositions with space at top for magazine's logo.
Text: Articles on all aspects of the personal water craft scene, but submit 100-word synopsis in the first instance.
Overall freelance potential: Good for action coverage.
Editor's tips: Exclusive material is preferred.
Fees: Pictures according to use. Text around £100 per 1,000 words.

PRACTICAL BOAT OWNER

IPC Magazines Ltd, Westover House, West Quay Road, Poole, Dorset BH15 1JG. Tel: 0202 680593.
Editor: George Taylor.
Monthly magazine for yachtsmen, sail and power.
Illustrations: B&W and colour. Pictures of pleasure craft, sail and power, and their equipment. Shots relating to their use, including sea marks such as light houses, harbour, etc. No "mood" pictures. Covers: colour pictures of pleasure boating subjects; happy with strong colours.
Text: Features and associated illustrations must be of real use to the people who own boats. Subjects can cover any boating facet on which reader might take action, from raising the money to buying a boat, through insurance to navigation, seamanship, care and maintenance etc. No narrative yarns please.
Overall freelance potential: About 60 per cent bought from contributors.
Fees: Good; on a rising scale according to size of reproduction or length of feature.

RYA NEWS

Royal Yachting Association, RYA House, Romsey Road, Eastleigh, Hampshire SO5 4YA. Tel: 0703 629962.
Editor: Carol Baker.
Quarterly publication for all personal members of the RYA, affiliated clubs and class associations.
Illustrations: B&W and colour. Pictures of boats, yachting events and personalities, used either in their own right or as illustrations for reports and articles. Covers: seasonal/topical colour shots of yachting subjects.
Text: Reports and articles on yachting.
Overall freelance potential: Moderate.
Fees: By arrangement.

REGATTA

Amateur Rowing Association, 6 Lower Mall, London W6 9DJ. Tel: 081-748 3632.
Editor: Christopher Dodd.
Ten editions annually. Covers rowing and sculling, competitive, recreational and technical.
Illustrations: B&W and colour. Action pictures of rowing, and rowing in scenic settings.
Text: Short, illustrated articles on all aspects of rowing. Particular emphasis on competitive rowing

and technical topics such as coaching, training and boat-building.
Overall freelance potential: Good.
Fees: Variable, around £25 for a short feature, £30 for cover picture.

SPORTS BOAT AND WATERSKI INTERNATIONAL

JPI Ltd, Brinkworth House, Brinkworth, Chippenham, Wiltshire SN15 5DF. Tel: 0666 510811.
Editor: Catherine Gunn-Taylor.
Published monthly during March–October; alternate-monthly from November–February. Aimed at all levels of waterskier (beginner, intermediate, advanced) and covering sportsboats from 14–60ft.
Illustrations: B&W and colour. Top quality action shots of small sports boats and the large Mediterranean range up to 60ft. Also stylish pictures that show boats as glamorous and exciting. All types of waterskiing – coverage of competitions, tournaments and events; news and personality pictures. Commissions may be available to illustrate major features. Covers: colour action shots with plenty of impact.
Text: Illustrated articles on all aspects of sports boats and waterskiing will always be considered. 500–3,000 words.
Overall freelance potential: Excellent.
Fees: By negotiation.

SURF MAGAZINE

Top Floor, DRG Building, Longmoor Lane, Breaston, Derbyshire DE7 3BQ. Tel: 0332 874731.
Editor: Mark Griffiths.
Quarterly surfing magazine.
Illustrations: B&W and colour. Anything relevant to surfing and the ocean environment, including events coverage.
Text: General features on topical surf-related subjects.
Overall freelance potential: Good for those who can produce good action material.
Fees: B&W 10; colour around £25.

WATERSKI ILLUSTRATED

Cambridge Style Ltd, 45 Grafton Street, Cambridge CB1 1DS. Tel: 0223 460490.
Editor: Chris Boiling.
Heavily-illustrated monthly for the recreational waterskier. Features kneeboards, wakeboards, hot-dogging and lots of action photography.
Illustrations: B&W and colour. Dramatic action shots, "tip" sequences and anyone having fun behind a boat.
Text: Illustrated articles always of interest, but submit ideas only in the first instance.
Overall freelance potential: Very good.
Fees: By negotiation.

WATERWAYS WORLD

Waterway Productions Ltd, Kottingham House, Dale Street, Burton-on-Trent DE14 3TD. Tel: 0283 64290.
Editor: Hugh Potter.
Monthly magazine that covers all aspects of canal and river navigations (not lakes) in Britain and abroad. Aimed at inland waterway enthusiasts and holiday boaters.
Illustrations: B&W and colour inside. Pictures of inland waterway subjects, e.g. interesting buildings; locks, preferably with boating activity if on a navigable waterway; canal scenes. No close-ups or artistic shots. Covers: colour pictures of canal or river scenes with boating activity prominently in the foreground; 6x6cm minimum.
Text: Features on inland waterways, 500–2,000 words. Send s.a.e. for contributors' guide.
Overall freelance potential: Around 20 per cent contributed.
Fees: B&W £10 minimum; colour £12 minimum; Cover, £33.

WINDSURF MAGAZINE
Arcwind Ltd, The Blue Barn, Tew Lane, Wootton, Woodstock, Oxon OX7 1HA. Tel: 0993 811181.
Editor: Mark Kasprowicz.
Published ten times a year. Aimed at the enthusiast and covering all aspects of windsurfing.
Illustrations: B&W and colour. Single pictures and photo sequences of windsurfing action. Top quality shots always considered on spec.
Text: Illustrated articles on any aspect of windsurfing.
Overall freelance potential: Excellent.
Fees: £5–£15 for B&W reproductions; up to £35 for full-page colour; £60 for centre-spread; £60 for covers.

YACHTING MONTHLY
IPC Magazines Ltd, Room 2315, King's Reach Tower, Stamford Street, London SE1 9LS. Tel: 071-261 6040.
Editor: Geoff Pack.
Monthly magazine for cruising yachtsmen.
Illustrations: Colour only. News pictures for immediate use; general cruising and location pictures for stock; pictures illustrating seamanship, navigation and technical subjects. Covers: top quality colour shots showing active cruising; people working boats; cruising boats at sea; yachts in harbour. Original transparencies used almost exclusively.
Text: Articles relevant to cruising yachtsmen, and short accounts of cruising experiences. 1,000–2,250 words.
Overall freelance potential: Around 40 per cent comes from outside contributors.
Fees: Dependent upon size of reproduction or length of feature. Normally around £40–£95 for colour; £150 for covers. Text from £100 per 1,000 words.

YACHTING WORLD
IPC Magazines Ltd, King's Reach Tower, Stamford Street, London SE1 9LS. Tel: 071-261 6800.
Editor: Andrew Bray. **Art Editor**: Robert Owen.
Monthly magazine for informed yachtsmen, experienced and with their own boats.
Illustrations: Colour. Pictures of general yachting techniques or types of boat; pictures of events and occasions. Covers: colour pictures of yachts – on board, at sea or general harbour pictures. Atmosphere shots. No dinghies.
Text: Informative or narrative yachting articles; technical yachting features; short humorous articles; and news. 1,000–1,500 words and 2,000–2,500 words.
Overall freelance potential: Around 30 per cent comes from freelances.
Editor's tips: Articles should be accompanied by colour illustrations and should not exceed noted lengths. Send for writers guidelines.
Fees: Text, up to: £100 per 1,000 words; covers, up to: £250; inside pictures on a scale according to size.

YACHTS AND YACHTING
Yachting Press Ltd, 196 Eastern Esplanade, Southend-on-Sea, Essex SS1 3AB. Tel: 0702 582245.
Editor: Frazer Clark.
Fortnightly publication covering all aspects of racing, including dinghies and offshore racers.
Illustrations: B&W and colour. Pictures of racing dinghies, yachts and general sailing scenes. Covers: colour action shots.
Text: Features on all aspects of the sailing scenes. 1,000–2,000 words.
Overall freelance potential: Quite good.
Fees: Negotiable.

Building and Engineering

ARCHITECTURE TODAY
Architecture Today plc, 33 Newman Street, London W1P 3PD. Tel: 071-436 6916.
Editors: Ian Latham and Dr Mark Swenarton.
Independent monthly for the architecture profession.
Illustrations: B&W and colour. Most photography is commissioned, but interesting pictures of current architectural projects are always of interest on spec.
Text: Illustrated articles of genuine interest to a professional readership; submit ideas only first. 800–2,000 words.
Overall freelance potential: Reasonable scope for specialists.
Editor's tips: Potential contributors must contact the editors before submitting anything.
Fees: £100 per 1,000 words; photography by arrangement.

BATHROOMS AND BEDROOMS: THE MAGAZINE
Maclean Hunter Ltd, Maclean Hunter House, Chalk Lane, Cockfosters Road, Barnet, Hertfordshire EN4 0BU. Tel: 081-975 9759.
Editor: Richard Moss.
Monthly trade journal for bathroom, bedroom and kitchen specialist retailers, builders' merchants, distributors, manufacturers, importers, installers, builders, developers, architects, local authorities, etc.
Illustrations: B&W and colour. Pictures of bathroom and kitchen units, bedroom furniture and fittings, built-in appliances, sinks, taps, worktops, tiles, floor and wall coverings, accessories, ceilings, blinds, etc.
Text: Only after prior consultation. Up to 1,000 words usually.
Overall freelance potential: Fairly good for the contributor with a specialised knowledge of the subject.
Fees: Good; on a rising scale according to the size of reproduction or length of article.

BUILD IT
Build It Publications Ltd, 37 High Street, Kingston-upon-Thames, Surrey KT1 1LQ. Tel: 081-549 2166.
Editor: Rosalind Renshaw.
Monthly magazine devoted to the self-build market, those people who build or have built a one-off home.
Illustrations: Colour only. Commissions available to experienced photographers to cover sites, construction, buildings and interiors. Some interest in stock photographs of housing and interior decoration subjects.
Text: Authoritative features on building, landscaping and interior design, plus specialised articles on finance, legal issues, weatherproofing, etc. Also well-illustrated celebrity features concerning well-known people who have built their own home.
Overall freelance potential: Excellent for the experienced contributor in the architecture and interiors field.
Fees: £140 per 1,000 words for text; photographs by negotiation.

BUILDING SERVICES
Building Services Publications Ltd, Builder House, 1 Millharbour, London E14 9RA. Tel: 071-537 2222.
Editor: Roderic Bunn. **Art Editor**: Alison Buckland.
Monthly publication for engineers and senior management involved with installing heating, air conditioning, ventilation, lighting, lifts, hot and cold water systems etc. into buildings.

Illustrations: B&W and colour. Good quality pictures of building services. Pictures used for caption stories and for stock. Covers: colour, but usually commissioned.
Text: Ideas for articles on the above subjects. 2,500 words maximum.
Overall freelance potential: Good, since very few pictures of this subject are offered.
Editor's tips: Examples of building photographs should be sent to the art editor.
Fees: By negotiation.

BUILDING SERVICES AND ENVIRONMENTAL ENGINEER
Batiste Publications Ltd, Pembroke House, Campsbourne Road, London N8 7PE. Tel: 081-340 3291.
Editor: Ken Sharpe.
Monthly publication for the building services industry, particularly heating, ventilating and air conditioning.
Illustrations: Colour only. Pictures on building services themes. Covers: colour pictures of similar subjects; 6x6cm minimum.
Text: Features of interest to the readership detailed above. 1,000–1,500 words.
Overall freelance potential: Limited.
Fees: Text, around £90 per 1,000 words; pictures by negotiation.

DESIGN ENGINEERING
Morgan-Grampian (Publishers) Ltd, 30 Calderwood Street, Woolwich, London SE18 6QH. Tel: 081-316 3410.
Editor: David Wilson.
Monthly publication aimed at engineering designers and design management. Contains case histories, background features and data, surveys, products and news stories.
Illustrations: Colour only. Usually only to accompany specific features and news stories. Covers: colour pictures associated with editorial inside.
Text: Features on subjects such as mechanical and electrical engineering, CAD/CAM, fluid power, electronics, materials, etc. Only from experts in their fields. 500–4,000 words.
Overall freelance potential: Mainly for specialists.
Editor's tips: Send synopsis first.
Fees: Covers, up to £200; text and pictures inside by negotiation.

ENERGY IN BUILDINGS & INDUSTRY
Industrial Trade Journals Ltd, Stakes House, Quebec Square, Westerham, Kent TN16 1TD. Tel: 0959 564212.
Editor: Mark Thrower.
Monthly magazine concerned with the use and conservation of energy in large buildings and the industrial environment. Aimed at architects, energy managers, building services engineers and energy consultants.
Illustrations: Mainly B&W. Pictures of relevant and interesting installations.
Text: Some scope for writer/photographers who have good knowledge of the energy business.
Overall freelance potential: Very limited unless contributors have connections within the field.
Fees: £15–£20 per picture; £70 per 1,000 words for text.

THE ENGINEER
Morgan Grampian Ltd, 30 Calderwood Street, Woolwich, London SE18 6QH. Tel: 081-855 7777.
Editor: Chris Barrie.
Magazine for engineering management, publishing 34 isues per year.
Illustrations: B&W and colour. Pictures showing new technology in action – must have a news angle. Covers: colour news pictures relating to the engineering industry.
Text: News of manufacturing industries and personnel, plus articles on technology trends. Up to 800 words.

Overall freelance potential: Scope only for freelances in close contact with engineering matters.
Fees: By agreement.

ENGINEERING

The Design Council, 28 Haymarket, London SW1Y 4SU. Tel: 071-839 8000.
Editor: Andy Pye.
Monthly magazine dealing with all areas of manufacturing engineering from a design point of view.
Illustrations: B&W and colour. Photographs depicting all aspects of design in industrial engineering, from aerospace and computers to energy management and waste disposal. Much from manufacturers but some by commission. Covers: mostly graphic illustration, but with some "artistic" photography.
Text: Short illustrated news items up to major design features. 250–2,000 words.
Overall freelance potential: Good for commissioned work.
Fees: £100 per published page for text. Covers £300–£400. Other commissioned photography around £120 per day.

H&V NEWS

EMAP Maclaren Ltd, PO Box 109, Maclaren House, Scarbrook Road, Croydon CR9 1QH. Tel: 081-688 7788.
Editor: Jack McDavid.
Weekly publication to all those who purchase or specify in organisations connected with heating, ventilating and air conditioning equipment.
Illustrations: B&W only inside. Action pictures of installations and equipment in use, preferably with human interest. Covers: colour pictures of relevant subjects.
Text: News stories, installation stories regarding heating, ventilating and air conditioning equipment, stories on companies and people. 200–300 words. Longer features by negotiation.
Overall freelance potential: Good scope for newsworthy material.
Editor's tips: The more current the information supplied, the better its chance of success.
Fees: £12 per 100 words; pictures by negotiation.

HOUSE BUILDER

House Builder Publications Ltd, 82 New Cavendish Street, London W1M 8AD. Tel: 071-580 5588.
Editor: Phillip Cooke.
Monthly journal of the House Builders Federation. Aimed at key decision makers, managers, technical staff, marketing executives, architects and local authorities.
Illustrations: B&W and colour. Some scope for housebuilding coverage, but only by prior consultation with the editor.
Text: Features on marketing, land and planning, government liaison, finance, materials, supplies, etc. All to be discussed before submission. 1,000 words.
Overall freelance potential: Around 50 per cent comes from freelances.
Editor's tips: Authoritative articles and news stories only. No PR "puffs".
Fees: £130 per 1,000 words; pictures by agreement.

MARINE ENGINEERS REVIEW

Marine Management (Holdings), Institute of Marine Engineers, 76 Mark Lane, London EC3R 7JN. Tel: 071-481 8493.
Editor: John Butchers.
Monthly publication for marine engineers.
Illustrations: B&W and colour. Showing ships and marine machinery.
Text: Articles on shipping and marine engineering, including naval and offshore topics. Up to 2,000 words.
Overall freelance potential: Good, but enquire before submitting.
Fees: £80 per 1,000 words. Pictures by negotiation.

NEW CIVIL ENGINEER
Thomas Telford Ltd, Telford House, 1 Heron Quay, London E14 4JD. Tel: 071-987 6999.
Editor: Mike Winney.
Weekly news magazine for professional civil engineers.
Illustrations: B&W and colour. Up-to-date pictures depicting any civil engineering project. Must be well captioned and newsworthy.
Text: By commission only.
Overall freelance potential: Limited.
Fees: On a rising scale according to size of reproduction or length of text.

PROCESS ENGINEERING
Morgan Grampian (Process Press) Ltd, 30 Calderwood Street, Woolwich, London SE18 6QH. Tel: 081-855 7777.
Editor: Mike Spear.
Monthly publication for process engineers. Read by chemical plant contractors, senior engineers and management employed in the chemical and process industries responsible for the design, construction, operation and maintenance of process plant, control systems and equipment.
Illustrations: B&W and colour. Pictures of process engineering applications. Covers: colour pictures of a similar subject; 6x6cm minimum.
Text: Features on process engineering and management articles. Up to 2,000 words.
Overall freelance potential: Small at present.
Editor's tips: Telephone if more background is required.
Fees: By agreement.

PROFESSIONAL ENGINEERING
Mechanical Engineering Publications Ltd, PO Box 24, Northgate Avenue, Bury St Edmunds, Suffolk IP32 6BW. Tel: 0284 763277.
Editor: Keld Fenwick.
Monthly publication for members of the Institution of Mechanical Engineers and decision-makers in industry.
Illustrations: B&W and colour. Pictures of general and specific mechanical engineering management subjects, preferably showing action; new equipment, applications, etc. Covers: would consider colour pictures of above subjects.
Text: Features with a general engineering bias at a fairly high management level, e.g. management techniques, new equipment, processes, materials applications, etc. 1,500 words maximum.
Overall freelance potential: A considerable amount of the magazine is freelance-contributed.
Fees: Not less than around £175 per 1,000 words published; pictures by agreement.

PROFESSIONAL LANDSCAPER AND GROUNDSMAN
Gladeside-Ardent Ltd, PO Box 45, Dorking, Surrey RH5 5YZ. Tel: 0306 712712.
Editor: Tony Ellis.
Bi-monthly magazine for landscapers, contractors, foresters, architects and environmental designers.
Illustrations: B&W and colour. Some scope for covers, only of subjects likely to be of interest to the magazine's professional readership.
Text: Well-illustrated articles dealing with technical or practical landscaping matters, forestry, and general environmental and conservation issues.
Overall freelance potential: Limited.
Fees: By negotiation.

RIBA JOURNAL
The Builder Group, Builder House, 1 Millharbour, London E14 9RA. Tel: 071-537 2222.
Editor: John Welsh.
Monthly magazine of the Royal Institute of British Architects. Covers general aspects of architectural

practice as well as criticisms of particular buildings; profiles and interviews.
Illustrations: B&W and colour. Pictures of building, old, new and refurbished. Covers: colour pictures connected with main feature inside.
Text: Features on architectural subjects and criticisms of buildings.
Overall freelance potential: Fair.
Fees: By arrangement.

Business

ACCOUNTANCY AGE
VNU Business Publications, 32–34 Broadwick Street, London W1A 2HG. Tel: 071-439 4242.
Editor: Robert Outram.
Weekly publication for qualified accountants.
Illustrations: B&W and colour. All commissioned but new photographers are always welcome.
Text: News and features coverage for accountants. Synopsis preferred in first instance. 1,200 words.
Overall freelance potential: Fairly good for commissioned photography. About 50 per cent of the features come from freelances.
Editor's tips: To gain acceptance, articles must contribute something which cannot be provided by the in-house staff.
Fees: By agreement.

AFRICA ECONOMIC DIGEST
Aare Abiola House, 26–32 Whistler Street, Highbury, London N5 1NH. Tel: 071-359 5335.
Editor: Eddie Momoh.
Fortnightly review of African business and general economic developments. Aimed at senior executives of banks, trading and manufacturing companies etc.
Illustrations: B&W only inside. Pictures of African economic, political and business life, including major development projects, agriculture, transport, ports, shipping, buildings, personalities and economic "events". Covers: colour pictures of similar subjects, plus more general African shots. No sunsets, lions or tribal dancers.
Text: Commissioned feature on above subjects considered. Contact editor first. Up to 1,000 words.
Overall freelance potential: A lot of material comes from AED correspondents, but freelance approaches welcome.
Fees: Negotiable.

THE AUTHOR
The Society of Authors, 84 Drayton Gardens, London SW10 9SB. Tel: 071-373 6642.
Editor: Derek Parker.
Quarterly publication dealing with the business of authorship, e.g. financial, contractual, social and historical side of writing.
Illustrations: B&W only. Only occasional portraits of authors.
Text: Features on the sides of authorship detailed above. Up to 1,200 words.
Overall freelance potential: About 50 per cent of the editorial is contributed.
Fees: By arrangement.

BARCLAYS NEWS
Barclays Bank plc, Johnson Smirke Building, 4 Royal Mint Court, London EC3N 4HJ. Tel: 071-626 1567 Ext. 4146.
Editor: Kevin O'Neill.
Bi-monthly magazine for Barclays Group staff worldwide.
Illustrations: Colour. Pictures that relate to the bank, its staff and customers. Also the bank's

history, travel, motoring.
Text: Features with a specific interest to Barclays Bank, its customers and staff. 300–500 words.
Overall freelance potential: The magazine has its own team of journalists, but they are always on the lookout for items of interest throughout the country that might not have come to their attention.
Editor's tips: Check first and a direct indication of interest will be given.
Fees: Negotiable.

CA MAGAZINE

Institute of Chartered Accountants of Scotland, 27 Queen Street, Edinburgh EH2 1LA. Tel: 031-225 5673.
Editor: Neil Fitzgerald. **Art Editor**: Jane Greig.
Scottish financial and business magazine incorporating monthly journal of The Institute of Chartered Accountants in Scotland.
Illustrations: B&W and colour. Pictures of industrial scenes, building developments, senior figures who are currently in the financial news.
Text: Articles on accounting and auditing, company law, finance, taxation, management topics, company/personal profiles, the financial and business & accounting scene in the UK and overseas countries, investment, computer science, etc. Length: 1,200–3,000 words.
Overall freelance potential: Fair for business journalists.
Fees: By arrangement.

COMMERCE MAGAZINE

Station House, Station Road, Newport Pagnell, Milton Keynes MK16 0AG. Tel: 0908 614477.
Group Editor: Bryan Jones.
Monthly regional business magazines aimed at "decision makers". Sold mainly by direct mail and some subscription. Editions for North Home Counties, M4/M40 Corridor, West Midlands, East Midlands, East Anglia, South West and South Wales, Yorkshire and Humberside, Central South.
Illustrations: Mainly B&W. Business and commerce subjects; faces well-known nationally and locally in the area – politicians, industrial leaders, etc. Covers: colour of similar subjects.
Text: Features on business and commerce subjects. Around 800 words. An advance features list is always available.
Overall freelance potential: Around 10 per cent comes from outside freelances.
Editor's tips: Always contact the magazine and talk over ideas before submission.
Fees: Negotiable.

COMPUTER WEEKLY

Reed Business Publishing Ltd, Quadrant House, The Quadrant, Sutton, Surrey SM2 5AS. Tel: 081-652 3122.
Editor: John Lamb.
News magazine aimed at professional computer staff and managers.
Illustrations: B&W and colour. News pictures, plus general shots of people involved in computer usage situations for general illustration purposes.
Text: Illustrated features on professional and business applications and issues in information technology. Length around 1,200 words.
Overall freelance potential: Main scope is for specialists.
Fees: By negotiation.

DIRECTOR

The Director Publications Ltd, Mountbarrow House, Elizabeth Street, London SW1W 9RB. Tel: 071-730 6060.
Editor: Stuart Rock. **Art Director**: Steve Devane.
Monthly journal for members of the Institute of Directors.
Illustrations: B&W and colour. Pictures showing overseas business areas (New York, Singapore,

Tokyo, etc.) for illustration of area surveys. Top quality portraits of chairmen or major business personalities. Covers: colour portraits of personalities, or top quality business/industry subjects.
Text: Interviews; management advice; company profiles; business controversies; EC affairs.
Overall freelance potential: Good.
Fees: By negotiation.

EXPORT TIMES
I.G.A. Ltd, 4 New Bridge Street, London EC4V 6AA. Tel: 071-583 0077.
Editor: Tony Bush.
Monthly newspaper covering all aspects of overseas marketing for British exporters.
Illustrations: B&W and colour. Captioned news pictures covering foreign trade, overseas development, and everyday life and work overseas. Areas of most interest: Western and Eastern Europe; USA; Middle and Far East.
Text: News stories or short features about exporting.
Overall freelance potential: Limited; most material comes from regular contributors.
Editor's tips: Always best to telephone first. If going on a trip abroad, make contact beforehand not upon your return.
Fees: £70 per 1,000 words; pictures according to size of reproduction.

MEED (MIDDLE EAST ECONOMIC DIGEST)
EMAP Business Information Ltd, 21 John Street, London WC1N 2BP. Tel: 071-404 5513
Editor: Edmund O'Sullivan.
Weekly business journal covering the affairs of Middle Eastern countries.
Illustrations: Mainly B&W. Pictures of current major construction projects in the Middle East and stock shots of important personalities (politicians, leading businessmen) in the region. Recent general views of particular locations occasionally used. Covers: colour pictures of contemporary Middle East subjects, preferably with an obvious business flavour.
Text: Specialist articles on relevant business matters.
Overall freelance potential: Limited.
Fees: On a rising scale according to size of reproduction or length of text.

MANAGEMENT ACCOUNTING
Chartered Institute of Management Accountants, 63 Portland Place, London W1N 4AB. Tel: 071-637 2311.
Editor: John Hillary.
Monthly publication for members and students of the Institute.
Illustrations: B&W and colour. Small market for top quality general industrial/commercial subjects with a financial bias. Covers: colour pictures of industrial and commercial subjects, computers, plus some "abstracts".
Text: Occasional freelance market for articles on management/accountancy subjects.
Overall freelance potential: Limited.
Fees: Covers, up to £300; inside pictures by agreement.

MARKETING
Haymarket Business Publications Ltd, 30 Lancaster Gate, London W2 3LP. Tel: 071-413 4150.
Editor: Mike Hewitt.
Weekly publication for senior marketing management.
Illustrations: Mainly B&W. Commissioned photography of people and subjects relating to marketing.
Text: News and features with a marketing angle and objective case histories.
Overall freelance potential: All pictures are freelance contributed; around 20 per cent of the text comes from freelances.
Editor's tips: A synopsis in the first instance is very important.
Fees: Variable.

POST MAGAZINE: THE INSURANCE WEEKLY
Buckley Press Ltd, 58 Fleet Street (entrance 3 Pleydell Street), London EC4Y 1JU. Tel: 071-583 0986.
Editor: Alyson Rudd.
Weekly publication covering insurance at home and abroad.
Illustrations: B&W and colour. Pictures of motoring, traffic, houses, offices, building sites, construction projects, damage (including fire and motoring accidents), shipwrecks or aviation losses, aircraft, etc.
Text: News and features on insurance, including life assurance, general insurance, reinsurance, pensions, financial services, savings, unit trusts, investment, offices and personnel areas.
Overall freelance potential: Most news and features are contributed by freelances.
Fees: By negotiation.

PROMOTIONS & INCENTIVES
Haymarket Marketing Publications Ltd, 22 Lancaster Gate, London W2 3LP. Tel: 071-413 4366/4128.
Editor: Caroline Marshall.
Monthly publication for brand managers, SP managers, incentive managers etc. Concerned with incentive ideas for staff motivation and sales promotion campaigns, aids and general marketing themes.
Illustrations: B&W and colour. Pictures limited to the marketing and/or promotions profession. Covers: highly creative colour pictures, usually linked to the main feature inside.
Text: Authoritatively written articles on technical aspects of the marketing and/or promotions profession. 1,500–2,000 words.
Overall freelance potential: Up to 30 per cent bought from freelances.
Editor's tips: Contact the magazine first.
Fees: By negotiation, depending on ability and subject matter.

Camping & Caravanning

CAMPING MAGAZINE
Link House Magazines Ltd, Link House, Dingwall Avenue, Croydon CR9 2DA. Tel: 081-686 2599.
Editor: David Roberts.
Monthly magazine covering all aspects of camping. Emphasises the range of activities that camping makes available.
Illustrations: B&W and colour. Photographs showing campers engaged in various activities; do not have to include a tent but must have an "outdoor" feel. Possible scope for atmospheric landscape shots. Covers: usually tied to a feature inside, but strong images of camping activities and destinations will be considered.
Text: Picture-led features that show camping as "a means to an end" and illustrate the range of people and lifestyles that camping embraces. News stories also welcome.
Overall freelance potential: Excellent.
Editor's tips: Pictures should not be dominated by tents and camping clutter. Call first and have a chat about your ideas.
Fees: Colour, from £20; B&W, from £10. Text £90 per 1,000 words.

CAMPING AND CARAVANNING
The Camping and Caravanning Club, Greenfields House, Westwood Way, Coventry CV4 8JH. Tel: 0203 694995.
Editor: Peter Frost.
Monthly magazine concerning camping and caravanning holidays in Britain.
Illustrations: Mainly colour. Usually only required in conjunction with feature articles.
Text: Illustrated features on camping and caravanning holidays, around 1,200 words. Contact the edi-

tor with ideas only in the first instance.
Overall freelance potential: Modest.
Fees: By agreement.

CARAVAN BUSINESS
A. E. Morgan Publications Ltd, Stanley House, 9 West Street, Epsom, Surrey KT18 7RL. Tel: 0372 741411.
Editor: David Ritchie.
Monthly publication for manufacturers, traders, suppliers and park operators in the caravan industry.
Illustrations: B&W and colour. Pictures of new caravan park developments, new models, new dealer depots, etc. Covers: occasional colour shot may be used.
Text: Company profiles on park owners and their businesses, traders and manufacturers. 900–1,200 words.
Overall freelance potential: Up to 30 per cent of the content comes from freelance contributors.
Fees: By agreement.

CARAVAN PLUS
Future Publishing Ltd, Beauford Court, 30 Monmouth Street, Bath BA1 2BW. Tel: 0225 442244.
Editor: Paul Elmer. **Art Editor**: Jane Toft.
Monthly general caravanning magazine.
Illustrations: Mainly colour. Scope only for photographers with experience of caravan photography.
Text: Approaches from experienced writers will be considered.
Overall freelance potential: Limited; a band of regular contributors produces most of the coverage.
Fees: By negotiation.

MOTOR CARAVAN WORLD
Stone Leisure Group Ltd, Andrew House, 2A Granville Road, Sidcup, Kent DA14 4BN. Tel: 081-302 6150/6069 and 081-300 2316.
Editor: Chris Burlace.
Monthly magazine for motor caravan owners and would-be owners. Details of travel, sites, road tests, etc.
Illustrations: B&W only. Photographs related to above subjects.
Text: Features on travel and motor caravanning. 750–1,500 words with pix.
Overall freelance potential: Good.
Editor's tips: Preference for copy that requires a minimum of subbing or rewriting.
Fees: £15–£20 for photographs; text negotiable.

PRACTICAL CARAVAN
Haymarket Publishing Ltd, 38–42 Hampton Road, Teddington, Middlesex TW11 0JE. Tel: 081-943 5021.
Editor: Jacki Buist. **Art Editor**: Laurence Gerrard.
Monthly magazine aimed at touring caravanners with the emphasis on the practical aspects of touring, sites and places.
Illustrations: Colour. General distinctive travel pictures, landscapes and sights from all areas of the UK, France, Italy, Spain and Germany. Must be exceptional quality as they are often used across a spread. Caravan park pics only useful with details included.
Text: Illustrated articles about the practical aspects of touring Britain or Europe, and personal caravanning experiences.
Overall freelance potential: Fair.
Fees: Variable.

Children & Teenage

BIG!
EMAP Metro Publications Ltd, 5th Floor, Mappin House, 4 Winsley Street, London W1N 7AR. Tel: 071-436 1515.
Editor: Dawn Bebe.
Fortnightly magazine for 8–16 year olds, concentrating on celebrities from pop music, film and TV.
Illustrations: All colour. Exclusive news pictures and pin-up shots of suitable current stars, but little accepted on spec.
Text: Little scope.
Overall freelance potential: Only for those closely involved in this scene.
Fees: By negotiation.

THE BROWNIE
Girl Guides Association, 17–19 Buckingham Palace Road, London SW1W 0PT. Tel: 071-834 6242.
Editor: Marion Thompson.
Monthly publication for Brownies in the 7–10 age group.
Illustrations: B&W and colour. Action pictures featuring Brownie subjects.
Text: Articles with Brownie themes. 500–800 words.
Overall freelance potential: Around 10 per cent is contributed.
Fees: By arrangement; tend to be on the low side.

CHECK IT OUT!
Consumers' Association, 2 Marylebone Road, London NW1 4DF. Tel: 071-486 5544.
Editor: Sue Harvey. **Art Editor**: Derick Balment.
Monthly consumer research magazine for the 10–15 age group.
Illustrations: Colour only. Commissions available to cover a varied range of subjects. Photographers who feel they could produce suitable material should make an appointment to show their portfolio. Some scope for stock and celebrity shots – send lists of relevant material available.
Text: No scope.
Overall freelance potential: Quite good for commissioned work.
Editor's tips: Portfolios should show good variation, lots of creativity and a sense of style.
Fees: £400 per day for studio work; £100–£300 for location jobs.

GUIDE PATROL
Girl Guides Association, 17–19 Buckingham Palace Road, London SW1W 0PT. Tel: 071-834 6242.
Editor: Mary Richardson.
Monthly publication on Guiding activities for girls in the 10–14 age group.
Illustrations: B&W and colour. Action pictures showing Guiding subjects. Cover: Colour pictures showing Guiding activities.
Text: Stories with Guiding themes – 1,000 words. Practical articles telling guides how to do activities like craftwork and sport – 800 words.
Overall freelance potential: Around 10 per cent comes from freelances.
Fees: By arrangement; tend to be on the low side. £40 per 1,000 words.

GUIDING
Girl Guides Association, 17–19 Buckingham Palace Road, London SW1W 0PT. Tel: 071-834 6242.
Editor: Nora Warner.
Illustrations: B&W and colour. Action pictures on Guiding subjects. Cover: Colour transparencies of Rainbows, Brownies, Guides, Rangers or Young Leaders in action.
Text: Articles allied to work with young people in various fields. 750–1,500 words.

Overall freelance potential: Suitable material from freelances welcome.
Fees: By arrangement but governed by the Association's charitable status.

JUST SEVENTEEN
EMAP Womens Group, 20 Orange Street, London WC2H 7ED. Tel: 071-957 8383.
Editor: Toni Rogers. **Picture Editor**: Sue Miles.
Weekly magazine for teenage girls in the 12–18 age group.
Illustrations: B&W and colour. Almost entirely by commission to accompany features.
Text: Articles and features on topics of interest to fashion-conscious teenage girls, always by commission. Features on current pop music stars.
Overall freelance potential: Restricted to the experienced contributor to this field.
Fees: £110 per 1,000 words for text. Commissions £300 per day.

LOOK-IN
Southbank Group, King's Reach Tower, Stamford Street, London SE1 9LS. Tel: 071-261 6385.
Editor: Frank Hopkinson. **Picture Editor**: John Bickerton.
Weekly junior *TV Times*. Concerned with children's TV, pop and film.
Illustrations: Mainly colour. Pictures of pop, sport, celebrities. Covers: colour pictures of same.
Text: Features on subjects detailed above.
Overall freelance potential: Very limited.
Fees: Depending on material and use.

MG
Southbank Group, IPC Magazines, King's Reach Tower, Stamford Street, London SE1 9LS. Tel: 071-261 6349.
Editor: Frank Hopkinson.
Weekly magazine for teenage girls in the 14–18 age group.
Illustrations: B&W and colour. Pop pin-ups (usually only studio shots), fashion and beauty. Occasional need for photo-story work.
Text: Features of interest to teenage girls. 1,000 words. Quizzes and fiction.
Overall freelance potential: Some photo stories and features come from freelance sources, but much of it is commissioned from known workers.
Editor's tips: Photographers must be able to work quickly with powerful bounce flash while directing up to seven models from a script. They will need to find their own models, props, locations. Car and teenage model contacts essential.
Fees: By agreement.

MIZZ
IPC Magazines Ltd, King's Reach Tower, Stamford Street, London SE1 9LS. Tel: 071-261 5000.
Editor: Simon Geller. **Art Editor**: Linda Ward.
Monthly magazine aimed at young women in the 15–19 age group.
Illustrations: B&W and colour. Some scope for single captioned pictures of a humorous nature. Celebrity pictures always of interest. Most other photography by commission, to illustrate specific features.
Text: Lively illustrated features on almost any topic that could be of interest to young women in the target age group. Text should be informative as well as entertaining. A detailed synopsis should always be submitted in the first instance.
Overall freelance potential: Good for the experienced contributor to the women's press.
Fees: By negotiation.

SCOUTING
The Scout Association, Baden-Powell House, Queen's Gate, London SW7 5JS. Tel: 071-584 7030.
Editor: David Easton.

Monthly publication, concerning practical programme and activity ideas for Scout Groups, plus supplements for Leaders and articles of general interest to Members of the Scout Movement and its supporters. All material should be Scouting related or relevant to Scouting.

Illustrations: B&W and colour. Pictures of Scouting activities, preferably action shots. Covers: colour action and head and shoulder shots of Beaver Scouts, Cub Scouts, Scouts, Venture Scouts.

Text: Features on activities, competitions and interesting and unusual news stories suitable for a national readership.

Overall freelance potential: Very high proportion of pictures and around 60 per cent of the editorial comes from freelances.

Editor's tips: Note that where uniform is used, it should the the correct uniform. Also, if the pictures are of adventurous or hazardous activities, the correct safety rules must be seen to be observed and the correct safety equipment and precautions must be evident.

Fees: By agreement.

County & Country

CORNISH LIFE

45 Queen Street, Exeter, Devon EX4 3SR. Tel: 0392 216766.

Editor: N. Hutchinson.

Monthly magazine concerned with Cornish people and businesses, fashion, motoring, wining and dining, etc. Aimed at general family readership.

Illustrations: B&W and colour. Mostly used with articles, but willing to consider Cornish landscapes, seascapes, people and events. Covers: colour pictures of subjects detailed above. 6x6cm minimum for transparencies, but prints preferred.

Text: Features on anything happening in Cornwall or about the county generally. 700–1,500 words.

Overall freelance potential: Always happy to receive freelance material.

Fees: Negotiable.

COTSWOLD LIFE

West One House, 23 St Georges Road, Cheltenham, Gloucestershire GL50 3DT. Tel: 0242 226367/226373.

Editor: John Drinkwater.

Monthly county magazine with emphasis on tradition and nostalgia.

Illustrations: B&W only inside. Pictures of local scenes and events, preferably with some life in them. Covers: 6x6cm transparencies of lively local scenes, with clear space at top left for magazine title.

Text: Illustrated articles of varying lengths, on local people, places, crafts, etc. Historical and nostalgic items.

Overall freelance potential: About half published material is from freelances.

Fees: Cover shots £40. Articles and other illustrations negotiable.

COUNTRY

Country Gentlemen's Association, Hill Crest Mews, London Road, Baldock, Hertfordshire SG7 6ND. Tel: 0462 490206.

Editor: Tony Bush.

Monthly magazine of the CGA.

Illustrations: B&W and colour. Good stock shots of attractive British landscapes, wildlife, farming, historic houses and gardens. Also coverage of game shooting, fishing and other field sports, but excluding hunting. Covers: striking colour shots of wildlife, shooting, cricket, sailing and polo.

Text: Illustrated articles on British subjects of interest to a traditional but up-market male readership.

Overall freelance potential: Excellent scope for the right type of material.

Editor's tips: Material must be of top class quality and of genuine relevance and interest for the readership.

Fees: By arrangement, according to use.

COUNTRY LIFE

IPC Magazines Ltd, Kings Reach Tower, Stamford Street, London SE1 9LS. Tel: 071-261 7058.

Editor: Clive Aslet. **Picture Editor**: Michael Lyons.

Weekly magazine for a general readership.

Illustrations: B&W and colour. Pictures of British countryside. Covers: colour pictures of landscape, rural and urban. Wildlife, interiors, country pursuits. 6x6cm acceptable, but 5x4in preferred.

Text: No scope.

Overall freelance potential: Around 20 per cent of the magazine comes from freelance sources.

Fees: Good; on a rising scale according to size of reproduction. Covers, £170.

COUNTRY WALKING

EMAP Pursuit Publications Ltd, Bretton Court, Bretton, Peterborough PE3 8DZ. Tel: 0733 264666.

Editor: Lynne Barber.

Monthly magazine for ramblers, hill-walkers, and backpackers.

Illustrations: B&W and colour. B&W pictures of walkers out and about, and stock shots of flora and fauna. Colour pictures depicting walkers in attractive locations, and top quality landscapes of suitable parts of the country.

Text: Well-illustrated articles and features on any walking or countryside topics. Strong emphasis on "where to go, what to see" type material.

Overall freelance potential: Excellent.

Editor's tips: The emphasis should always be on getting more enjoyment from walking and the countryside.

Fees: £8 upwards for B&W; £15 upwards for colour. Colour covers around £60.

THE COUNTRYMAN

The Countryman Ltd, Sheep Street, Burford, Oxfordshire OX18 4LH. Tel: 0993 822258.

Editor: Christopher Hall.

Six times a year, covering all matters of countryside interest other than blood sports.

Illustrations: B&W only. Sequences of pictures about particular places, crafts, customs, farming practices, kinds of wildlife, etc. Must be accompanied by ample caption material. Only limited scope for single stock pictures. Covers: colour, must fit small (120mm x 112mm) space and still be noticeable on bookstalls.

Text: Well-illustrated articles of around 1,200 words, on such subjects as mentioned above.

Overall freelance potential: Excellent; almost all photographs, and most articles, are from freelance contributors.

Fees: £10 upwards for photographs. Text according to length and merit.

DEVON LIFE

45 Queen Street, Exeter, Devon EX4 3SR. Tel: 0392 216766.

Editor: N. Hutchinson.

Monthly magazine concerned with Devon people and businesses, fashion, motoring, wining and dining, etc. Aimed at general family readership.

Illustrations: B&W and colour. Mostly used with articles, but willing to consider Devon landscapes, seascapes, people and events. Covers: colour pictures of subjects detailed above. 6x6cm minimum, but prints preferred.

Text: Features on anything happening in Devon, or about the county generally. 700–1,500 words.

Overall freelance potential: Always happy to receive freelance material.

Fees: Negotiable.

DORSET LIFE – THE DORSET MAGAZINE
Dorset County Magazines Ltd, Trinity Lane, Wareham, Dorset BH20 4LN. Tel: 0929 551264.
Editor: John Newth.
Monthly magazine for the Dorset area.
Illustrations: B&W and colour. Interesting and original photographs, but usually required as part of an article, not in isolation. Covers: 6x6cm transparencies of local scenes, suitable for upright reproduction. Must be original.
Text: Well-illustrated articles on any topic relating to Dorset, around 1,000 words.
Overall freelance potential: Most contributions come from regular freelance contributors but new contributors always considered.
Fees: According to size of reproduction and length of text.

ESSEX COUNTRYSIDE
Market Link House, Elsenham, Bishops Stortford, Hertfordshire CM22 6DY. Tel: 0279 647555.
Editor: Suzanne Kuyser.
Monthly county magazine for the named area.
Illustrations: B&W and colour. People, places, and events in the county. Covers: transparencies of local countryside views; action shots preferred.
Text: Topical articles on any aspect of the county.
Overall freelance potential: Limited; much is supplied by regular freelance contributors.
Fees: £40 for cover. B&W, inside colour and text by negotiation.

THE FIELD
Harmsworth Active, 10 Sheet Street, Windsor, Berkshire SL4 1BG. Tel: 0753 856061.
Editor: Jonathan Young.
Monthly publication concerned with all country and sporting interests.
Illustrations: Colour only. Good pictures illustrating relevant articles. Covers: colour pictures of same.
Text: Illustrated features on country and sporting subjects. Length according to article.
Overall freelance potential: Around 50 per cent comes from outside contributors, most of whom are specialists.
Fees: According to merit.

GLOUCESTERSHIRE & AVON LIFE
34 Berlington Court, Redcliff Mead Lane, Bristol BS1 6FB. Tel: 0272 252052.
Editor: Neil Pickford.
Monthly county magazine majoring on country and local topics, arts and leisure interests.
Illustrations: B&W and colour. Pictures only to illustrate features. Covers: colour pictures of places of interest usually by commission.
Text: Features of local, topical or historical interest. Up to 1,800 words.
Overall freelance potential: About 50 per cent of the magazine comes from freelance sources, but much of that is from regular contributors.
Fees: By negotiation.

THE GREAT OUTDOORS
George Outram and Co. Ltd, The Plaza Tower, The Plaza, East Kilbride, Glasgow G74 1LW. Tel: 03552 46444.
Editor: Cameron McNeish.
Monthly magazine for walkers in the UK. Covers hill and mountain walking, lowland areas, other countryside topics and environmental issues.
Illustrations: Colour transparencies for stock, mostly landscapes, no towns or churches. Plus pictures to illustrate features. Covers: colour pictures in upright format considered independently of internal content. Photographs of walkers, backpackers, fell walkers.

Text: Features on the subjects mentioned above. 1,200–1,500 words.
Overall freelance potential: Most of the magazine comes from freelance sources.
Editor's tips: Too many freelances send material which is outside the area covered by the magazine.
Fees: Articles, £80–£150 depending on length and number of illustrations; covers, £60.

HERTFORDSHIRE COUNTRYSIDE
Beaumonde Publications, 4 Mill Bridge, Hertford SG14 1PY. Tel: 0992 553571.
Editor: Sandra Small.
Monthly county magazine for the named area.
Illustrations: B&W and colour. People, places, and events in the county. 6x6cm required in the case of colour. Covers: 6x6cm transparencies of local countryside views.
Text: Topical articles, of a cultural nature, on any aspect of the county.
Overall freelance potential: Limited; much is supplied by regular freelance contributors.
Fees: By negotiation.

LAKESCENE–THE COUNTY MAGAZINE FOR CUMBRIA
Scenic Publications, Townfoot Industrial Estate, Brampton, Carlisle, Cumbria CA8 1SW. Tel: 06977 3898.
Editor: Nigel Williamson.
Monthly publication for tourists and residents in the Lake District. Gives details of events and diary dates for the area.
Illustrations: Mainly B&W. Pictures of the Lake District. Covers: colour prints of Cumbrian leisure scenes.
Text: Articles about leisure activities, personalities and places to visit in Cumbria. 500 words and longer.
Overall freelance potential: Very good if material is suitable.
Fees: By negotiation.

LANCASHIRE LIFE
Town and County Magazines, Oyston Mill, Strand Road, Preston PR1 8UR. Tel: 0772 722022.
Editor: Brian Hargreaves.
Monthly up-market county magazine including national as well as regional features.
Illustrations: B&W and colour. Pictures of the Lancashire region, mainly to accompany features. Pictures of nationally known personalities with a Lancashire connection. Covers: top quality regional scenes; 6x6cm preferred.
Text: Articles and features on regional and national topics. Always consult the editor in the first instance.
Overall freelance potential: Good; around 75 per cent is from freelance sources.
Editor's tips: The magazine is not interested in the merely parochial.
Fees: By negotiation.

LINCOLNSHIRE LIFE
County Life Ltd, PO Box 8, Newark, Nottinghamshire NG23 7AJ. Tel: 0522 778567.
Executive Editor: Jenny Walton.
Monthly magazine, dealing with county life past and present from the Humber to the Wash.
Illustrations: B&W and colour. Pictures of people and places within the county of Lincolnshire. No current social events. Covers: colour pictures of landscapes, buildings, street scenes, etc. 35mm acceptable, but medium format preferred.
Text: Features on people and places within the appropriate area. No more than 1,000 words.
Overall freelance potential: Virtually the whole magazine comes from freelance sources.
Fees: By agreement.

MANX LIFE
Trafalgar Press Ltd, 14 Douglas Street, Peel, Isle of Man. Tel: 0624 843881.
Editor: Ian Faulds.
Monthly magazine exclusively interested in Manx subjects, e.g. current affairs, personalities, consumer interests and freshly researched historical and cultural material.
Illustrations: B&W and colour inside. Pictures used only as illustrations to features. Covers: colour pictures of views and activities in the Isle of Man. Vertical format.
Text: Features of strictly Manx interest. Mostly factual articles, occasionally fiction and poems. 1,000–2,500 words.
Overall freelance potential: Approximately 80 per cent of material is contributed, but only from freelances with detailed and accurate knowledge of Manx affairs.
Editor's tips: Check first to see if your chosen subject has already been covered.
Fees: Text, £20 per 1,000 words; B&W pictures, up to £5; colour, £10.

NORTH EAST TIMES COUNTY MAGAZINE
Chris Robinson (Publishing) Ltd, Tattler House, Beech Avenue, Fawdon, Newcastle-upon-Tyne NE3 2RN. Tel: 091-284 4495.
Editor: Chris Robinson.
Monthly up-market county magazine.
Illustrations: B&W only. Any general interest pictures connected with the North-East of England.
Text: Features on fashion, property, motoring, wining and dining, sport, etc. all with North-East connections. Around 750 words with two pictures.
Overall freelance potential: Very good.
Fees: By agreement.

OUTDOOR
Mark Allen Publishing Ltd, 286A-288 Croxted Road, London SE24 9BY. Tel: 081-671 7521.
Editor: Moira Crawford.
Monthly magazine for walking and outdoor enthusiasts.
Illustrations: Colour only. Nice views of British landscapes, most specifically of hill-walking areas. Prefer dramatic pictures that make Britain look exciting. Covers: "stunning" cover shots considered, though most produced in-house.
Text: Illustrated articles on aspects of walking, both practical, how-to-do-it pieces on tents, navigation, etc, and pieces which describe a particular walking area in detail. Length 1,200 – 1,500 words. The latter must be accompanied by a thorough "fact file" on places to stay, transport, recommended pubs, etc, plus relevant addresses and phone numbers. Prefer to discuss ideas first.
Overall freelance potential: Excellent.
Editor's tips: Photographs are generally used to illustrate articles about specific areas, so in the first instance photographers should simply send details of available coverage with a few samples.
Fees: Photographs negotiable; text around £100 per 1,000 words.

RAMBLING TODAY
The Ramblers' Association, 1–5 Wandsworth Road, London SW8 2XX. Tel: 071-582 6878.
Editor: Annabelle Birchall.
Quarterly journal for the 90,000 members of the Ramblers' Association.
Illustrations: B&W and colour. Any scenic views of the countryside, preferably but not necessarily with ramblers. Also pictures of problems encountered when walking in the countryside, e.g. damaged bridges, locked gates, obstructed footpaths, etc.
Text: Articles on the work of the Ramblers' Association. Any issues affecting the countryside or walkers' interests. General articles on walking. Maps, news, letters, book reviews.
Overall freelance potential: Limited.
Editor's tips: Photos without articles should not be sent without prior agreement with the editor.
Fees: By agreement.

THE SCOTS MAGAZINE
D. C. Thomson and Co. Ltd, 2 Albert Square, Dundee DD1 9QJ. Tel: 0382 23131.
Editor: John Rundle.
Monthly magazine for Scots at home and abroad, concerned with Scottish subjects.
Illustrations: Mostly colour. Scottish scenes, but avoid the obvious. Non-Highland subjects particularly welcome. Scenics with one or more figures, often preferred to "empty pictures".
Text: Features on all aspects of Scottish life past and present. 2,000–3,500 words.
Overall freelance potential: Around 80 per cent of the magazine comes from freelances.
Editor's tips: Nothing on sport, politics, household, beauty or fashion.
Fees: Variable.

SCOTTISH FIELD
Outram Magazines, The Plaza Tower, East Kilbride, Glasgow G74 1LW. Tel: 03552 46444.
Editor: Peter Evans.
Monthly magazine reflecting the quality of life in Scotland today and yesterday for Scots at home and abroad.
Illustrations: Mainly colour. Must be accompanied by appropriate text. Covers always related to internal matter.
Text: Features with a Scottish dimension. Submit only ideas initially, rather than completed articles. 850, 1,200, 1,500 words.
Overall freelance potential: Most articles are commissioned and there are limited openings for new contributors.
Editor's tips: Market study is essential.
Fees: Above average.

SCOTTISH WORLD
Oban Times Publishing Group, PO Box 1, Oban, Argyll PA34 5PY. Tel: 0631 63058.
Editor: Archie Mackenzie.
Quarterly general interest magazine for Scots at home and abroad.
Illustrations: Mostly B&W. News pictures and pictures for stock and general illustration, depicting life in Scotland today.
Text: Short news items and longer general interest features, but always contact the editor before submitting.
Overall freelance potential: Good.
Fees: Photographs by negotiation; £40 per 1,000 words for text.

SOMERSET AND AVON LIFE
34 Berlington Court, Redcliff Mead Lane, Bristol BS1 6FB. Tel: 0272 252052.
Editor: Neil Pickford.
General interest county magazine for the Somerset and Avon area.
Illustrations: B&W and colour. Local views; landscapes; curiosities; events; people. Covers: colour shots of local interest.
Text: Illustrated articles on anything relating to the area. 900–2,000 words.
Overall freelance potential: 20–30 per cent comes from freelance contributors.
Fees: By negotiation.

THE SOMERSET MAGAZINE
Smart Print Publications Ltd, 23 Market Street, Crewkerne, Somerset TA18 7JU. Tel: 0460 78000.
Editor: Jack Rayfield.
Monthly magazine for the Somerset area.
Illustrations: B&W and colour. Interesting and original photographs of the area, but usually required as part of an article, not in isolation. 6x6cm or larger transparencies for d.p.s. features and covers.

Text: Well-illustrated articles on any topic relating to Somerset, around 1,000 words.
Overall freelance potential: Most material comes from regular freelance contributors but new contributors always considered.
Fees: According to size of reproduction and length of text.

SUSSEX LIFE
Brownhart Publishing Ltd, 30A Teville Road, Worthing, West Sussex BN11 1UG. Tel: 0903 204628.
Editor: Chris Harvey.
Monthly magazine on all aspects of Sussex.
Illustrations: B&W only inside. Stock photographs always welcomed, but complete illustrated articles are preferred. Covers: medium format transparencies of Sussex scenes, usually depicting landscapes, houses, activities, interiors also welcome.
Text: Well illustrated features on any topic relevant to the county. 1,000–2,000 words.
Overall freelance potential: Quite good.
Fees: By negotiation.

THIS ENGLAND
This England International Ltd, PO Box 52, Cheltenham, Gloucestershire GL50 1HT. Tel: 0242 577775.
Editor: Roy Faiers.
Quarterly magazine on England, mainly its people, places, customs and traditions. Aimed at those who love England and all things English.
Illustrations: B&W and colour. Town, country and village scenes, curiosities, craftsmen at work, nostalgia, patriotism, prefer people in the picture. Dislike cars, boats, modernity, etc. Pictures for stock or use in their own right.
Text: Illustrated articles on all thing English. 1,500–2,000 words.
Overall freelance potential: Around 70 per cent comes from freelance sources.
Fees: Colour page, £20; B&W, £15. Covers, £60.

TRAIL WALKER
EMAP Pursuit Publishing Ltd, Bretton Court, Bretton, Peterborough PE3 8DZ. Tel: 0733 264666.
Editor: David Ogle.
Monthly magazine aimed at the younger, more adventurous walker.
Illustrations: Colour only. Well-composed pictures of walkers and backpackers in suitable landscapes, UK or overseas. High viewpoints preferred. Covers: "stunning" colour shots as above.
Text: Illustrated articles on any aspect of long-distance walking and backpacking, but always discuss ideas with the editor in the first instance.
Overall freelance potential: Good.
Fees: From £15 – £50; £70 for covers.

Cycling & Motorcycling

BACK STREET HEROES
Myatt McFarlane plc, PO Box 28, Altrincham, Cheshire WA15 8SH. Tel: 061-928 3480.
Editor: Caz Carroll.
Monthly magazine for custom bike enthusiasts.
Illustrations: B&W and colour. Pictures of individual machines and coverage of custom bike meetings and events, but the style of photography must be tailored to fit the style of the magazine. Covers: usually commissioned.
Text: Some freelance market.
Overall freelance potential: Good for those who can capture the flavour and style of the custom

bike scene.

Editor's tips: This is something of a "lifestyle" magazine, and it is essential that the stylistic approach be absolutely right.

Fees: By negotiation.

BIKE

EMAP National Publications Ltd, 20–22 Station Road, Kettering, Northants NN15 7HH. Tel: 0536 416416.

Editor: Martyn Moore.

Monthly motorcycling magazine aimed at all enthusiasts in the 18–80 age group.

Illustrations: B&W and colour. Sporting pictures for file. Action pictures, "moody" statics and shots that are strong on creative effects. Reportage/documentary shots of events/people.

Text: Features on touring, long term reports on bikes, incidents of interest to the readership. 1,000–3,000 words.

Overall freelance potential: All photography comes from freelances; 20 per cent of the words are contributed.

Editor's tips: "Check out the magazine first. Photography has to be brilliant."

Fees: By agreement.

BRITISH BIKE MAGAZINE

Green Designs, PO Box 19, Cowbridge, South Glamorgan CF7 7YD. Tel: 0446 775033.

Editor: Tim Holmes and Rebekka Smith.

Monthly magazine devoted to British motorcycles from vintage to the present day.

Illustrations: B&W and colour. Top quality action and still pictures of British motorcycles. Offbeat pictures. Covers: colour shots of motorcycles, always related to the contents.

Text: Articles of a technical or mechanical nature – maintenance, rebuilding, modifications. Also travel material with a motorcycle connection, preferably long-distance trips. Length: 1,500–3,000 words.

Overall freelance potential: Fair.

Fees: Text, £50 per 1,000 words; pictures, by negotiation.

CLASSIC BIKE

EMAP National Publications Ltd, Bushfield House, Orton Centre, Peterborough PE2 5UW. Tel: 0733 237111.

Editor: John Pearson.

Monthly magazine dealing with thoroughbred and classic motorcycles from 1900 to the early 1970s with special emphasis on 1945–70.

Illustrations: B&W and colour. Pictures of rallies, races, restored motorcycles.

Text: Technical features, histories of particular motorcycles, restoration stories, profiles of famous riders, designers etc. 500–2,000 words.

Overall freelance potential: Around 50 per cent of the magazine is freelance contributed.

Fees: By agreement and on merit.

THE CLASSIC MOTOR CYCLE

EMAP National Publications Ltd, Bushfield House, Orton Centre, Peterborough PE2 5UW. Tel: 0733 237111.

Editor: Phillip Tooth.

Monthly publication that specialises in veteran, vintage and post-war classic motor cycles and motorcycling.

Illustrations: B&W and colour. Pictures that cover interesting restoration projects, unusual machines, personalities with a background story, etc. Covers: colour pictures, usually a well-restored and technically interesting motor cycle, always with editorial. 35mm acceptable.

Text: Features on subjects detailed above. 1,500–2,500 words.

Overall freelance potential: Around 60 per cent of the magazine comes from freelances, but much of it is commissioned.

Editor's tips: Potential contributors must have a good technical knowledge of the field.

Fees: Good; on a rising scale according to size of reproduction or length of article.

CYCLE SPORT

IPC Magazines Ltd, King's Reach Tower, Stamford Street. London SE1 9LS. Tel: 071-261 5588.

Editor: Andrew Sutcliffe.

Monthly devoted to professional cycle sport, offering a British perspective on this essentially Continental sport.

Illustrations: Colour only. High quality, topical photographs relating to professional cycle racing.

Text: Illustrated features on the professional scene, but always query the editor before submitting. 2,000–4,000 words.

Overall freelance potential: Good for those with access to the professional scene, but most coverage comes from specialists based on the Continent.

Editor's tips: Most interested in "the news behind the news".

Fees: Pictures according to nature and use. Text £100–£200 per 1,000 words.

CYCLING PLUS

Future Publishing Ltd, Beauford Court, 30 Monmouth Street, Bath BA1 2BW. Tel: 0225 442244.

Editor: Andy Ide.

Monthly magazine aimed at recreational cyclists, covering all aspects including top level racing.

Illustrations: Mainly colour. Photographs that capture the excitement and dynamics of cycle sport. Speculative submissions welcomed; commissions also available.

Text: Little freelance scope; most is produced by a team of regular writers.

Overall freelance potential: Very good for photographers.

Fees: By negotiation.

CYCLING WEEKLY

IPC Magazines Ltd, King's Reach Tower, Stamford Street, London SE1 9LS. Tel: 071-261 5588.

Editor: Andrew Sutcliffe.

News-biased weekly magazine covering all aspects of cycling; aimed at the informed cyclist.

Illustrations: B&W and colour. Good photographs of cycle racing and touring, plus any topical photographs of interest to cyclists. Covers: striking colour photographs of cycle racing; must be current.

Text: Well-illustrated articles on racing, touring and technical matters. Around 1,500 words.

Overall freelance potential: Fairly good.

Fees: According to use.

HEAVY DUTY

Power Play Publications Ltd, Parker House, Tan Yard Lane, Bexley, Kent DA5 1AH. Tel: 0322 555959.

Editor: Stuart Garland.

Monthly magazine for committed custom bike enthusiasts, with the emphasis on Harley-Davidson machines.

Illustrations: B&W and colour. Photographs of unusually interesting machines and related lifestyle material. Coverage of events throughout the Europe and America.

Text: Some scope for those with knowledge of this scene.

Overall freelance potential: Good for those in touch with the custom bike scene.

Fees: By negotiation.

MOTORCYCLE INTERNATIONAL

Myatt McFarlane plc, PO Box 666, Altrincham, Cheshire WA15 2UD. Tel: 061-928 3480.

Editor: Tom Isitt.

Monthly buyers' guide to the motorcycle market, including general motorcycling features.

Illustrations: Mostly colour. Sporting action at international level; off-beat pictures; examples of motorcycles being used in an unusual or unorthodox way; coverage of world trips by motorcycle. Covers: little scope.

Text: Illustrated articles on any motorcycling topic – sport, world trips, etc. Around 2,000 words.

Overall freelance potential: About 25 per cent of the magazine is contributed by freelances, but most of it is commissioned.

Editor's tips: Material must be composed imaginatively and be of first class technical competence.

Fees: By negotiation.

MOUNTAIN BIKING UK

Future Publishing Ltd, Beauford Court, 30 Monmouth Street, Bath BA1 2BW. Tel: 0225 442244.

Editor: Tym Manley. **Art Editor**: Paul Tudor.

Monthly magazine devoted to the sport of mountain biking.

Illustrations: B&W and colour. Spectacular or unusual shots of mountain biking, action pictures that convey a sense of both movement and height. General coverage of events and individual riders may be of interest.

Text: Well-illustrated articles that show good knowledge of the sport.

Overall freelance potential: Good scope for individual and original photography.

Fees: By negotiation.

PERFORMANCE CYCLIST

United Leisure Magazines, PO Box 3205, City Harbour, 4 Selsdon Way, London E14 9RZ. Tel: 071-712 0550.

Editor: Tony Doyle.

Monthly magazine combining coverage of the racing scene with reviews of "performance" cycling products. Aimed at club cyclists and racing enthusiasts.

Illustrations: Mainly colour. Good action photography of major races worldwide.

Text: Articles on any aspect of race cycling, especially behind the scenes coverage. Some technical articles. 3,000 words maximum.

Overall freelance potential: Quite good.

Editor's tips: Study several back issues for style and contact editor before submitting.

Fees: By negotiation.

SCOOTERING

PO Box 46, Weston-Super-Mare, Avon BS23 1AF. Tel: 0934 414785.

Editor: Stuart Lanning.

Monthly magazine for motor scooter enthusiasts.

Illustrations: B&W and colour. Pictures of motor scooters of the Lambretta/Vespa type – shows, meetings, "runs", racing, special paint jobs, "chopped" scooters, etc. Covers: usually staff-produced.

Text: Short illustrated articles of up to 500 words on any scootering topic. Contributors should be aware of the particular lifestyle and terminology attached to the scooter scene.

Overall freelance potential: Good scope for those who know the current scooter scene and its followers.

Editor's tips: The magazine being based in the South and able to cover events in its own locality, contributions from the North are particularly welcome.

Fees: By negotiation.

SUPERBIKE

Link House Magazines Ltd, Dingwall Avenue, Croydon CR9 2TA. Tel: 081-686 2599.

Editor: John Cutts.

Monthly magazine for motorcycle enthusiasts, aimed at the serious rider as well as newer motorcycle fans. Humour a speciality.

Illustrations: All colour. Pictures of unusual motorcycles, road-racing, drag-racing and other sports pictures of unusual interest or impact. Crash sequences. Motorcycle people. Covers: colour pictures with strong motorcycle interest.

Text: Features of general or specific motorcycle interest. 1,500–3,000 words.

Overall freelance potential: Around 30 per cent of the magazine is contributed from outside sources.

Fees: Dependent on size and position in magazine.

Defence

DEFENCE
Argus Business Publications, Queensway House, 2 Queensway, Redhill, Surrey RH1 1QS. Tel: 0737 768611.

Editor: George Paloczi-Horvath.

Monthly publication covering military equipment, e.g. guns, tanks, ships, aircraft and electronics, as well as military topics of world interest.

Illustrations: B&W and colour. Pictures showing a whole system (gun, tank, ship or aircraft) clearly, or a portion of the system which is of particular interest. Also good action shots. Covers: colour pictures in close-up of military equipment in use; 6x6cm minimum.

Text: Limited market for features on defence matters.

Overall freelance potential: Around 5 per cent is contributed from outside sources.

Editor's tips: The magazine is always on the lookout for a different approach to a subject.

Fees: Pictures inside, £10 for B&W, £25 for colour.

DEFENCE HELICOPTER WORLD
Shephard Press Ltd, 111 High Street, Burnham, Buckinghamshire SL1 7JZ. Tel: 0628 604311.

Editor: Frank Colucci.

Bi-monthly publication concerned with military helicopters and their applications.

Illustrations: B&W and colour. Pictures of military helicopters anywhere in the world. Must be accurately captioned. Covers: high quality colour pictures of military helicopters. Should preferably be exclusive and in upright format. No "sterile" pictures; must be action shots.

Text: Knowledgeable articles on any aspect of military helicopter use and technology. 1,500–2,500 words.

Overall freelance potential: Good.

Fees: By negotiation.

LEGION
The Royal British Legion, 48 Pall Mall, London SW1Y 5JY. Tel: 071-973 0633.

Editor: Bill Kingdon.

Bi-monthly official journal of The Royal British Legion.

Illustrations: B&W and colour. Any subject relating to The Royal British Legion or the ex-service community. Covers: colour shots concerned with the Legion.

Text: Short news stories and features concerned with the Legion or with military matters.

Overall freelance potential: Limited.

Fees: Fair. On a rising scale according to size of reproduction or length of article.

MILITARY FIRE FIGHTER
Kennedy Communications Ltd, Unit 8, The Old Yarn Mills, Westbury, Sherborne, Dorset DT9 3RG. Tel: 0935 816030.

Editor: Aidan Turnbull.

Quarterly magazine for those involved in military firefighting.

Illustrations: Mostly B&W. Pictures of anything involving military firefighting services – major fires,

accidents, crashes, extrications, fire and accident victims – and firefighting personnel in action.
Covers: Powerful colour images of the same.
Text: No scope for non-specialists.
Overall freelance potential: Fair.
Fees: Negotiable, but generally good. Up to £200 for a really good cover picture.

NAVY INTERNATIONAL
Maritime World Ltd, 'Hunters Moon', Hogspudding Lane, Newdigate, Dorking, Surrey RH5 5DS. Tel: 0306 631442.
Editor: Anthony Watts.
Bi-monthly magazine for professional decision makers in Naval defence. Concerns latest developments in warship design and manufacture, weapons and electronic warfare systems. Provides an independent medium for free discussion of maritime strategic issues which impinge on the freedom of the seas.
Illustrations: B&W and colour. Mainly as illustrations for features. Covers: colour pictures of naval vessels at sea.
Text: Features on maritime affairs on an international level. 2,000 words.
Overall freelance potential: Over 60 per cent of the magazine comes from freelance sources.
Fees: £75 per 1,000 words; pictures by agreement.

Education

JUNIOR EDUCATION
Scholastic Publications Ltd, Villiers House, Clarendon Avenue, Leamington Spa, Warwickshire CV32 5PR. Tel: 0926 887799.
Editor: Mrs Terry Saunders.
Monthly publication for junior school teachers.
Illustrations: Mostly B&W. Good unposed pictures of children in the 7–12 age range in school. Situation pictures that can be used symbolically, or where the child cannot be identified, are particularly useful. Covers: colour pictures as above, but usually commissioned.
Text: Willing to consider good, practical curriculum ideas for work in the junior classroom. 1,000 words.
Overall freelance potential: Around 60 per cent of the pictures come from freelances or agencies.
Fees: By agreement.

PRACTICAL ENGLISH TEACHING
MGP International, 140 Freston Road, London W10 6TR. Tel: 071-792 3644.
Editor: Janet Olearski.
Quarterly publication featuring practical teaching ideas plus news and information for teachers of English as a foreign language in European secondary schools.
Illustrations: B&W inside. Pictures of language teaching activities being carried out in classes or teacher training sessions. Classes should be of the 9–19 age group. Also "freeze-frame" style photos – unusual images for the Visual Ideas section. Covers: colour pictures of language teachers in action, pupils participating in learning activities, teachers demonstrating a language teaching technique, etc.
Text: Articles on language teaching techniques and issues of current interest in EFL teaching. Outlines only considered in the first instance. Articles of 400 words (Teaching Tips), 900 and 1,400 words.
Overall freelance potential: Fairly high.
Fees: Text, £30 per published page; B&W pictures, £15 plus; covers, £75 plus.

RIGHT START
Needmarsh Ltd, 71 Newcomen Street, London SE1 1YT. Tel: 071-403 0840.
Editor: Anita Bevan. **Art Editor**: Julia Illingworth.
Alternate-monthly magazine for parents of pre-school and primary school age children, covering health, behaviour and education.
Illustrations: B&W and colour. Mostly by commission. Some scope for good stock coverage of children in educational and learning situations; send only lists or details of coverage available in the first instance.
Text: Opportunities for education and child care specialists. Approach with details of ideas and previous experience.
Overall freelance potential: Limited.
Fees: By negotiation.

SAFETY EDUCATION
The Royal Society for the Prevention of Accidents, Cannon House, The Priory Queensway, Birmingham B4 6BS. Tel: 021-200 2461.
Editor: Carole Peart.
Published three times per year and aimed at teachers and educationalists in local authorities.
Illustrations: B&W and colour. Pictures depicting road safety, home safety, playground safety, industrial safety and water safety subjects; predominantly aimed at children. Covers: colour pictures of similar subjects.
Text: Features on topics detailed above. 1,000–3,000 words.
Overall freelance potential: Pictures, 10 per cent of the magazine; articles, 60–70 per cent.
Fees: On a rising scale according to the size of reproduction or length of article.

THE TEACHER
National Union of Teachers, Hamilton House, Mabledon Place, London WC1H 9BD. Tel: 071-388 6191.
Editor: Mitch Howard.
Official magazine of the National Union of Teachers. Published eight times a year.
Illustrations: B&W and colour. News pictures concerning any educational topic, especially those taken in schools and colleges. Coverage of union activities, personalities, demonstrations, etc.
Text: Short articles and news items on educational matters.
Overall freelance potential: Good.
Editor's tips: Consult the editor before submitting.
Fees: According to use.

YOUNG PEOPLE NOW
National Youth Agency, 17–23 Albion Street, Leicester LE1 6GD. Tel: 0533 471200.
Editor: Jackie Scott.
Monthly publication for youth workers, social workers, young volunteer organisers, careers officers, teachers, supervisors on youth unemployment schemes, youth counsellors and policy makers in the youth affairs field.
Illustrations: B&W and colour. Pictures of young people, aged between 13 and 21, involved in group activities of a formal or informal nature, e.g. street activities such as shopping, transport, relationships with police, inter-generational groups, positive images of young people. Covers: colour pictures relating to the above.
Text: Small proportion of copy is from freelance contributors.
Overall freelance potential: About 10 per cent of the illustrations come from general freelances and another 50 per cent from specially commissioned freelances.
Fees: From £10 per picture used. From £45 per 1,000 words.

Electrical & Electronics

CITIZEN'S BAND
Argus Specialist Publications Ltd, Argus House, Boundary Way, Hemel Hempstead, Herts HP2 7ST. Tel: 0442 66551.
Editor: Tony Hetherington.
Monthly magazine for CB radio enthusiasts and anyone else interested in the world of two-way communications.
Illustrations: B&W only. Pictures connected with the CB world. Prefers to commission work.
Text: Features on CB and two-way radio systems. News and reviews of equipment, clubs, etc. 1,000–2,000 words.
Overall freelance potential: Between 30 and 50 per cent comes from freelances.
Editor's tips: The magazine is always on the lookout for features on new and novel uses for CB or short news items on how CB might have been used to report accidents, crime or traffic problems, etc.
Fees: £30 per published page.

ETI
Argus Specialist Publications Ltd, Argus House, Boundary Way, Hemel Hempstead, Herts HP2 7ST. Tel: 0442 66551.
Editor: Paul Freeman.
Monthly magazine aimed at professional electronics engineers, advanced hobbyists, hi-fi enthusiasts and general scientific interest.
Illustrations: B&W and colour. Photographs of technical subjects are invariably tied to specific articles. A wide range of related subjects are required to illustrate some articles, e.g. three-dimensional cutaway drawings. Some humorous captioned photos are occasionally used. Covers: colour shots, usually commissioned to tie in with leading article.
Text: Technical articles of general scientific and electronic nature, and related items of more general interest to the readership. Humorous items with a technical bias. 700–5,000 words.
Overall freelance potential: Most material is supplied by working technical journalists and specialists.
Editor's tips: It is useful to have samples of work and details of specialisation, so that commissions may be offered.
Fees: Negotiable.

ELECTRICAL AND RADIO TRADING
Reed Business Publishing, Quadrant House, The Quadrant, Sutton, Surrey SM2 5AS. Tel: 081-661 3500.
Editor: Ray Taylor.
Weekly publication, designed to bring its readers opinion, in-depth coverage of news, trade politics, products, people, markets, marketing and statistics concerning the electrical consumer durables industries. Slightly biased towards the independent retailer.
Illustrations: B&W and colour. Very limited scope for one-off pictures.
Text: Articles mainly on marketing of and developments in domestic appliances and/or consumer electronic products. Illustrated where necessary. 1,000 words.
Overall freelance potential: Good, but highly specialised.
Editor's tips: Contact magazine before submitting, since requirements are specialised.
Fees: £100 per 1,000 words. Pictures by negotiation.

ELECTRICAL TIMES
Reed Business Publishing, Quadrant House, The Quadrant, Sutton, Surrey SM2 5AS. Tel: 081-652 3115.
Editor: Bill Evett.

Monthly publication for electrical contractors in the public and private sectors, wholesalers, architects, commercial and industrial users of electricity and the electricity supply industry.
Illustrations: B&W and colour. Pictures of new technical products, site installation work, electrical-related exhibitions, personalities, electronic equipment, computers, etc.
Text: Technical articles are usually commissioned. Some openings for business-related articles on the electrical industry. 750–1,000 words.
Overall freelance potential: Limited.
Fees: By negotiation.

ELECTRONICS WORLD & WIRELESS WORLD
Reed Publishing Group, Quadrant House, The Quadrant, Sutton, Surrey SM2 5AS. Tel: 081-652 3128.
Editor: Frank Ogden.
Monthly technical journal covering electronics, computing, broadcasting, audio and video at a professional level.
Illustrations: B&W and colour. Mainly for use with features. Covers: colour pictures of any subject in the area detailed above. No blatant advertising shots.
Text: Illustrated features on subjects detailed above. 4,000 words.
Overall freelance potential: Limited; mainly from professional engineers.
Fees: £90 per printed page. Covers by agreement.

INFOMATICS
VNU Business Publications, 32–34 Broadwick Street, London W1A 2HG. Tel: 071-439 4242.
Editor: Phil Jones.
Monthly magazine concerned with computers, electronics and telecommunications.
Illustrations: B&W and colour inside. Pictures of politicians and heads of computer companies; invariably commissioned.
Text: Features on computers, electronics and telecommunications.
Overall freelance potential: All pictures are taken by freelances.
Fees: Commissioned photography, £45 for half-day; £80 for full day.

PRACTICAL PC
Alban House Publishing Ltd, Edinburgh House, 82-90 London Road, St Albans, Hertfordshire AL1 1TR. Tel: 0727 844555.
Editor: John Taylor.
Monthly consumer magazine for users of budget personal computers costing under £1,500.
Illustrations: B&W and colour. Usually by commission only to illustrate specific articles.
Text: Practical articles on aspects of using cheaper PCs either for work or recreation. Style should be popular and jargon-free. Contact the editor with ideas in the first instance.
Overall freelance potential: Good for those with experience of the subject.
Editor's tips: Contributors should have "hands on" experience of PCs.
Fees: Around £70 for photographs used inside; £250–£300 for covers. £120 per published page for text.

PRACTICAL WIRELESS
PW Publishing Ltd, Arrowsmith Court, Station Approach, Broadstone, Dorset BH18 8PW. Tel: 0202 659910.
Editor: Rob Mannion. **Art Editor**: Steve Hunt.
Monthly magazine covering all aspects of radio of interest to the radio amateur and enthusiast.
Illustrations: B&W only inside. Usually only required to illustrate specific articles. Covers: radio-related subjects; B&W or colour.
Text: Articles on amateur radio or short wave listening, or on aspects of professional radio systems of interest to the enthusiast. 1,000–5,000 words.
Overall freelance potential: Little scope for individual photographs; complete articles welcome.
Fees: By negotiation.

PRO SOUND NEWS
Spotlight Publications Ltd, 8th Floor, Ludgate House, 245 Blackfriars Road, London SE1 9UR. Tel: 071-620 3636.
Editor: Joe Hosken.
Monthly news magazine for professionals working in the European sound production industry. Covers recording, live sound, post-production and broadcasting.
Illustrations: Mainly B&W. News pictures on all aspects of the industry, from equipment manufacture to live sound shows and concert performances.
Text: Illustrated news items, reviews and features (800–1,000 words) on any aspect of the industry, but always check with the editor before submitting.
Overall freelance potential: Good for those with contacts in the audio and music business.
Fees: £100–150 per 1,000 words for text; photographs according to use.

WHAT HI-FI?
Haymarket Magazines Ltd, 38–42 Hampton Road, Teddington, Middlesex TW11 0JE. Tel: 081-943 5000.
Editor: Rahiel Nasir. **Art Editor**: Trisha Mitchell-Vargas.
Monthly magazine with emphasis on equipment reviews and ideas, particularly in the lower-priced areas of the market.
Illustrations: B&W and colour. Pictures from hi-fi shows, providing they are submitted quickly after the show. Pictures also used to illustrate articles.
Text: Features on hi-fi equipment. Interested in contacting freelances in the London area with access to and the ability to test equipment. Also general features on the subject, 1,500–3,000 words.
Overall freelance potential: An average of 50 per cent comes from freelances, but most of these are long-standing contributors.
Editor's tips: Photographers should be able to inject life into essentially "boring" black boxes. Potential reviewers should have the ability to listen to hi-fi critically, plus a technical knowledge of the subject, good product knowledge, and must be able to write clearly and accurately.
Fees: Text, from £40 per piece of equipment tested, £80–£100 per page for general articles; pictures, by negotiation.

Equestrian

EQUESTRIAN TRADE NEWS
Equestrian Management Consultants Ltd, Wothersome Grange, Bramham, Nr. Wetherby, Yorkshire LS23 6LY. Tel: 0532 892267.
Editor: Antony Wakeham.
Monthly publication for business people and trade in the equestrian world.
Illustrations: B&W and colour. Pictures covering saddlery, feedstuffs, new riding schools and business in the industry. Also people connected with the industry, e.g. people retiring, getting married, etc.
Text: Features on specialist subjects and general articles on retailing, marketing and business. 1,000 words.
Overall freelance potential: Around 50 per cent comes from freelances.
Editor's tips: Only stories with a business angle will be considered. No general horsey or racing material.
Fees: Text, £25 per 1,000 words; pictures by arrangement.

HORSE AND PONY
EMAP Pursuit Publications Ltd, Bretton Court, Bretton, Peterborough PE3 8DZ. Tel: 0733 264666.
Editor: Sarah Haw.

Fortnightly magazine reflecting the dedication and enthusiasm of people who love horses.
Illustrations: Colour. Amusing or unusual pictures of horses at work and play.
Text: Picture caption articles on the practical side of the subject.
Overall freelance potential: Around 10 per cent is contributed from outside.
Editor's tips: Possible news stories – check with office (by telephone) beforehand if possible or immediately after event. Awareness of magazines style and needs advantageous.
Fees: Negotiable.

HORSE REVIEW

Ivanhoe Publishing Ltd, 13 Kings Meadow, Ferry Hinksey Road, Oxford OX2 0DP. Tel: 0865 791006.
Editor: Pamela W Young.
Upmarket alternate-monthly covering all forms of equestrian sport.
Illustrations: Colour only. Top quality coverage of dressage, eventing, showjumping, distance-riding, carriage driving, polo, racing, travel and sporting art.
Text: High quality articles on any of the above subjects. Potential contributors should begin by submitting examples of previous work alongside their ideas. Gossip column items also welcomed.
Overall freelance potential: Excellent for the equestrian specialist.
Editor's tips: Speculative photographic contributions are welcome but check with the editor before submitting. Little real scope for polo coverage as this is handled by regulars.
Fees: Photographs from £12.50 (diary pics) up to £100 (full page). £150 per 1,000 words. Payment on publication.

HORSE AND RIDER

D. J. Murphy (Publishers) Ltd, 296 Ewell Road, Surbiton, Surrey KT6 7AQ. Tel: 081-390 8547.
Editor: Alison Bridge.
Monthly magazine aimed at adult horse-riders.
Illustrations: B&W and colour inside. Off-beat personality shots and pictures for photo stories illustrating equestrian subjects, e.g. plaiting up, clipping, etc. Also general yard pictures, riding pictures, people and horses. Covers: colour pictures of anything equestrian and a little out of the ordinary.
Text: Illustrated features on stable management, instructional and anything on horses. 1,500 words.
Overall freelance potential: A good possibility for freelances who show an understanding of the market.
Editor's tips: Material must be technically accurate, i.e. riders must be shown wearing the correct clothes, especially hats; horses must be fit and correctly tacked.
Fees: B&W pictures, £15; colour, £25–£60. Text, £65 per 1,000 words.

PONY

D. J. Murphy (Publishers) Ltd, 296 Ewell Road, Surbiton, Surrey KT6 7AQ. Tel: 081-390 8547.
Editor: Kate Austin.
Monthly magazine about horses, ponies and riding. Aimed at 8–16 age group.
Illustrations: Mainly B&W. High quality, close-up shots to illustrate features on ponies, stable management and riding. Must be technically accurate. Inside colour poster spreads: "pretty" pictures and atmospheric shots; medium format preferred. Covers: striking close-up colour shots of ponies, usually with teenage riders.
Text: Short picture stories on ponies or foals. Illustrated features about horses and the care of them. Fiction with a strong, contemporary plot. 800 words.
Overall freelance potential: Good quality freelance work is always welcome.
Fees: B&W pictures, £15; covers, £50; text around £65 per 1,000 words.

RIDING

Corner House, Foston, Grantham, Lincolnshire NG32 2JU. Tel: 0400 82032.
Editor: Helen Scott.
Monthly magazine aimed at the "grass roots" of the equestrian world. Contains informative and

instructional articles on riding and horse care; breeding; news and reports on equestrian events and competitions at all levels; riding clubs; and matters of general interest to this market.

Illustrations: B&W and colour. Anything as detailed above, including major events. Particularly interested in pictures of unusual events or incidents for news pages.

Text: Instructional articles and equestrian experiences of general interest to readers in any equestrian field. 1,000–2,000 words.

Overall freelance potential: A substantial amount of freelance work is used each month.

Fees: Good; on a rising scale, according to the size of reproduction or length of feature.

Farming

CROPS

Reed Farmers Publishing Group, Quadrant House, The Quadrant, Sutton, Surrey SM2 5AS. Tel: 081-652 4080.

Editor: Debbie Beaton.

Fortnightly magazine catering exclusively for the arable farmer.

Illustrations: Colour only. News pictures depicting anything of topical, unusual or technical interest concerning crop farming and production. Captions must be precise and detailed.

Text: Limited scope for short topical articles written by specialists.

Overall freelance potential: Good for farming specialists.

Fees: By negotiation.

DAIRY FARMER

Morgan Grampian Farming Press Ltd, Wharfedale Road, Ipswich IP1 4LG. Tel: 0473 241122.

Editor: David Shead.

Monthly technical journal for dairy farmers.

Illustrations: Mainly B&W. Captioned pictures for use as fillers. Pictures of a positive interest, technical or maybe historical. No "pretty-pretty" pictures.

Text: Features on technical advances and other notable achievements in dairying.

Overall freelance potential: Around 50 per cent comes from outside sources, but that includes several regular contributors.

Fees: By arrangement.

DAIRY INDUSTRIES INTERNATIONAL

Wilmington Publishing Ltd, Wilmington House, Church Hill, Wilmington, Dartford, Kent DA2 7EF. Tel: 0322 277788.

Editor: Sarah McRitchie.

Monthly publication for the dairy processing industry.

Illustrations: Colour. Pictures relating to the industry.

Text: Features on the technology of dairy processing, new dairy products and overseas developments.

Overall freelance potential: Around 5 per cent comes from freelance sources.

Fees: By agreement.

FARMERS WEEKLY

Reed Business Publishing Ltd, Quadrant House, The Quadrant, Sutton, Surrey SM2 5AS. Tel: 081-652 4911.

Editor: Stephen Howe.

Weekly covering all matters of interest to farmers.

Illustrations: Colour only. News pictures relating to the world of farming. Pictures stories on technical aspects.

Text: Tight, well-written copy on farming matters and anything that will help the farmer to run his

business more efficiently.
Overall freelance potential: Fair.
Fees: By negotiation.

INTERNATIONAL MILLING FLOUR AND FEED
Turret Group plc, 171 High Street, Rickmansworth, Herts WD3 1SN. Tel: 0923 777000.
Editor: Susan Fraser.
Monthly international business journal for the flour milling and feed compounding industries. Covers news, marketing, products, government policies and market reports on flour, wheat and animal feeds, new technology.
Illustrations: B&W and colour. Explosions/fires in milling plants, etc.
Text: Market reports, opinion polls, articles, new milling technology. Off-beat features which will create discussion. 1,500 words.
Overall freelance potential: The magazine uses a lot of freelance work. Especially of interest are articles on new mills (incl. Third Word countries), and innovative technology.
Editor's tips: Phone before submission, or send synopsis.
Fees: Pictures by negotiation. Text £55 per 1,000 words.

THE LANDWORKER
Rural, Agricultural and Allied Workers National Trade Group (TGWU), Transport House, Smith Square, London SW1P 3JB. Tel: 071-828 7788.
Editor: Bridget Henderson.
Six issues per year, dealing with politics and agriculture. Aimed mainly at rural workers.
Illustrations: B&W and colour. Pictures of all types of farm work, forestry, food processing, rural employment and union activity.
Text: Features on subjects detailed above. Up to 800 words.
Overall freelance potential: Limited.
Fees: On a rising scale according to size of reproduction or length of article.

PIG FARMING
Farming Press Ltd, Wharfedale Road, Ipswich, Suffolk IP1 4LG. Tel: 0473 241122.
Editor: Bryan Kelly.
Monthly publication for pig farmers.
Illustrations: B&W and colour. Pictures showing specific points of pig production, new ideas, systems, etc. Occasional off-beat pictures of pigs used.
Text: Technical and practical articles on modern pig production, covering the industry from breeding through to products ready for the shop. Some general interest features. Maximum 1,200 words.
Overall freelance potential: Limited.
Fees: By arrangement.

POULTRY WORLD
Reed Business Publishing, Quadrant House, Sutton, Surrey SM2 5AS. Tel: 081-652 4021.
Editor: John Farrant.
Monthly publication aimed at the UK, EC and worldwide commercial poultry industries. Includes Pure Breeds and Game Birds sections.
Illustrations: B&W and colour. News pictures relating to the poultry industry.
Text: News items and ideas for features always considered.
Overall freelance potential: Limited.
Fees: By negotiation.

TRACTOR AND FARM MACHINERY TRADER
Wordsworth Trade Press Ltd, 39 Church Road, Harold Wood, Romford, Essex RM3 0JX. Tel: 07083 47276.

Editor: Richard Lee.

Monthly publication for farm machinery dealers.

Illustrations: B&W only. Pictures of farm machinery dealers standing, with a few of their key staff members, in front of their premises, to illustrate short reports on the people involved.

Text: Short reports (100 words) on above pictures detailing the dealer's main agencies and the situation with current trade. Illustrated short features (300 words) on dealers at county shows.

Overall freelance potential: Over 50 per cent comes from freelances.

Fees: Short reports with pictures, £20; illustrated features with five or six pictures, £40. Other features by arrangement.

Food & Drink

HOTEL & RESTAURANT MAGAZINE

Quantum Publishing Ltd, 29/31 Lower Coombe Street, Croydon CR9 1LX. Tel: 081-681 2099.

Editor: Annie Stephenson.

Monthly magazine for the restaurant trade, dealing with the top end of the market.

Illustrations: Mainly colour. News pictures featuring openings, expansions, refurbishments, trade personalities, etc.

Text: Illustrated features on areas of development, profiles of individual restaurateurs and their establishments. Coverage from outside London particularly welcome, but always contact the editor first.

Overall freelance potential: Good for those with connections in the trade.

Editor's tips: Remember that this is a business journal and avoid consumer type material. The magazine deals with restaurants at the top end of the market and there is no interest in fast food outlets etc.

Fees: By negotiation.

INDEPENDENT CATERER

IML Group Ltd, Blair House, 184–186 High Street, Tonbridge, Kent TN9 1BQ. Tel: 0732 359990.

Editor: Caroline Scoular.

Monthly magazine for the independent catering sector.

Illustrations: B&W for news pages; B&W and colour for feature illustrations. News pictures with stories relating to independent caterers in mainly small to medium-sized operations in hotels, restaurants and pubs.

Text: Illustrated articles that would interest or amuse caterers in smaller businesses, including practical advice that would assist in the successful running of such operations. 1,000–1,200 words.

Overall freelance potential: Quite good.

Fees: £100 per 1,000 words for text; photographs by negotiation.

THE JEWISH VEGETARIAN

The International Jewish Vegetarian Society, 853/855 Finchley Road, London NW11 8LX. Tel: 081-455 0692.

Editorial contact: Shirley Labelda.

Quarterly publication concerned with vegetarianism, its ethics, nutritional value and health benefits.

Illustrations: B&W only inside. Pictures showing ecology, animal welfare and proper land use. Pictures with an emotional interest between man (especially children) and animals. Covers: colour pictures of same.

Text: No freelance market.

Overall freelance potential: Quite good.

Fees: By agreement.

PUBLICAN
Quantum Publishing Ltd, 29/31 Lower Coombe Street, Croydon CR9 1LX. Tel: 081-681 2099.
Editor: Andrew Palmer.
Weekly independent newspaper for publicans throughout the UK.
Illustrations: B&W and colour. Pictures of pub interiors and exteriors; cellar equipment; anything concerning brewery management and publicans. Must be newsworthy or have some point of unusual interest.
Text: News items and picture stories about publicans – humorous, unusual, or controversial. Stories that have implications for the whole pub trade, or that illustrate a problem. Original ways of increasing trade. News items up to 250 words maximum; features around 500–800 words.
Overall freelance potential: Good for original in-depth material, especially from outside London and the South East.
Editor's tips: Forget charity bottle smashes and pub openings, and forget pictures of people pulling or holding pints – hundreds of these are received already.
Fees: On a rising scale according to size of reproduction or length of text.

SCOTTISH LICENSED TRADE NEWS
Peebles Publishing Group, Berguis House, Clifton Street, Glasgow G3 7LA. Tel: 041-331 1022.
Editor: Patrick Duffy.
Fortnightly publication for Scottish publicans, off-licensees, hoteliers, caterers, restaurateurs, drinks executives, drinks companies.
Illustrations: B&W only. Pictures connected with the above subjects.
Text: News and features of interest to the Scottish trade.
Overall freelance potential: Limited.
Fees: By agreement.

TASTE
HHL Publishing, Greater London House, Hampstead Road, London NW1 7QQ. Tel: 071-388 3171.
Editor: Drew Smith.
Monthly, up-market food and drink magazine that aims to appeal to both consumers and catering professionals.
Illustrations: Colour only. Original photo essays on aspects of the food chain may be considering on spec. Otherwise all photography commissioned to accompany specific articles.
Text: Top quality features on food subjects, usually by commission. 2,000–3,000 words.
Overall freelance potential: Good for specialists only.
Editor's tips: Study the magazine first and don't submit mediocre material.
Fees: By negotiation.

VQ
The Vegetarian Society (UK) Ltd, Parkdale, Dunham Road, Altrincham, Cheshire WA14 4QG. Tel: 061-928 0793.
Editor: Carol Timperley.
Quarterly magazine of the Vegetarian Society.
Illustrations: B&W and colour. Relevant news pictures; photographs of farm animals and poultry, in both intensive/battery and free-range conditions.
Text: General articles on vegetarianism, animal welfare and environmental issues.
Overall freelance potential: Good.
Fees: Photographs according to use. Text around £75 per 1,000 words.

VEGETARIAN LIVING
HHL Publishing Group Ltd, Greater London House, Hampstead Road, London NW1 7QQ. Tel: 071-388 3171.
Editor: Nicola Graimes.

Monthly publication for vegetarians and anyone interested in the subject.

Illustrations: B&W and colour. Stock pictures of farm animals and poultry in free range, "old fashioned" or modern units so that the types can be contrasted. Also, well-known vegetarian personalities.

Text: Articles on animal rights and vegetarianism. Interviews with vegetarian personalities; travel; environmental/conservation issues; cookery features.

Overall freelance potential: Between 30 and 40 per cent of the magazine is contributed by freelances.

Fees: Text, negotiable up to £120 per 1,000 words.

WINE AND SPIRIT INTERNATIONAL

The Evro Publishing Co, 60 Waldegrave Road, Teddington, Middlesex TW11 8LG. Tel: 081-943 5943.

Editor: Eluned Jones.

Monthly trade magazine for the wine and spirit industry. Aimed principally at the international wine and spirit trade, buyers, marketing directors, management, producers, quality control, etc.

Illustrations: Colour for covers only: vertical format shots of wine and spirit subjects – no bottles.

Text: Features on marketing and production in the wine and spirits industry worldwide. 1,000–2,000 words.

Overall freelance potential: Around 40 per cent of the publication comes from freelance sources.

Editor's tips: Telephone before submitting.

Fees: Negotiable.

Gardening

AMATEUR GARDENING

IPC Magazines Ltd, Westover House, West Quay Road, Poole, Dorset BH15 1JG. Tel: 0202 680586.

Editor: Graham Clarke.

Weekly magazine for the amateur gardener.

Illustrations: Colour. Little scope for speculative submissions, but the editor will always be interested in receiving lists of subjects available from freelances.

Text: Illustrated out-of-the-ordinary features from contributors with a good knowledge of the subject.

Overall freelance potential: Limited to the specialist contributor.

Fees: By arrangement.

BBC GARDENERS' WORLD MAGAZINE

Redwood Publishing Ltd, 101 Bayham Street, London NW1 0AG. Tel: 071-331 8000.

Editor: Adam Pasco.

Monthly magazine for gardeners at all levels of expertise.

Illustrations: Colour only. No speculative submissions. Photographers with specialist gardening collections should send lists of material available. Commissions may be available to photograph individual gardens; the editor will always be pleased to hear from photographers who can bring potential subjects to his attention.

Text: No scope.

Overall freelance potential: Mainly for specialists.

Editor's tips: Always looking for interesting "real" gardens for possible coverage.

Fees: By negotiation.

THE GARDEN

The Royal Horticultural Society, 80 Vincent Square, London SW1 2PE. Tel: 071-834 4333.

Editor: Ian Hodgson.

Monthly journal of the Royal Horticultural Society. Publishes articles on plants and specialist aspects and techniques of horticulture.

Illustrations: B&W and colour of identified plants and specific gardens.
Text: Little freelance market.
Overall freelance potential: Limited.
Fees: £35–£60, according to size of reproduction; cover £100.

GARDEN ANSWERS
EMAP Apex Publications Ltd, Apex House, Oundle Road, Peterborough PE2 9NP. Tel: 0733 898100.
Managing Editor: Adrienne Wild.
Monthly magazine for the enthusiastic amateur gardener.
Illustrations: Colour. Little scope for speculative submissions, but the editor is always interested in receiving lists of subjects available from photographers accompanied by up to 24 transparencies and an SAE.
Text: Experienced gardening writers may be able to obtain commissions.
Overall freelance potential: Limited to the experienced gardening contributor.
Editor's tips: Practical gardening pictures are required, rather than simple shots of plants.
Fees: By arrangement.

GARDEN NEWS
EMAP Apex Publications Ltd, Apex House, Oundle Road, Peterborough PE2 9NP. Tel: 0733 898100.
Editor: Andrew Blackford.
Weekly consumer magazine for gardeners.
Illustrations: B&W and colour. Pictures of general horticultural subjects. Practical photographs to illustrate gardening techniques. Colour portraits of trees, shrubs, flowers and vegetables.
Text: Features of interest to gardeners.
Overall freelance potential: Fair.
Fees: By agreement.

GARDEN TRADE NEWS INTERNATIONAL
EMAP Apex Publications Ltd, Apex House, Oundle Road, Peterborough PE2 9NP. Tel: 0733 898100.
Editorial direct line: 0536 402341.
Editor: Mike Wyatt.
Monthly trade publication containing news, features and advice for growers, garden centres, wholesalers and manufacturers of horticultural products.
Illustrations: B&W and colour. Pictures for illustrated features.
Text: Articles about, or of interest to garden centres and garden shops. Max. 600 words.
Overall freelance potential: Limited.
Editor's tips: Remember, this is a trade magazine, not a consumer publication.
Fees: £8 per 100 words; pictures on a rising scale according to size of reproduction.

THE GARDENER
HHL Publishing Ltd, Greater London House, Hampstead Road, London NW1 7QQ. Tel: 071-388 3171.
Editor: Cathy Buchanan.
Up-market gardening magazine published monthly.
Illustrations: Colour, always by commission. Top quality pictures of all gardening subjects.
Text: Practical articles and inspirational features, usually by commission form experienced contributors.
Overall freelance potential: Limited to the experienced contributor to the gardening press, or to features with an unusual bias.
Fees: By negotiation.

GARDENS ILLUSTRATED
John Brown Publishing Ltd, The Boathouse, Crabtree Lane, Fulham, London SW6 8NJ. Tel: 071-381 6007.

Editor: Rosie Atkins. **Art Director**: Claudia Zeff.
Alternate-monthly, heavily-illustrated magazine with a practical and inspirational approach.
Illustrations: Colour only. Usually commissioned, but high quality submissions may be considered on spec. Photography should have a narrative and journalistic slant rather than just pretty pictures of gardens. The gardens should be depicted in relation to the landscape, houses and the people who own or work them. Coverage from outside UK welcome.
Text: Scope for experienced gardening writers – submit samples of previously published work first.
Overall freelance potential: Very good for the right material.
Editor's tips: Material previously featured elsewhere is not of interest.
Fees: By negotiation.

HORTICULTURE WEEK

Haymarket Publishing Ltd, 38–42 Hampton Road, Teddington, Middlesex TW11 0JE. Tel: 081-943 5000.
Editor: Stovin Hayter.
Weekly aimed at commercial growers of ornamental plants and those employed in landscape work, garden centres, public parks and gardens.
Illustrations: B&W and colour. Captioned news and feature pictures relating to commercial horticulture, landscaping, public parks, garden centres.
Text: Short news items about happenings affecting the trade.
Overall freelance potential: Limited.
Editor's tips: Contact the news or features editor first.
Fees: By arrangement.

NURSERYMAN AND GARDEN CENTRE

Bouverie Publishing Co Ltd, 147–151 Temple Chambers, Temple Avenue, London EC4Y 0BP. Tel: 071-583 3030.
Editor: Peter Dawson.
Fortnightly publication for nurserymen, garden centre operators, manufacturers of garden products, gardening journalists, educational establishments in the field, landscape designers and contractors, groundsmen, etc.
Illustrations: B&W and colour. Fully captioned single pictures of subjects of interest to the readership.
Text: Features on all aspects of garden centre and nursery work, and the equipment used. New developments at home and abroad. 1,000–1,500 words.
Overall freelance potential: Fair.
Fees: By negotiation.

PRACTICAL GARDENING

EMAP Apex Publications Ltd, Apex House, Oundle Road, Peterborough PE2 9NP. Tel: 0733 898100.
Editor: Adrienne Wild.
Monthly guide to inspired ideas for the garden, written by experts for enthusiastic, but not specialist, gardeners.
Illustrations: Colour only. Top quality plant portraits, groups and garden scenes.
Text: Practical articles on all gardening topics.
Overall freelance potential: Quite good.
Fees: By agreement.

YOUR GARDEN

IPC Magazines Ltd, Westover House, West Quay Road, Poole, Dorset BH15 1JG. Tel: 0202 680586.
Editor: Graham Clarke.
Monthly practical magazine for the amateur gardener. Somewhat more up-market sister to *Amateur Gardening*.

Illustrations: Colour only. Generally relies on the same contributors as its sister title, but freelances who can offer a fresh approach always welcome.
Text: Illustrated features from contributors with a good knowledge of the subject.
Overall freelance potential: Only for specialists.
Fees: By arrangement.

General Interest

ACTIVE LIFE
Aspen Specialist Media, Christ Church, Cosway Street, London NW1 5NJ. Tel: 071-262 2622.
Editor: Helene Hodge.
Quarterly general interest magazine for the over-55s.
Illustrations: Mainly colour. Positive images of older people; usually to accompany specific articles but some scope for stock material.
Text: Illustrated articles on a wide range of topics, offering a positive view of the retired lifestyle. Should contain plenty of informative details. Style should be simple and punchy, running from 500–1,000 words.
Overall freelance potential: Fair.
Editor's tips: "Try not to write as though readers are only fit for the knackers yard!"
Fees: £100 per 1,000 words for text; pictures by negotiation.

THE AMERICAN
British American Newspapers Ltd, 114–115 West Street, Farnham, Surrey GU9 7HL. Tel: 0252 713366.
Editor: Bob Pickens.
Fortnightly publication for American residents in the UK and short-term US visitors.
Illustrations: B&W only. Pictures of Americans or American activities in the UK.
Text: Features on Americans or American activities in the UK. Human interest and "people" stories work best, particularly if they involve business, education, arts or sports.
Overall freelance potential: Good. Several regular freelance columns plus at least one general freelance piece in each issue.
Editor's tips: Currently increasing the number of stories on Americans in the UK. Phone queries are OK, but should be followed by a query letter and manuscript within two weeks. Seasonal material should be submitted three months in advance.
Fees: 50p per column centimetre printed; pictures from £15.

ANTIQUES TODAY
Stanley Gibbons Ltd, 5 Parkside, Christchurch Road, Ringwood, Hampshire BH24 3SH. Tel: 0425 472363.
Editor: Hugh Jefferies.
Monthly tabloid covering all aspects of antiques and collectibles for the ordinary collector.
Illustrations: B&W only. Relevant news pictures always of interest, though much comes from PR sources, auction houses, etc. Photographers with good stock coverage of specific antiques and collectibles may find it worthwhile to supply lists of subjects available.
Text: Illustrated news items, and articles on all aspects of antique collecting of 1,000 words or more.
Overall freelance potential: Limited.
Fees: Text around £50 per 1,000 words.

CHOICE
Choice Publications Ltd, 2 St John's Place, St John's Square, London EC1M 4DE. Tel: 071-490 7070.
Editor: Wendy James. **Picture Researcher**: Claire Hoffman.

General interest monthly for the over-50s.

Illustrations: Colour. Photographs mainly used to illustrate specific features. Top quality stock shots of older people enjoying various activities may be of interest, but send lists of material available in the first instance.

Text: Ideas for articles on any suitable topic always welcome.

Overall freelance potential: Fair.

Fees: By negotiation.

EXPRESSION

Redwood Publishing Ltd, 101 Bayham Street, London NW1 0AG. Tel: 071-331 8000.

Editor: Sue Thomas.

Bi-monthly general interest magazine for American Express cardmembers.

Illustrations: B&W and colour. Mostly commissioned, but always interested in hearing from photographers with good stock library of mostly travel-related subjects. Also occasional need for stock shots of cars and personalities.

Text: Articles invariably commissioned, but will consider proposals from experienced freelances. Travel, the arts, general interest.

Overall freelance potential: Limited.

Fees: Good; on a rising scale according to the size of the illustration of the length of the feature.

FORUM

Northern & Shell plc, Northern & Shell Tower, PO Box 381, City Harbour, London E14 9GL. Tel: 071-987 5090.

Editor: Elizabeth Coldwell. **Art Director**: Linda Brodie.

Monthly magazine dealing with all aspects of sex, i.e. social, medical, problematical, political, relationships, etc. Aimed at intelligent, aware, educated men and women.

Illustrations: B&W only. Pictures are taken only to illustrate articles. All pictures must be tasteful despite the subject matter, which can be anything from fetishes to problems with love and marriage.

Text: Factual, social and medical features with a keen sex relevance. No porn.

Overall freelance potential: Nearly all material comes from freelance sources.

Editor's tips: Study recent issues of the magazine and then submit only a synopsis or outline in the first instance.

Fees: By arrangement, but reasonably good.

GREEN MAGAZINE

PO Box 3205, City Harbour, 4 Selsdon Way, London E14 9GL. Tel: 071-712 0550.

Editor: Alistair Townley.

Monthly magazine covering all "green" and environmental issues.

Illustrations: Mainly colour. Good stock pictures and picture stories on any environmental and ecological subjects, ranging from politics to wildlife.

Text: Well-illustrated features and investigative articles on any "green" issue, but always query with the editor in the first instance.

Overall freelance potential: Good; many contributions are freelance

Fees: By negotiation.

HARRINGTON KILBRIDE PUBLISHING GROUP

The Publishing House, Highbury Station Road, Islington, London N1 1SE. Tel: 071-226 2222.

Picture Editor: Nick Rose.

Major magazine publishing group, producing over 80 titles per annum. Publications include specialist European and international business magazines as well as consumer magazines on a wide range of subjects.

Illustrations: Mostly colour; some B&W. Colour pictures to illustrate the whole range of the company's products. Major subjects of interest: babies, food, healthcare, agriculture, industry, conservation, pollution, travel and royalty. Sports coverage of special interest. B&W archive material of foreign

countries, royalty and politicians. Send a few samples plus lists of subjects available, or make an appointment to show portfolio.
Text: No scope.
Overall freelance potential: Excellent.
Fees: Variable according to use, from £35 upwards.

THE ILLUSTRATED LONDON NEWS
The Illustrated London News & Sketch Ltd, 20 Upper Ground, London, SE1 9PF. Tel: 071-928 2111.
Editor: James Bishop.
Bi-monthly general interest magazine with particular relevance to living in London.
Illustrations: B&W and colour. Picture stories about Britain and particularly on London.
Text: Articles on Britain and particularly London. Also, general material on the arts, entertainment, etc.
Overall freelance potential: Good, but most material is commissioned.
Editor's tips: "We are actively seeking new and innovative photographic work. We are especially interested in pictures that lead to stories, although pictures may often stand on their own."
Fees: Negotiable; good.

OK! MAGAZINE
OK! Magazines Ltd, Northern & Shell Tower, City Harbour, London E14 9GL. Tel: 071-987 5090.
Editor: Ann Wallace. **Art Director**: Andy Becker. **Picture Editor**: Gregory King.
Fortnightly, picture-led magazine almost entirely devoted to celebrities.
Illustrations: Colour only. Shots of celebrities of all kinds considered on spec – submit to the picture editor. Commissions available to experienced portrait workers – contact the art director.
Text: Exclusive stories/interviews with celebrities always of interest.
Overall freelance potential: Excellent for the right type of material.
Fees: Negotiable; depends on nature of the material or assignment.

PREDICTION
Link House Magazines plc, Link House, Dingwall Avenue, Croydon, CR9 2TA. Tel: 081-686 2599.
Editor: Jo Logan.
Monthly magazine covering astrology and all aspects of the occult. Regular features on Tarot, palmistry, graphology etc.
Illustrations: Colour only for cover use. Must be pertinent to general contents of the magazine. 6x6cm minimum.
Text: Articles with an occult slant, i.e. mythology, magic, alternative therapies, ESP, telepathy, UFOs, earth mysteries, dowsing, etc. 1,500–2,000 words.
Overall freelance potential: Very good for articles; 95 per cent of content is contributed.
Fees: Variable.

READER'S DIGEST (British Edition)
The Reader's Digest Association Ltd, Berkeley Square House, Berkeley Square, London W1X 6AB. Tel: 071-629 8144.
Editor: Russell Twisk.
Monthly magazine for a general interest readership.
Illustrations: B&W and colour. Pictures of general interest, usually to illustrate specific features.
Text: High quality features on all topics.
Overall freelance potential: Very limited opportunities for new freelance contributors.
Fees: By agreement.

SAGA MAGAZINE
Saga Publishing Ltd, The Saga Building, Middelburg Square, Folkestone, Kent CT20 1AZ. Tel: 0303 711523.

Editor: Paul Bach.

Monthly general interest magazine aimed at retired people.

Illustrations: Colour only. Usually required to illustrate articles or as part of a complete feature package. Picture features on hobbies or collecting of nostalgic items, heritage, nostalgia, crafts and natural history and celebrities/achievers of interest/relevance to the age group.

Text: Illustrated articles with general appeal to an older readership. Usually commissioned, but freelance suggestions are welcome.

Overall freelance potential: Good scope for top quality photo features.

Fees: By negotiation.

SAINSBURY'S THE MAGAZINE

New Crane Publishing Ltd, 4 Bargehouse Crescent, 28 Upper Ground, London SE1 9PD. Tel: 071-633 0266.

Editor: Michael Wynn Jones. **Picture Editor**: Suzie Hamilton.

Monthly general interest magazine produced for the Sainsbury's supermarket chain.

Illustrations: Colour only. Commissions available for general features illustration in the areas of portraiture, interior design, gardening, fashion, health and beauty.

Text: Could be some scope for experienced contributors.

Overall freelance potential: Quite good for the experienced specialist.

Editor's tips: Although the magazine is biased towards food and drink topics, food photographers are *not* required; this area is well covered.

Fees: Negotiable, but photographers' day rate around £250.

SKY MAGAZINE

Hachette Emap, Mappin House, 4 Winsley Street, London W1 7AR. Tel: 071-436 1515.

Editor: Angela Holden. **Art Editor**: Sean Cook.

Monthly youth culture magazine aimed at both sexes in the 18–24 age group. Major subjects covered include music, films, fashion, style, news stories and sport.

Illustrations: Mostly colour. Pictures to illustrate articles and features. Mainly commissioned work in the fields of music, fashion, still life and portraiture. Top quality speculative submissions always considered.

Text: Lively and very topical articles on any subject of interest to an intelligent young readership, invariably by commission. Ideas are always welcome.

Overall freelance potential: Good for top quality work.

Fees: Photographic fees based on a page rate of £150. Covers around £250; colour spreads around £300. Text by arrangement.

TITBITS MAGAZINE

Caversham Communications Ltd, 2 Caversham Street, London SW3 4AH. Tel: 071-351 4995.

Editor: Leonard Holdsworth.

Monthly general interest publication with the accent on men's interests.

Illustrations: Colour only. Main scope for celebrity pictures, but there is some scope for dramatic and off-beat pictures. Also saucy news items.

Text: Articles of general interest, preferably dramatic or off-beat, or of "adult" interest.

Overall freelance potential: More scope for complete articles than single pictures.

Editor's tips: Potential contributors are strongly advised to consult the publication itself *before* submitting material. Also note the publication is full-colour throughout.

Fees: By agreement.

YOURS

Yours Publishing Co Ltd, Apex House, Oundle Round, Peterborough PE2 9NP. Tel: 0733 555123.

Editor: Neil Patrick.

Monthly publication aimed at the over-sixties. Aims to be entertaining as well as informing the retired generation of their rights and entitlements.

Illustrations: B&W and colour. Pictures showing old people's achievements, holidays, housing, etc., plus general features likely to be of particular interest to an older readership.

Text: Articles and features on above subjects. 750–1,000 words.

Overall freelance potential: Fair.

Fees: By negotiation.

Health & Fitness

CARERS WORLD
A. E. Morgan Publications Ltd, 9 West Street, Epsom, Surrey, KT18 7RL. Tel: 0372 741411.

Editor: Chris Cattrall.

Bi-monthly magazine for carers and the elderly, taking a positive approach to coping with disability. Includes good coverage of leisure topics.

Illustrations: B&W only. Photographs showing the positive achievements of handicapped people. Disabled people at work, taking part in sport, on holiday, and so on. Covers: colour pictures usually related to a major feature inside the magazine.

Text: Illustrated articles and features, from 250 words upwards, concentrating on self-help and the positive approach. General leisure topics from the disabled point of view.

Overall freelance potential: An intelligent and sensitive approach to the subject will pay off.

Editor's tips: Avoid a patronising or negative approach.

Fees: £5 for black and white pictures; up to £30 for suitable cover shots. Payments for articles by prior agreement.

HEALTH & EFFICIENCY (H+E)
Peenhill Ltd, 28 Charles Square, Pitfield Street, London N1 6HT. Tel: 071-253 4037.

Editor: Kate Sturdy.

Monthly naturist/nudist magazine. Also quarterly and bi-annual editions.

Illustrations: B&W and colour. Attractive photos of naturists. Male and female nudes, single or groups, young (18+) to mature. Also travel and scenic shots used.

Text: Short illustrated articles about naturists, resorts, human relationships.

Overall freelance potential: Very good.

Editor's tips: Recent policy change provides much wider scope for photographers. Guidelines on request.

Fees: £20+ per page and pro rata for colour; £10 per page and pro rata for black and white. "Increased rates negotiable for top quality submissions."

HEALTH & FITNESS MAGAZINE
Headway, Home and Law Publishing Group Ltd, Greater London House, Hampstead Road, London NW1 7QQ. Tel: 071-388 3171.

Editor: Sharon Walker. **Art Director**: Grant Turner.

Glossy monthly covering all aspects of fitness, health and nutrition, aimed at women.

Illustrations: Mostly colour; some B&W. Captioned news pictures, and photographs for use in illustrating articles and features. Covers: outstanding and striking colour shots, usually featuring an obviously healthy young woman in close-up, or a young, healthy male and female couple.

Text: Articles and features on suitable topics, with an appeal to women generally. No "health fads and hypochondria" type material.

Overall freelance potential: Little scope for non-specialists.

Editor's tips: Always query the editor before submitting.

Fees: By negotiation.

HERE'S HEALTH
EMAP Elan, Victory House, Leicester Place, London WC2H 7BP. Tel: 071-437 9011.
Editor: Mandy Francis.
Monthly publication covering anything that relates to good health, from vitamin and mineral supplements to ecology and conservation. Accent is on the practical. Aimed at people who want to help themselves to total health, physical, mental and spiritual.
Illustrations: B&W and colour. Mainly to illustrate specific features.
Text: Features on all forms of health, alternative medicine, therapies, travel, food.
Overall freelance potential: Around 50 per cent is contributed from outside sources, though this includes regular contributors. Always room for good freelance articles and pictures.
Fees: On a rising scale, according to quality and size.

Hobbies & Crafts

THE AQUARIST AND PONDKEEPER
Dog World Ltd, 9 Tufton Street, Ashford, Kent TN23 1QN. Tel: 0233 621877.
Editor: John Dawes.
Monthly fishkeeping magazine dealing with tropical, freshwater, marine and coldwater fish; water gardening, aquarium keeping and all allied subjects, e.g. reptiles and amphibians, conservation, etc.
Illustrations: B&W and colour. Any picture connected with indoor or outdoor keeping of pet fish, reptiles and amphibians, and water gardening. *Not* fishing or angling. Covers: colour pictures of tropical, coldwater or marine fish.
Text: Features on the keeping of indoor or outdoor fish, aquatic plants, expeditions, conservation and herpetological subjects. All articles should be illustrated, either by photographs or with line drawings. 1,200–1,500 words.
Overall freelance potential: Very good; over 90 per cent comes from outside contributors.
Fees: By arrangement.

BIRD KEEPER
IPC Magazines, King's Reach Tower, Stamford Street, London SE1 9LS. Tel: 071-261 5000.
Editor: Peter Moss.
Alternate-monthly magazine for bird keepers and breeders, particularly aimed at the newcomer to the hobby.
Illustrations: B&W and colour. Good pictures of British cage birds, budgerigars, canaries and parrots, plus any more general pictures illustrating news or developments in aviculture. Covers: top quality colour of individual birds.
Text: Most contributed by known experts, but some scope for photo features of about 1,500 words.
Overall freelance potential: Quite good.
Fees: By negotiation.

CAGE & AVIARY BIRDS
IPC Magazines Ltd, King's Reach Tower, Stamford Street, London SE1 9LS. Tel: 071-261 6116.
Editor: Brian Byles.
Weekly journal covering all aspects of birdkeeping and breeding, aimed at enthusiasts of all ages.
Illustrations: B&W and colour. Mostly as illustrations to features. Others should cover avicultural subjects in general. Covers: colour of birds mentioned below.
Text: Features on all aspects of breeding birds such as British birds, budgerigars, canaries, pheasants, foreign birds, waterfowl and birds of prey. Any reasonable length.
Overall freelance potential: Very good. Most material comes from freelances.
Fees: Good; on a rising scale according to size of reproduction or length of feature.

CAR NUMBERS MAGAZINE
PO Box 100, Devizes, Wiltshire SN10 4TE. Tel: 0380 818181.
Editor: Tony Hill.
Bi-monthly publication for all those interested in personalised car number plates.
Illustrations: B&W only inside. Particularly interested in pictures of well known people with their car and personalised number plate. Covers: colour pictures of same.
Text: Short articles concerning number plates and associated subjects. Particular interest in legal angles. 200–300 words.
Overall freelance potential: Small at the moment but growing.
Fees: £50 for colour or B&W of famous owners; other B&W pictures around £10; £15–£30 per article.

THE CLOCKMAKER
TEE Publishing, Edwards Centre, Regent Street, Hinckley, Leicestershire LE10 0BB. Tel: 0455 616419/637173.
Editor: C. L. Deith.
Bi-monthly magazine concerned with clockmaking and restoring.
Illustrations: B&W only. Photographs only used in conjunction with specific news items or articles. No market for stock photos. Covers: B&W photographs on any subject related to clocks.
Text: Well-illustrated articles and features on all aspects of clockmaking. Must be of a serious and technical nature.
Overall freelance potential: Only for those who can offer serious coverage of the subject.
Editor's tips: This is a highly specialised field and articles must have good technical content.
Fees: Negotiable.

CLOCKS
Argus Specialist Publications, Argus House, Boundary Way, Hemel Hempstead, Herts HP2 7ST. Tel: 0442 66551.
Editor: John Hunter.
Monthly magazine for clock enthusiasts generally, i.e. people interested in building, repairing, restoring and collecting clocks as well as watches.
Illustrations: B&W and colour. Pictures of anything concerned with clocks, e.g. public clocks, clocks in private collections, clocks in museums, clock movements and parts, people involved in clock making, repairing or restoration. Detailed captions essential. Covers: colour pictures as detailed above.
Text: Features on clockmakers, repairers or restorers; museums and collections; clock companies. 1,000–2,000 words.
Overall freelance potential: Around 90 per cent of the magazine is contributed by freelances.
Editor's tips: Pictures unaccompanied by textual descriptions of the clocks, or articles about them, are rarely used.
Fees: By arrangement.

ENGINEERING IN MINIATURE
TEE Publishing, Edward Centre, Regent Street, Hinckley, Leicestershire LE10 0BB. Tel: 0455 616419/637173.
Editor: C. L. Deith.
Monthly magazine concerned with model engineering and working steam models.
Illustrations: B&W only. Photographs only used in conjunction with specific news items or articles. No stock photos required. Covers: colour photographs on any subject related to steam or model engineering.
Text: Well-illustrated articles and features on all aspects of model engineering and serious modelling, and on full size railways and steam road vehicles. Must be of a serious and technical nature. There is no coverage of model railways below '0' gauge, or of plastic models.
Overall freelance potential: Some 80 per cent of contributions come from freelances.
Editor's tips: This is a highly specialised field and articles must have good technical content.
Fees: Negotiable.

FISHKEEPING ANSWERS

EMAP Pursuit Publishing Ltd, Bretton Court, Bretton, Peterborough PE3 8DZ. Tel: 0733 264666.
Editor: Sue Parslow.
Monthly magazine aimed mainly at newcomers to the hobby.
Illustrations: Colour only. Good stock shots of aquarium fish and other fishkeeping subjects.
Text: Well-illustrated practical articles on any fishkeeping topic, up to 1,500 words. Send suggestions or synopsis in the first instance.
Overall freelance potential: Good.
Fees: Photographs according to size or reproduction, from a minimum of £20. Text by negotiation.

GOOD WOODWORKING

Future Publishing Ltd, Beauford Court, 30 Monmouth Street, Bath BA1 2BW. Tel: 0225 442244.
Editor: Nick Gibbs. **Art Editor**: Dean Wilson.
Monthly magazine for the serious amateur woodworker.
Illustrations: Mostly colour. By commission only. Assignments available to cover specific projects – contact the art editor.
Text: Ideas and suggestions welcome, but writers must have good technical knowledge of the subject. Commissions available to interview individual woodworkers.
Overall freelance potential: Good for those with knowledge of the subject.
Fees: Photography by negotiation. Text around £150 per 1,000 words.

MODEL BOATS

Argus Specialist Publications Ltd, Argus House, Boundary Way, Hemel Hempstead, Herts HP2 4ST. Tel: 0442 66551.
Editor: John Cundell.
Monthly magazine that covers any facet of model boating plus occasional material on full-size subjects of interest to modellers.
Illustrations: B&W and colour. All model boating subjects, including regattas. Sharp colour prints preferred. Covers: colour transparencies of model boating subjects. Medium format preferred, but will consider 35mm if vertical format.
Text: News items, illustrated articles and plans on wide range of ship and boat modelling, e.g. scale, electric, internal combustion, steam, sail, etc. Other maritime subjects considered if there is some connection with modelling. Up to 3,000 words.
Overall freelance potential: Good; 30 per cent bought from outside contributors.
Editor's tips: Send SAE with a request for a contributor's guide before submitting. Prints should be well captioned.
Fees: Approximately £20 per published page.

MODEL ENGINEER

Argus Specialist Publications Ltd, Argus House, Boundary Way, Hemel Hempstead, Herts HP2 7ST. Tel: 0442 66551.
Editor: E. J. Jolliffe.
Twice monthly magazine aimed at the serious model engineering enthusiast.
Illustrations: B&W and limited colour. No stock shots required; all pictures must be part of an article. Covers: medium format transparencies depicting models of steam locomotives and traction engines; metalworking equipment and home workshop scenes; some full size vintage vehicles.
Text: Well-illustrated articles from specialists.
Overall freelance potential: Considerable for the specialist.
Fees: Negotiable.

MODEL RAILWAYS

Argus Specialist Publications Ltd, Argus House, Boundary Way, Hemel Hempstead, Herts HP2 7ST. Tel: 0442 66551.

Editor: Roy Johnstone.

Monthly magazine for the model railway enthusiast.

Illustrations: B&W and colour. Pictures used only as illustrations to features. Covers: colour pictures connected with an inside feature.

Text: Illustrated features on layouts, techniques and new innovations in the model railway world. Best supplied by a freelance with a good contacts in the hobby.

Overall freelance potential: Quite good for the right material, but all regular contributors are well established in the hobby.

Editor's tips: Very specialised field. Require features of a modelling or prototypical nature, not toys.

Fees: By agreement.

POPULAR CRAFTS

Argus Specialist Publications Ltd, Argus House, Boundary Way, Hemel Hempstead, Herts HP2 7ST. Tel: 0442 66551.

Editor: Brenda Ross.

Monthly magazine for everyone interested in crafts.

Illustrations: B&W and colour. Pictures used as illustrations for features, or with news items. Covers: colour pictures linked with feature inside.

Text: All types of craft with strong emphasis on how to do it. 500–2,000 words. Also news items up to 300 words.

Overall freelance potential: Around 85 per cent of the magazine is contributed.

Editor's tips: Articles should have a strong practical bias, helped by step-by-step pictures, or should be interesting profiles of craftspeople.

Fees: Approximately £40 per published page.

PRACTICAL FISHKEEPING

EMAP Pursuit Publishing Ltd, Bretton Court, Bretton, Peterborough PE3 8DZ. Tel: 0733 264666.

Editor: Steve Windsor.

Monthly magazine for all freshwater, marine and coldwater fishkeepers, aimed at every level from hobbyist to expert.

Illustrations: Colour. Pictures of all species of tropical, marine and coldwater fish, plants, tanks, ponds and water gardens. Prefer to hold material on file for possible future use.

Text: Emphasis on instructional articles on the subject. 1,000–1,500 words.

Overall freelance potential: Most is supplied by contributors with a specific knowledge of the hobby. Freelance material is considered on its merit at all times.

Editor's tips: Telephone first to give a brief on the intended copy and/or photographs available. Caption all fish clearly and get names right.

Fees: Negotiable.

SCALE MODEL TRAINS

Kristall Productions Ltd, 71b Maple Road, Surbiton, Surrey KT6 4AG. Tel: 081-399 9656.

Editor: Chris Ellis.

Monthly magazine for railway modellers.

Illustrations: B&W only. Pictures showing real railway activity in the UK or overseas, or railway modelling activity.

Text: No freelance market.

Overall freelance potential: Fair.

Fees: By agreement.

SCALE MODELS INTERNATIONAL

Argus Specialist Publications Ltd, Argus House, Boundary Way, Hemel Hempstead, Herts HP2 7ST. Tel: 0442 66551.

Editor: Kelvin Barber.

Monthly magazine for serious modellers of any type of scale model.

Illustrations: B&W and colour. Pictures of unusual and original scale models, but usually only as part of an article.

Text: Well-illustrated articles written for serious and experienced modellers. A style sheet is available for potential contributors.

Overall freelance potential: Good for those in touch with the modelling scene.

Editor's tips: Contributors should have good working knowledge of the field.

Fees: By negotiation.

STAMP MONTHLY

Stanley Gibbons Ltd, 5 Parkside, Christchurch Road, Ringwood, Hampshire BH24 3SH. Tel: 0425 472363.

Editor: Hugh Jefferies.

Monthly magazine for stamp collectors.

Illustrations: B&W and colour. Pictures inside only as illustrations for articles. Covers: colour pictures of interesting or unusual stamps.

Text: Features on stamp collecting. 1,000 words.

Overall freelance potential: Most of the editorial comes from freelance contributors.

Fees: £17 per 1,000 words (minimum).

TREASURE HUNTING

Greenlight Publishing, The Publishing House, Hatfield Peverel, Chelmsford, Essex CM3 2HF. Tel: 0245 381011.

Editor: Greg Payne.

Monthly magazine for metal detecting and local history enthusiasts.

Illustrations: B&W only inside. Only as illustrations for features as detailed below. Covers: colour pictures of people using metal detectors in a countryside or seaside setting.

Text: Illustrated features on club treasure hunts, lost property recovery, local history etc. News stories on the subject. News, 300–1,000 words; features, 1,000–3,000 words.

Overall freelance potential: Approximately 50 per cent of the magazine comes from freelance contributions.

Editor's tips: Advisable to telephone the magazine before attempting a cover.

Fees: Covers, £55; B&W pictures, £4; news, £10 per 1,000 words; features, £15 per 1,000 words.

WOODCARVING

Guild of Master Craftsman Publications Ltd, 166 High Street, Lewes, East Sussex BN7 1XU. Tel: 0273 477374.

Editor: Bernard Cooper.

Quarterly magazine aimed at both amateur and professional woodcarvers.

Illustrations: B&W and colour. Mostly to illustrate specific articles, but some scope for news pictures and shots of interesting pieces of work accompanied by detailed captions. Covers: striking colour shots of exceptional woodcarvings or woodcarvers in action.

Text: Illustrated articles on all aspects of serious woodcarving, including profiles of individual craftsmen.

Overall freelance potential: Limited.

Fees: £75 for covers, £25 for reproductions inside. £50 per published page for articles.

WOODTURNING

Guild of Master Craftsman Publications Ltd, 166 High Street, Lewes, East Sussex BN7 1XU. Tel: 0273 477374.

Editor: Nick Hough.

Bi-monthly magazine aimed at both amateur and professional woodturners.

Illustrations: B&W and colour. Mostly to illustrate specific articles, but some scope for unusual or

interesting single pictures. Covers: striking colour shots of turned items.
Text: Illustrated articles on all aspects of woodturning, including profiles of individual craftsmen.
Overall freelance potential: Good for the right material.
Fees: £75 for covers, £25 for reproductions inside. £50 per published page for articles.

WOODWORKER

Argus Specialist Publications Ltd, Argus House, Boundary Way, Hemel Hempstead, Herts HP2 7ST.
Tel: 0442 66551.
Editor: Zachary Taylor.
Monthly magazine for all craftspeople in wood. Readership includes schools and woodworking businesses, as well as individual hobbyists.
Illustrations: B&W and colour. Pictures relevant to woodworking and wood crafts. Mostly used as illustrations for features. Covers: colour pictures of fine furniture. 35mm acceptable but medium format preferred.
Text: Illustrated features on all facets of woodworking crafts. 1,500 words.
Overall freelance potential: Good, about 75 per cent bought from outside contributors.
Editor's tips: Clear, concise authoritative writing in readable, modern style essential.
Fees: Negotiable, but around £50–55 per published page.

Home Interest

COUNTRY HOMES AND INTERIORS

Southbank Publishing Group, King's Reach Tower, Stamford Street, London SE1 9LS. Tel: 071-261 6451.
Editor: Julia Watson. **Art Editor**: Gary Ottewill.
Monthly magazine concerning up-market country homes, interiors, and allied subjects.
Illustrations: Colour. Top quality coverage of architecture, interiors, gardens, landscapes, food, and personalities. Mostly by commission, but speculative submissions of picture features on specific country houses or gardens, or other country-based topics, may be considered if of the highest quality. No market for single pictures. Covers: always related to a major feature inside.
Text: Always by commission. Top level coverage of country lifestyle subjects and personality profiles.
Overall freelance potential: Good scope for top quality work.
Editor's tips: Photographers should always contact the editor in the first instance.
Fees: By negotiation.

DO-IT-YOURSELF MAGAZINE

Link House Magazines Ltd, Link House, Dingwall Avenue, Croydon CR9 2TA. Tel: 081-686 2599.
Editor: John McGowan.
Monthly magazine for home owners of all social classes interested in maintaining and improving their property.
Illustrations: B&W and colour. Pictures only by commission to illustrate features.
Text: Readers' success stories, showing work done on a property needing renovation or restoration. 600 words.
Overall freelance potential: Limited, since the magazine maintains an experienced staff.
Editor's tips: Contact the magazine first with ideas or, at the most, a synopsis.
Fees: By negotiation.

ELLE DECORATION

Hachette/EMAP Magazines Ltd, Victory House, 14 Leicester Place, London WC2H 7BP. Tel: 071-437 9011.
Editor: Ilse Crawford. **Art Editor**: Barbara Hajek.

Alternate-monthly, glossy interior decoration magazine aimed at a youthful readership (25–40).
Illustrations: Mostly colour. By commission only, but always interested in hearing from photographers experienced in this field.
Text: Ideas for features always of interest.
Overall freelance potential: Plenty of scope for the experienced freelance.
Editor's tips: Particular projects must always be discussed in detail beforehand to ensure that the magazine's specific styling requirements are observed.
Fees: £100 per page for photography; £250 per 1,000 words/page for text.

HERE'S HOW

RAP Publishing Ltd, 120 Wilton Road, London SW1V 1JZ. Tel: 071-834 8534.
Editor: Barbara Raine-Allen. **Art Director**: Martin Cotterell.
Monthly magazine concerned with home improvement projects.
Illustrations: Colour only. Commissions available for experienced workers in the home or DIY fields.
Text: Scope for contributors who can write knowledgeably and enjoyably on specific subjects, i.e. carpentry, plumbing, electrical, etc. Illustrated features on one particular project are required for regular "Open House" feature, but submit ideas only in the first instance.
Overall freelance potential: Very good for those with some experience in the field.
Fees: By negotiation.

HOMES & GARDENS

Southbank Publishing Group, IPC Magazines, King's Reach Tower, Stamford Street, London SE1 9LS.
Tel: 071-261 5098.
Editor: Amanda Evans. **Art Director**: Paul Ryan.
Monthly glossy magazine devoted to quality interior design and related matters.
Illustrations: Colour only. High quality commissioned coverage of interior decoration, gardens, furnishings and food.
Text: Features on subjects as above, invariably commissioned.
Overall freelance potential: Good for really top quality work.
Fees: By negotiation.

HOUSE BEAUTIFUL

National Magazine Company Ltd, 72 Broadwick Street, London W1V 2BP.Tel: 071-439 5000.
Editor: Pat Roberts. **Art Editor**: Mark Richardson.
Monthly magazine with the emphasis on practical home decorating ideas.
Illustrations: All colour. Usually by commission. Photographs of houses, interior decoration, furnishings, cookery and gardens. Complete picture features depicting houses and interiors of interest.
Text: Features on subjects as above, invariably commissioned, but possible scope for speculative features on suitable subjects.
Overall freelance potential: Quite good for experienced contributors in the home interest and interiors field.
Fees: By negotiation.

HOUSE & GARDEN

Condé Nast Publications Ltd, Vogue House, Hanover Square, London W1R OAD. Tel: 071-499 9080.
Editor: Robert Harling.
Monthly glossy magazine devoted to high quality homes and associated subjects.
Illustrations: Colour only. Almost entirely by commission. Photographs of interior decoration, architecture, furnishings, food and wine, and gardens. Complete picture features depicting a house or

apartment of interest and quality.

Text: Features on subjects as above, invariably commissioned.

Overall freelance potential: Reasonable scope for experienced architectural and interiors photographers to obtain commissions. Also some scope for non-commissioned features on houses, gardens and food.

Fees: By negotiation.

PERFECT HOME

DMG Home Interest Magazines, Times House, Station Approach, Ruislip, Middx HA4 8NB. Tel: 0895 677677.

Editor: Sarah Gale.

Monthly magazine for anyone interested in home improvements.

Illustrations: Colour. Pictures to accompany articles and features on interior decoration, home improvements, gardens, etc. Usually comissioned.

Text: Suggestions from experienced contributors always considered.

Overall freelance potential: Good for experienced contributors in this field.

Fees: By negotiation.

PERIOD LIVING

EMAP Elan, Victory House, 14 Leicester Place, London WC2H 7BP. Tel: 071-437 9011.

Editor: Isobel McKenzie-Price. **Art Director**: Deborah Baker.

Monthly magazine featuring homes from any period pre-1939.

Illustrations: Colour only. Commissions available to experienced interiors photographers, who should show portfolios in the first instance.

Text: No scope.

Overall freelance potential: Good for interior decoration specialists only.

Fees: By negotiation.

PRACTICAL HOUSEHOLDER

HHL Publishing Ltd, Greater London House, Hampstead Road, London NW1 9QQ. Tel: 071-388 3171.

Editor: Martyn Hocking.

Monthly magazine concerned with DIY and practical home improvements.

Illustrations: B&W and colour. Pictures to accompany articles and features on interior decoration and home improvement projects.

Text: Practical articles on home projects and interior design ideas. Technical and building matters discussed in a simple and straightforward manner. Basic DIY projects and personal experiences are sometimes of interest.

Overall freelance potential: Good for experienced contributors in this field.

Editor's tips: "Look at the magazine before writing an article – it saves your time and mine."

Fees: By negotiation.

THE WORLD OF INTERIORS

Condé Nast Publications Ltd, 234 Kings Road, London SW3 5UA. Tel: 071-351 5177.

Editor-in-Chief: Min Hogg.

Monthly magazine showing the best interior decoration of all periods and in all countries.

Illustrations: Mainly colour, occasional B&W. Subjects as above. Extra high standard of work required.

Text: Complete coverage of interesting houses; occasionally public buildings, churches, shops, etc. 1,000–2,000 words.

Overall freelance potential: Much of the work in the magazine comes from freelances.

Fees: Negotiable.

Industry

AEA TIMES

AEA Technology, 329 Harwell, Didcot, Oxfordshire OX11 0RA. Tel: 0235 432706.
Editor: Ms Lindsay Chandler.
Monthly newspaper for staff of AEA Technology. Both technical and non-technical readership.
Illustrations: B&W and colour. Pictures of social events involving employees and news affecting or involving the nuclear industry. News rather than feature pictures are preferred.
Text: Topical news coverage of events involving employees and nuclear industry. Up to 500 words.
Overall freelance potential: Around 10 per cent of the news pictures come from freelance photographers.
Fees: On a rising scale according to size of reproduction. Text by agreement.

APPAREL INTERNATIONAL

Apparel Publishers Ltd, The White House, 6 High Street, Potters Bar, Herts EN6 5AB. Tel: 0707 656828.
Editor: Mike Fairley.
Monthly publication for clothing and footwear manufacturers.
Illustrations: Mainly B&W. News pictures and pictures of individual processes in the trade.
Text: Features on manufacturing and marketing of clothing and footwear. 1,000 words.
Overall freelance potential: Limited, owing to specialist nature of the subject matter.
Fees: News pictures, £15; other pictures and words by arrangement.

BT TODAY

British Telecom, A233, BT Centre, 81 Newgate Street, London EC1A 7AJ. Tel: 071-356 5276.
Editor: Ken Runicles.
Monthly publication for all BT employees, plus pensioners, opinion formers, MPs, the media, etc.
Illustrations: B&W and colour. Pictures of all Telecom subjects, usually by commission.
Text: Features related to Telecom. About 300 words.
Overall freelance potential: Limited.
Fees: By agreement.

BROADCAST HARDWARE INTERNATIONAL

The Hardware Magazine Company Ltd, 48 The Broadway, Maidenhead, Berkshire SL6 1PE. Tel: 0628 773395.
Editor: David Sparks.
Alternate-monthly magazine for the television broadcast industry, aimed at senior engineers.
Illustrations: B&W and colour. Photographers of television broadcast studios, control rooms, outside broadcast vehicles and operations. Covers: normally by commission.
Text: Technical aspects of television production and post-production. 2,000–2,500 words.
Overall freelance potential: Quite good.
Editor's tips: Phone with ideas in the first instance.
Fees: Negotiable.

EUROPEAN RUBBER JOURNAL

Crain Communications Ltd, 2nd Floor, Cowcross Court, 75 Cowcross Street, London EC1M 6BP. Tel: 071-608 1116.
Editor: David Shaw.
Published 11 times per year for the rubber producing, processing and using industries.
Illustrations: B&W and occasional colour inside. Pictures of rubber and rubber applications of a technical nature, e.g. tyres, belting, etc. Also news and people pictures. Covers: top-class, graphically striking colour pictures of rubber-related subjects. Must have human interest as well as technical content.

Vertical format; 6x6cm minimum.

Text: Features on new applications of rubber, new product stories; new equipment, materials, processes information; business, marketing, personnel and technical news. Features up to 2,000 words.

Overall freelance potential: Around 25 per cent of the publication comes from freelances.

Editor's tips: All contributions must have a high news value or have sound technical content.

Fees: By arrangement.

FOOD INDUSTRY NEWS

Becon Publishing Ltd, 95 Bridger Way, Crowborough, East Sussex TN6 2XD. Tel: 0892 668172.

Editor: Stephen Blake.

Monthly publication covering the food production industry, aimed at managers and technicians.

Illustrations: B&W and colour. News pictures, which must be up-to-date and fully captioned. Some interest in stock pictures depicting specialist areas of food processing and technology. Commissions sometimes available to illustrate company profiles and special features.

Text: By commission, only from specialists.

Overall freelance potential: Limited.

Fees: Negotiable; around £120 per published page.

GAS WORLD INTERNATIONAL

The Petroleum Economist Ltd, PO Box 105, 25–31 Ironmonger Row, London EC1V 3PN. Tel: 071-251 3501.

Editor: Alan Bakalor.

Monthly journal aimed at middle and senior management in the engineering and commercial disciplines of the international gas supply, transmission and distribution industries, UK and overseas.

Illustrations: B&W and colour. Pictures of pipelines, compressor stations, liquefaction plants, gas equipment.

Text: Features on new developments in engineering, marketing, business and political fields. Up to 2,000 words.

Overall freelance potential: Around 50 per cent is bought from freelance contributors.

Fees: By arrangement.

GLASS AGE & WINDOW CONSTRUCTION

Spotlight Publications Ltd, Ludgate House, 245 Blackfriars Road, London SE1 9UR. Tel: 071-620 3636.

Editor: Richard Schwarz.

Monthly magazine for the flat glass and allied industries. Aimed at builders, architects, double glazing producers, shopfitters, glass merchants, stained glass artists and all glass-related workers.

Illustrations: B&W only. Particularly interested in pictures of glass in new buildings. Detailed captions essential.

Text: Features on glass in construction.

Overall freelance potential: Good opportunities for quality architectural photography.

Editor's tips: Make contact before submitting any material.

Fees: On a rising scale according to the size of reproduction or length of feature.

INDUSTRIAL DIAMOND REVIEW

De Beers Industrial Diamond Division (PTY) Ltd, Charters, Sunninghill, Ascot, Berkshire SL5 9PX. Tel: 0344 23456.

Editor: Paul Daniel.

Bi-monthly publication designed to promote a wider and more efficient use of diamond tools, i.e. grinding wheels, drill bits, saw blades, etc. in all branches of engineering.

Illustrations: B&W and colour. Pictures of any type of diamond tool in action.

Text: Case histories on the use of diamond tools in engineering, mining, etc. Up to 2,000 words for finished feature.

Overall freelance potential: Excellent but highly specialised.
Editor's tips: Technical case histories are welcome, but check acceptance with editor before submitting material. Potential contributors are advised to win the confidence of a diamond tool supplier or a major user in the industry.
Fees: Excellent; by arrangement.

INDUSTRIAL FIRE JOURNAL

Kennedy Communications Ltd, Unit 8, The Old Yarn Mills, Westbury, Sherborne, Dorset DT9 3RG. Tel: 0935 816030.
Editor: Aidan Turnbull.
Quarterly magazine concerning firefighting in the industrial sector.
Illustrations: Mostly B&W. Pictures of anything involving firefighting services in an industrial context, including firefighting personnel in action. Covers: powerful colour images of the same.
Text: No scope for non-specialists.
Overall freelance potential: Fair.
Fees: Negotiable, but generally good. Up to £200 for a really good cover picture.

INK AND PRINT

Batiste Publications Ltd, Pembroke House, Campsbourne Road, Hornsey, London N8 7PT. Tel: 081-340 3291 Ext. 260.
Editor: Dr Robert Leach.
Quarterly publication that provides a forum of communication between all involved in the manufacture of ink and development of ink technology. Produced for manufacturers and suppliers of printing companies, inplant printers, industry and commerce, advertising companies, government and local authorities, research establishments.
Illustrations: B&W and colour. Pictures of all printing subjects, i.e. machinery, ink, paper, raw materials, personalities etc. Covers: interesting or unusual shots of printing processes; 6x6cm minimum.
Text: Technical articles on the ink and print business. 1,500–2,500 words.
Overall freelance potential: Growing.
Fees: By agreement.

INTERNATIONAL REINFORCED PLASTICS INDUSTRY

Channel Publications Ltd, PO Box 1787, Gerrards Cross, Buckinghamshire SL9 0TD. Tel: 0753 890200.
Editor: David Pamington.
Bi-monthly publication issued to all moulders of fibre reinforced plastics, i.e. fibreglass. Aimed at management level in industry.
Illustrations: B&W and colour. Examples of components or completed structures manufactured from reinforced plastic materials, i.e. boats, aircraft, vehicles, chemical plant, pipes and building applications. Covers: colour pictures, preferably unpublished, of components or structures relating to the industry. 6x6cm minimum.
Text: Features describing the use of reinforced plastics materials in boat building, aircraft manufacture, vehicle construction, tank and vessel fabrication and cladding for buildings. 1,500–2,000 words.
Overall freelance potential: Around 15 per cent bought from outside.
Fees: By negotiation; around £40–£60 per 1,000 words; pictures by agreement.

MANUFACTURING CHEMIST

Morgan-Grampian (Process Press) Ltd, 30 Calderwood Street, Woolwich, London SE18 6QH. Tel: 081-855 7777.
Editor: Gerry Duggin.
Monthly journal for the chemical industry. Read by senior management involved in research, development reproduction and marketing of general chemicals, drugs, household products, cosmetics, toiletries and aerosol products.

Illustrations: B&W and colour. Pictures of any aspect of the fine chemical industry from general chemicals to drugs and cosmetics. Covers: colour pictures of same. 35mm acceptable, but medium format preferred.

Text: Features on any aspect of the chemical industry as detailed above. 2,000–3,000 words.

Overall freelance potential: Approximately 30 per cent is contributed by freelances.

Fees: Text, £100 per 1,000 words for features, £12 per 100 words for news stories; pictures by agreement.

NATURAL GAS

The Petroleum Economist Ltd, PO Box 105, 25–31 Ironmonger Row, London EC1V 3PN. Tel: 071-251 3501.

Editor: Alan Bakalor.

Bi-monthly publication concerned with the application of natural gas in commerce and industry with particular reference to efficient usage. Aimed at managing directors, chief engineers, architects and energy specialists, hotels, universities, schools, local authorities, hospitals, etc.

Illustrations: B&W and colour. Pictures of natural gas application in commerce and industry. Covers: colour pictures of same.

Text: General interest, well illustrated features with some reference to natural gas. Features on specific gas installations with particular reference to the economic use of gas. 600–1,500 words.

Overall freelance potential: Around 30 per cent bought from freelance sources.

Fees: Negotiable.

ROUSTABOUT MAGAZINE

Roustabout Publications, Suite 5, International Base, Greenwell Road, East Tullos, Aberdeen AB1 4AX. Tel: 0224 876582.

Editor: Lorna J. Anderson.

Monthly for oil industry personnel working on and off shore in the North Sea. Also covers Houston & business news.

Illustrations: B&W and colour. All pictures must be directly related to the North Sea oil industry. Minimum transparency size: 6x6cm.

Text: Articles related to the North Sea oil industry. 600–1,000 words.

Overall freelance potential: Limited because of extremely specialised subject.

Fees: By arrangement.

SIGN WORLD

A. E. Morgan Publication Ltd, Stanley House, 9 West Street, Epsom, Surrey KT18 7RL. Tel: 0372 741411.

Editor: Mike Connolly.

Monthly publication dealing with sign manufacturing and allied industries. Aimed at architects, town planners, surveyors, traffic and design engineers, shopfitters, sign manufacturers, trade suppliers, graphic designers, advertising agents, exhibition organisers and specifiers in major organisations.

Illustrations: Mainly B&W (also colour by arrangement). Only as illustrations to features.

Text: Features on new technological developments in the sign manufacturing industry. Information on relevant contracts at home and abroad. 1,000–1,500 words or by arrangement.

Overall freelance potential: Open to development for freelances with the right specialist knowledge

Editor's tips: Sample copies available – phone for details.

Fees: About £100 per 1,000 words; pictures by agreement.

STEEL TIMES

FMJ International Publications Ltd, Queensway House, 2 Queensway, Redhill RH1 1QS. Tel: 0737 768611.

Editor: Tim Smith.

Monthly publication for all those interested in the iron and steel industry.

Illustrations: B&W and colour. Topical pictures related to the industry, usually to illustrate specific features.
Text: Articles on new products, processes and contracts in the industry plus economic and review articles on the steel industry.
Overall freelance potential: Limited.
Fees: By negotiation.

TIMBER GROWER

Timber Growers United Kingdom Ltd. Editorial: Oakhurst, Crown Gardens, Fleet, Hampshire GU13 9PD. Tel: 0252 622301.
Editor: David Steers.
Quarterly publication for woodland owners, agents and managers, contractors and those interested in forestry as a land use and as an industry.
Illustrations: B&W and some colour. Pictures of forestry activity and people, relevant to articles and content.
Text: Features on forestry. 750 words.
Overall freelance potential: Limited.
Fees: By agreement.

TIN INTERNATIONAL

Market Information and Industrial Data, PO Box 2137, London NW10 6TN. Tel: 081-961 7487.
Editor: Robin Amlot.
Monthly publication covering all aspects of the production and consumption of tin, including can manufacture, canning, soldering, chemicals and alloys.
Illustrations: B&W and colour. Pictures illustrating any aspects of the mining of tin and its application in end uses.
Text: Features on subject detailed above. 1,000–2,000 words.
Overall freelance potential: Limited.
Fees: £100 per 1,000 words; pictures by agreement.

URETHANES TECHNOLOGY

Crain Communications Ltd, Cowcross Court, 2nd Floor, 75/77 Cowcross Street, London EC1M 6BP. Tel: 071-608 1116.
Editor: David Reed.
Alternate-monthly publication for the polyurethane producing, processing, and using industries.
Illustrations: B&W and occasional colour. Pictures of production, equipment, and application of polyurethane materials. Also news pictures and shots of trade personalities. Covers: top quality and graphically striking colour shots of polyurethane-related subjects. 6x6cm minimum.
Text: Features on new applications of polyurethanes; new products; new equipment and processing. Business, marketing, personnel and technical news items. Features, up to 2,000 words.
Overall freelance potential: Good scope for those with access to the industries involved.
Fees: By arrangement.

WORKS MANAGEMENT

Findlay Publications Ltd, Franks Hall, Horton Kirby, Kent DA4 9LL. Tel: 0322 222222.
Editor: John Dwyer. **Art Editor**: Roland Davies.
Monthly publication for managers and engineers who directly control or perform the works management function in selected manufacturing concerns.
Illustrations: B&W and colour. Occasional need for regional coverage of managers and workers in realistic work situations in factories. Mostly pictures are used only to illustrate features.
Text: Illustrated features of interest to management, e.g. productivity, automation in factories, industrial relations, employment law, finance, energy, maintenance, handling and storage, safety and welfare. Around 2,000 words.

Overall freelance potential: Up to 30 per cent is contributed by freelances.
Fees: By agreement.

WORLD TOBACCO
International Trade Publications Ltd, Queensway House, 2 Queensway, Redhill, Surrey RH1 1QS.
Tel: 0737 768611.
Editor: George Gay.
Alternate-monthly aimed at international manufacturers, dealers and suppliers to the tobacco processing and manufacturing industries.
Illustrations: B&W only. Pictures of tobacco growing, processing or manufacture from any part of the world.
Text: No scope.
Overall freelance potential: Fair.
Editor's tips: Pictures from remote parts of the world are particularly welcome.
Fees: By arrangement.

Local Government & Services

FIRE PREVENTION
Fire Protection Association, 140 Aldersgate Street, London EC1A 4HX. Tel: 071-606 3757.
Editor: Lynn Jackson.
Technical publication concerning fire safety. Aimed at fire brigades, fire equipment manufacturers, architects, insurance companies, and those with responsibility for fire safety in public sector bodies, commerce and industry. Published 10 times a year.
Illustrations: B&W and colour. Pictures of large and small fires to illustrate reports. Pictures showing different types of occupancy (offices, commercial premises, warehouses, etc) also welcome.
Text: Technical articles and news items on fire prevention and protection. Features 2,000–3,000 words.
Overall freelance potential: Good pictures of fires and unusual fire safety experiences are always welcome.
Fees: Pictures, negotiable from £15. Text, negotiable from £80 per 1,000 words.

FIRE AND RESCUE
Kennedy Communications Ltd, Unit 8, The Old Yarn Mills, Sherborne, Dorset DT9 3RG. Tel: 0935 816030.
Editor: Aidan Turnbull.
Quarterly magazine for all involved in municipal firefighting and emergency services.
Illustrations: Mostly B&W. Good shots of firefighting and emergency services personnel in action. Also pictures of major fires, accidents, vehicle crashes, extrications, fire and accident victims. Covers: Powerful colour images of the same.
Text: Scope only for those with expert knowledge of the subject.
Overall freelance potential: Fair.
Fees: Negotiable, but generally good. Up to £200 for a really good cover picture.

LEGAL ACTION
The Legal Action Group, 242 Pentonville Road, London N1 9UN. Tel: 071-833 2931.
Editor: Roger Smith.
Monthly publication for lawyers, experienced advice workers, law students and academics.
Illustrations: B&W only. Pictures of lawyers, judges, especially other than the standard head and shoulders shot. Courts. Plus pictures to illustrate features covering a wide range of subjects (e.g. housing, police, immigration, advice services).

Text: Features on legal services and professional issues, including the courts. High technical content required. Also information for news and feature material that can be written in-house.

Overall freelance potential: Rarely commissions new work but interested in knowing of photographers already holding suitable material.

Fees: By negotiation.

LOCAL GOVERNMENT NEWS

B&M Publications (London) Ltd, PO Box 13, Hereford House, Bridle Path, Croydon, Surrey CR9 4NL. Tel: 081-680 4200.

Editor: Phillip Cooper.

Monthly news magazine for professional officers, middle to higher grade, in all technical departments of local authorities, officers in water authorities and professional civil servants in relevant government departments.

Illustrations: B&W only. Pictures of architectural and building projects, road schemes, housing projects, national and local politicians and news pictures with local government angle.

Text: Features on any local government related story with exception of those dealing with education or social service policy matters. 750–1,000 words.

Overall freelance potential: More than 50 per cent of material comes from freelance sources.

Fees: By negotiation.

MUNICIPAL JOURNAL

Municipal Journal Ltd, 32 Vauxhall Bridge Road, London SW1V 2SS. Tel: 071-973 6400.

Editor: Michael Burton.

Weekly publication for senior local government officers, councillors, Whitehall departments and academic and other institutions.

Illustrations: B&W and colour. Personalities, vehicles, buildings, etc., general shots.

Text: Features on local government issues. 750–1,000 words.

Overall freelance potential: Very good.

Editor's tips: The articles and pictures must be on local government issues.

Fees: Good; on a rising scale according to the size of reproduction or length of feature.

MUNICIPAL REVIEW AND AMA NEWS

Association of Metropolitan Authorities, 35 Great Smith Street, London SW1P 3BJ. Tel: 071-222 8100.

Editor: Peter Smith.

Published 10 times a year for local authority elected members and chief officers, universities, MPs, etc. Contains news of the Association's policies and activities plus articles on urban and local government.

Illustrations: B&W only. Pictures of events involving metropolitan district authorities, or London boroughs. No stock pictures.

Text: No freelance market.

Overall freelance potential: The publication has a strong need for appropriate pictures about local authority activities, particularly in London, Merseyside, Greater Manchester, West Midlands, West Yorkshire, South Yorkshire and Tyne and Wear.

Editor's tips: Ring before submitting.

Fees: By negotiation.

POLICE REVIEW

Police Review Publishing Company Ltd, South Quay Plaza 2, 183 Marsh Wall, London E14 9FZ. Tel: 071-537 2575.

Editor: Brian Hilliard.

Weekly news magazine for the police service.

Illustrations: B&W and colour. All aspects of the police service. Particular interest in up-to-date news pictures covering the previous seven days. Some commissioned work available, with a need for more photographers to carry out regional work. Contact first to show portfolio.

Text: Limited scope because of specialist subject matter, but will consider any subject of contemporary interest to police officers, 1,000–1,500 words.

Overall freelance potential: Good.

Editor's tips: The magazine is published on Thursdays with a Wednesday morning deadline for news pictures. Photographs for features should be good photojournalism and reportage; we are not interested in "publicity style" photos.

Fees: Negotiable, minimum £75.

SOUTHAMPTON CITY NEWS

Southampton City Council, Public Relations Unit, Civic Centre, Southampton SO9 4XR. Tel: 0703 832000/832001.

Editor: Sarah Zyga.

Civic newspaper published six times a year – one of the largest and most comprehensive in Britain. Contains news on the council, features on the city and community news.

Illustrations: B&W with front and back page full colour. Any pictures concerning events, activities, objects, developments or people involved in the Southampton scene. Covers: mainly pictures of general subjects from the city and port of Southampton.

Text: No freelance market.

Overall freelance potential: Freelance photographers used on a regular, established basis. Most requirements are met by these and/or by council sources. The paper is always willing, however, to consider photographic contributions with pictorial impact, artistic or creative qualities.

Fees: Negotiable.

SPECIAL BEAT

Police Review Publishing Co Ltd, South Quay Plaza 2, 183 Marsh Wall, London E14 9FZ. Tel: 071-537 2575.

Editor: Ian MacQuillin.

Quarterly publication of the Special Constabulary, the volunteer reserve police force.

Illustrations: Colour preferred; prints acceptable. Pictures of members of the Special Constabulary in action at special events, engaged in public order or involved in any other newsworthy activities. Should be fully captioned with officer's name, force, location and role in the event depicted.

Text: No freelance scope.

Overall freelance potential: Very good. Virtually all photographs are commissioned. Looking to establish a roster of reliable and imaginative photographers around the country. Will also use good speculative news pictures.

Editor's tips: Specials can be identified by their flat caps and shoulder flash stating "Special Constabulary", although those in the Metropolitan Police and some other forces wear identical uniforms to regulars (including helmets) and are only identified by a small "SC" on their epaulettes. *Special Beat* is interested in good photojournalism, not publicity/recruiting style material.

Fees: Reproduction feee from £30. Commission fees negotiable.

Male Interest

CLUB INTERNATIONAL

Paul Raymond Publications Ltd, 2 Archer Street, London W1V 7HE. Tel: 071-734 9191.

Editor: Stephen Bleach.

Popular monthly for men.

Illustrations: Colour only; Kodachrome preferred. Requires top quality glamour sets of very attractive girls.

Text: Articles on sexual or humorous topics, or factual/investigative pieces. 1,000–2,000 words.

Overall freelance potential: Most of the published glamour material comes from freelances, but they are normally experienced glamour photographers.

Editor's tips: Study the magazine to appreciate style. As well as being very attractive girls featured must look contemporary and fashionable.

Fees: £500–£1,000 for glamour sets. Text up to £200 per 1,000 words.

ESCORT

Paul Raymond Publications Ltd, 2 Archer Street, London W1V 7HE. Tel: 071-734 9191.

Editor: Nevile Player.

Monthly for men; less sophisticated than the other Paul Raymond publications, *Men Only* and *Club International*.

Illustrations: Colour only; 35mm Kodachrome preferred. Looks for glamour sets of "normal, healthy, girl-next-door" types. Sets frequently run to fewer pages than is the case with other men's magazines. Each issue contains about eight glamour sets running to only two or three pages each. Covers: single colour shots required for the cover, back cover and centre spread.

Text: Articles of 1,000–2,000 words on sexual or humorous topics.

Overall freelance potential: Good.

Fees: £200 for glamour sets. Articles: £50–£100.

ESQUIRE

The National Magazine Company Ltd, 72 Broadwick Street, London W1V 2BP. Tel: 071-439 5000.

Editor: Rosie Boycott. **Picture Editor**: Sean Hogan.

Up-market general interest monthly aimed at intelligent and affluent men in the 25–44 age group.

Illustrations: Mainly colour. Top-quality material only, invariably by commission. Mostly portrait or fashion work with some photojournalism.

Text: Scope for "name" writers only.

Overall freelance potential: Good for photographers, but restricted to those experienced at the highest level of magazine work.

Fees: By negotiation.

FIESTA

Galaxy Publications Ltd, PO Box 312, Witham, Essex CM8 3SZ. Tel: 0376 510555.

Editor: J. D. Heard.

Monthly men's magazine, actually aimed at both men and women for whom nudity and sex are not too problematic.

Illustrations: Mainly colour. Glamour photo sets – ordinary settings in which a girl strips. Other picture subjects have included Soho strippers, the Alternative Miss World competition, girls who get wet/muddy, girls in uniform, sexy lingerie, etc.

Text: Features on all aspects of sex, humour, and related topics and what turns men and women on. 1,800–2,000 words. Fillers: 500–1,000 words.

Overall freelance potential: Freelances contribute a major part of the magazine.

Editor's tips: The subject is sex and rarely does the magazine deviate from the topic.

Fees: Photo sets, by negotiation up to £600; Features by negotiation.

GQ

Condé Nast Publications Ltd, Vogue House, Hanover Square, London W1R 0AD. Tel: 071-499 9080.

Editor: Michael VerMeulen. **Picture Editor**: Maryse Vassalo.

Up-market general interest magazine for men in the 20–45 age group.

Illustrations: Mainly colour. Top-quality illustrations for articles on a range of topics, invariably by commission.

Text: Top level investigative, personality, fashion and style features, plus articles on other subjects likely to be of interest to successful and affluent men.

Overall freelance potential: Only for the contributor experienced at the top level of magazine work.

Editor's tips: People can see from the magazine itself what sort of style and quality is required.
Fees: By negotiation.

KNAVE
Galaxy Publications Ltd, PO Box 312, Witham, Essex CM8 3SZ. Tel: 0376 510555.
Editor: David Spenser.
Monthly magazine for men.
Illustrations: Mainly colour. Glamour girl sets (minimum 100 transparencies). Feature illustrations by commission only.
Text: Sexy, humorous, factual articles. Plus pieces of male interest.
Overall freelance potential: Most of the magazine comes from freelances.
Fees: Glamour sets, £600; articles without pictures £200; articles with accompanying illustrations £300–£400.

MAYFAIR
Paul Raymond Publications Ltd, 2 Archer Street, London W1V 7HE. Tel: 071-734 9191.
Editor: Stephen Bleach.
Sophisticated monthly for men.
Illustrations: Colour only; 35mm preferred. Glamour sets taken in up-market surroundings. Only top quality material can be accepted. Backgrounds should be real-life locations, such as a luxury furnished flat. Outdoor material needs strong sunlight. Covers: always feature a girl, partly nude, though nipples not shown. Potential cover pictures should be sexy, provocative, natural and head-turning; an occasional touch of humour is allowable. Subject should be shot as a square composition, but allowing a further quarter depth above the composition for the title logo. Background should be reasonably plain and not variable so that the logo can either be projected on top or reversed out.
Text: Articles on general male interests.
Overall freelance potential: Good; all the photographs and major features are the work of freelance contributors.
Editor's tips: Thought should be given to the erotic use of clothing and suggestion of sex appeal or sexual situation, together with striking but simple colour co-ordination.
Fees: £250–£1,000 for glamour sets. Covers: £150 and up.

MEN ONLY
Paul Raymond Publications Ltd, 2 Archer Street, London W1V 7HE. Tel: 071-734 9191.
Editor: Nevile Player.
Sophisticated monthly for men.
Illustrations: Colour only; 35mm Kodachrome preferred. Glamour sets depicting beautiful girls in quality locations.
Text: Articles on sexual or humorous topics.
Overall freelance potential: Good; most of the published material comes from freelances.
Editor's tips: The emphasis is on contemporary sets featuring fresh, smiling, attractive and friendly girls. Photographers should pay close attention to bright summery colours, sexy and colourful clothing, realistic locations and a story-line in which the girl begins fully dressed.
Fees: £500–£1,000 for glamour sets.

PENTHOUSE
Northern and Shell plc, Northern & Shell Tower, City Harbour, London E14 9GL. Tel: 071-987 5090.
Editor: Deric Botham.
Sophisticated monthly aimed mainly at men between the ages of 18 and 30.
Illustrations: Colour only; 35mm Kodachrome preferred. Requires top quality glamour sets of very beautiful girls. Sets normally run to between six and ten pages.
Text: General features of male interest.
Overall freelance potential: Good; but only those experienced in glamour photography are likely to

get work accepted here.

Editor's tips: Submit a few sample shots in the first instance, so that the editor can judge whether the particular girl would be suitable for a full-scale glamour set.

Fees: Minimum rate: £75 per published page.

Medical

AFRICA HEALTH

FSG Communications Ltd, Vine House, Fair Green, Reach, Cambridge CB5 0JD. Tel: 0638 743633.

Editor: Paul Chinnock.

Bi-monthly publication for doctors and senior health administrators in English-speaking black African countries.

Illustrations: B&W and occasional colour. Pictures from Africa, specifically medical or general lifestyle where this relates to health, e.g. water supplies, urban deprivation, etc.

Text: Features on anything appertaining to health developments in Africa, plus UK-originating stories of research advances which might be of benefit to African. Emphasis is mainly clinical but some community health coverage.

Overall freelance potential: Fair for material from Africa.

Fees: By agreement.

DENTAL LABORATORY

The Dental Laboratories Association Ltd, Chapel House, Noel Street, Nottingham NG7 6AS. Tel: 0602 704321.

Editor: William L Courtney.

Trade magazine aimed at dental laboratory owners with strong emphasis on small business legislation and new products.

Illustrations: Mainly B&W, occasionally colour. Subjects related to the dental laboratory.

Text: Any items of specific interest to dental laboratories or small businesses, but *not* dental surgeries. Features with a loosely connected dental technician interest will be considered, especially if illustrated. 2,000 words maximum.

Overall freelance potential: Good, though very little is used at present.

Editor's tips: A continuing series would be considered for inclusion in each of the year's issues.

Fees: Negotiated per item, dependent on content.

THE DENTAL TECHNICIAN

A.E. Morgan Publications Ltd, Stanley House, 9 West Street, Epsom, Surrey KT18 7RL. Tel: 0372 741411.

Editor: David Ritchie.

Monthly newspaper for dental technicians.

Illustrations: B&W and colour. Pictures of dental technicians engaged in activities, either within or outside their normal work.

Text: Illustrated articles on new laboratories, new techniques, etc. 800–1,200 words.

Overall freelance potential: Limited, due to lack of experienced contributors in this field.

Fees: By agreement.

FAR EAST HEALTH

71 Lauderdale Tower, Barbican, London EC2Y 8AB. Tel: 071-920 0723.

Editor: Wendy Clare.

Monthly publication for doctors and health administrators in South East Asia.

Illustrations: B&W and colour. Pictures of new hospitals, hospital projects, health ministers and top doctors in the designated region.

Text: Features on medicine and medical equipment, latest technology. 1,200 words.
Overall freelance potential: Limited, but always interested in news stories from the region.
Fees: Good; on a rising scale according to the size of reproduction or length of article.

FINANCIAL PULSE
Morgan Grampian Ltd, 30 Calderwood Street, London SE18 6QH. Tel: 081-855 7777.
Editor: Steve Toon.
Fortnightly publication concerned with the financial and management side of general practice medicine.
Illustrations: Colour only. Commissions available for high quality portraiture, especially outside the London area.
Text: No scope.
Overall freelance potential: Good for portrait specialists.
Editor's tips: Most interested in photographers who can produce original and creative portrait work.
Fees: Negotiable, around £150 per day.

GENERAL PRACTITIONER
Medical Publications Ltd, 30 Lancaster Gate, London W2 3LP. Tel: 071-413 4032.
Editor: Stephen Lederer.
Weekly newspaper for family doctors.
Illustrations: B&W and colour. Pictures of general practitioners involved in news stories, and clinical/scientific pictures.
Text: News stories, up to 400 words, preferably by prior arrangement with the news editor; features, always by prior arrangement with the features editor.
Overall freelance potential: The paper uses a lot of pictures from freelances.
Fees: By negotiation, but around £30 for 300 words, and £75 for half-day photographic session.

JOURNAL OF ALTERNATIVE AND COMPLEMENTARY MEDICINE
Mariner House, 53A High Street, Bagshot, Surrey GU19 5AH. Tel: 0276 451522.
Editor: Leon Chaitow.
Monthly publication for health care professionals in the alternative and complementary fields.
Illustrations: B&W and colour. Pictures illustrating treatments and techniques in acupuncture, chiropractic, homeopathy, naturopathy, osteopathy, and any other such forms of therapy. Practitioners at work and patients undergoing treatment.
Text: Articles by specialists on suitable topics. 1,500–2,000 words.
Overall freelance potential: Modest.
Fees: Photographs by negotiation; £100 per 1,000 words for text.

MIMS MAGAZINE WEEKLY
Medical Publications Ltd, 30 Lancaster Gate, London W2 3LP. Tel: 071-413 4379.
Editor: Peter Chambers.
Therapeutics journal for general practitioners, covering developments in pharmaceuticals and the use of drugs.
Illustrations: B&W and colour. Good conceptual and scientific pictures always in demand. Covers: top quality colour pictures, usually by commission.
Text: News and features concerning drug information and therapeutics. 1,500 words.
Overall freelance potential: Modest.
Fees: By agreement.

MIDDLE EAST HEALTH
71 Lauderdale Tower, Barbican, London EC2Y 8AB. Tel: 071-920 0723.
Editor: Wendy Clare.
Monthly publication for senior medical and health care personnel in the Middle East.

Iilustrations: B&W and colour. Pictures showing health care practice in the Middle East, e.g. treatment at hospitals and clinics. Also clinical photographs, e.g. disease conditions, surgery, etc.
Text: Articles of a clinical or technical nature, written by medically qualified people or those in allied professions.
Overall freelance potential: About 25 per cent is commissioned, usually from known freelances.
Fees: On a rising scale, according to the size of reproduction or length of article.

OPTOMETRY TODAY

Association of Optometrists. Editorial Office: Unit 4, Station Approach, Fleet, Hampshire GU13 8QY. Tel: 0252 816266.
Editor: Maureen Hunter.
Fortnightly publication for the optometric and dispensing profession in the UK.
Illustrations: B&W and colour. News pictures of eminent people in the profession. Other pictures to illustrate articles. Covers: Colour news pictures.
Text: Articles of technical interest to the profession. 1,000–2,000 words.
Overall freelance potential: Limited.
Fees: £100 per 1,000 words.

PRACTICE NURSE

Reed Health Communications Ltd, Quadrant House, The Quadrant, Sutton, Surrey SM2 5AS. Tel: 081-652 8432.
Editor: Carolyn Scott.
Fortnightly magazine for nurses in general practice.
Illustrations: Colour only. Relevant news pictures and good stock coverage of GP (not hospital) nursing.
Text: Illustrated features on aspects of GP nursing.
Overall freelance potential: Fair.
Fees: By negotiation.

PRACTICE NURSING

Mark Allen Publishing Ltd, Croxted Mews, 288 Croxted Road, London SE24 9DA. Tel: 081-671 7521.
Editor: Moira Crawford.
Fortnightly magazine for general practice nurses.
Illustrations: Colour only. News pictures concerning general practice nursing, accompanied by 100–300 word stories.
Text: Usually contributed by health professionals.
Overall freelance potential: Limited.
Fees: According to use.

PULSE

Morgan-Grampian (Professional Press) Ltd, 30 Calderwood Street, London SE18 6QH. Tel: 081-855 7777.
Editor: Howard Griffiths.
Weekly newspaper for family doctors.
Illustrations: Colour. Pictures with captions, involving family doctors.
Text: News and topical features about family doctors.
Overall freelance potential: Good.
Fees: Negotiable.

THERAPY WEEKLY

Macmillan Magazines Ltd, 4 Little Essex Street, London WC2R 3LF. Tel: 071-379 6144.
Editor: Simon Crompton.
Weekly newspaper for physiotherapists, occupational therapists and speech and language therapists.

Illustrations: B&W and colour. Pictures of anything connected with the above professions.
Text: News and features on the professions detailed above. 750–1,000 words.
Overall freelance potential: Limited.
Fees: Good; on a rising scale according to the size of reproduction or length of feature.

Motoring

AMERICAN CAR WORLD
CH Publications Ltd, PO Box 75, Tadworth, Surrey KT20 7XF. Tel: 0895 623612.
Editor: Tony Beadle.
Alternate-monthly covering the US car scene in Europe. Covers vehicles of all periods up to the present day.
Illustrations: B&W and colour. Photographs and photo-features on especially interesting or unusual cars. Racing coverage – drag strip, circuit or oval. Also pictures of related Americana: jukeboxes, fashion, diners, etc. Some opportunities for experienced car photographers to produce commissioned work for major features.
Text: Illustrated articles on any suitable subject, but always discuss ideas with the editor first.
Overall freelance potential: Very good.
Fees: By negotiation.

AUTO EXPRESS
United Consumer Magazines, Ludgate House, 245 Blackfriars Road, London SE1 9UX. Tel: 071-928 8000.
Editor: Andrew Bordiss.
Popular weekly magazine, aimed at the average motorist rather than the car enthusiast.
Illustrations: Colour only. Any general motoring subjects with impact, news pictures, humorous shots, etc.
Text: Features on any motoring topic, to appeal to a general readership. Articles may be practical but should not be too technical. 1,000–2,000 words.
Overall freelance potential: Reasonable.
Editor's tips: Writers should always submit a synopsis in the first instance. Although a popular non-technical title, accuracy is essential.
Fees: Photographs from £52.50–£124.40, depending upon size. Text usually £200 per 1,000 words.

AUTOCAR AND MOTOR
Haymarket Publishing Ltd, 38–42 Hampton Road, Teddington, Middlesex TW11 0JE. Tel: 081-943 5013.
Editor: Michael Harvey. **Art Editor**: Martin Tullett.
Weekly magazine on general motoring topics. Includes road tests, historical features, information on new cars, coverage of motor shows, etc.
Illustrations: B&W and colour. Unusual or special cars, especially pre-production models under test.
Text: Illustrated features on unusual or special cars. Veteran or vintage car features with contemporary pictures. 1,000–2,000 words.
Overall freelance potential: Around 20 per cent of features and pictures come from freelance sources.
Editor's tips: Technical accuracy is essential. Full information on the cars featured must be detailed. Colour features stand a better chance if accompanied by B&W pictures as well. Feature, news and photographic ideas welcome.
Fees: Features by negotiation.

THE AUTOMOBILE

Enthusiast Publishing Ltd, Holmerise, Seven Hills Road, Cobham, Surrey KT11 1ES. Tel: 0932 864212.

Editor: Brian Heath.

Monthly publication featuring veteran, vintage, and pre-1950 motor vehicles.

Illustrations: B&W and colour. Not much scope for single pictures unless of particular interest. The main requirement is for well-illustrated articles concerning any pre-1950 motor vehicle; not only cars but also commercial vehicles. Of particular interest are good restoration features, with both "before" and "after" pictures showing what can be achieved. Also limited room for coverage of race meetings, exhibitions or other events at which old motor vehicles are present.

Text: Informative illustrated articles as above.

Overall freelance potential: Although limited there is scope for illustrated features – consult the editor before starting on feature.

Editor's tips: There is absolutely no point in submitting material concerning any post-1950 vehicles.

Fees: By negotiation.

AUTOMOTIVE MANAGEMENT

Leading Edge Publishing Ltd, 5 Blenheim Centre, Locks Lane, Mitcham, Surrey CR4 2JX. Tel: 081-687 2340.

Editor: Mark Bursa.

Fortnightly publication for the retail motor trade, concentrating on the franchise dealer scene.

Illustrations: Mostly B&W. News photographs covering the motor trade generally. Some scope for commissions to photograph industry figures.

Text: Regional news items and good "grass roots" features about the franchise dealer scene.

Overall freelance potential: Good for those with contacts in the trade.

Fees: By negotiation.

CAR AND ACCESSORY TRADER

Haymarket Publishing Ltd, 60 Waldegrave Road, Teddington, Middlesex TW11 8LG. Tel: 081-943 5827.

Editor: Murdo Morrison.

Monthly magazine for traders involved in the selling of car parts and accessories.

Illustrations: B&W and colour. Captioned news pictures, concerning new products, openings of new premises, handover of sales awards, etc. Much is commissioned. Covers: excellent relevant photographs considered.

Text: Varied subjects of interest to the trade, by commission only.

Overall freelance potential: About 50 per cent of contributions are from freelance sources.

Fees: £100 per £1,000 words. Photographs negotiable.

CAR CHOICE

Haymarket Motoring Magazines, 38–42 Hampton Road, Teddington, Middlesex TW11 0JE. Tel: 081-943 5703.

Editor: Hugh Poulter. **Art Editor**: Steve Moore.

Monthly magazine offering advice for buyers of both new and used cars.

Illustrations: Pictures to illustrate advice features on all aspects of car purchase.

Text: Features on all aspects of choosing, purchasing, running and financing new and used cars.

Overall freelance potential: Reasonable for motoring specialists.

Fees: By negotiation.

CAR WEEK

EMAP National Publications Ltd, Abbot's Court, 34 Farringdon Road, London EC1R 3AV. Tel: 071-216 6200.

Editor: Gavin Green. **Art Editor**: Peter Charles.

General, news-led motoring weekly.

Illustrations: B&W and colour. Hard news pictures plus pictures of newsy, motoring-related subjects and situations: traffic jams, accidents, humorous pictures, wacky events, etc. Commissions available to photographers who can produce original and interesting work.

Text: Only for experienced motoring writers.

Overall freelance potential: Very good.

Editor's tips: "Our style is quite different from that used in most monthlies or in advertising photography; the approach is less glossy and much more photojournalistic."

Fees: By negotiation and according to use.

CARS AND CAR CONVERSIONS

Link House Magazines (Croydon) Ltd, Link House, Dingwall Avenue, Croydon CR9 2TA. Tel: 081-686 2599.

Editor: Nigel Fryatt.

Monthly magazine concentrating on technical matters, performance tuning and motor sport.

Illustrations: B&W and colour. Coverage of motor sport events involving both saloon and sports cars, such as saloon car racing, rallying, etc. Picture stories concerning interesting or unusual car modifications. Covers: good colour action shots.

Text: General or technical articles about high performance cars, modification, and racing. 1,500 words upwards.

Overall freelance potential: Around 20 per cent is contributed by freelances.

Fees: Negotiable.

CLASSIC AMERICAN

Myatt McFarlane plc, Trident House, Heath Road, Hale, Altrincham, Cheshire WA14 2UD. Tel: 061-928 3480.

Editor: Steve Myatt.

Bi-monthly magazine concerning American cars and motorcycles of the 50s, 60s and 70s.

Illustrations: Mainly colour. Striking or unusual pictures of classic US vehicles. However, much of the photography is commissioned from regulars or staff-produced.

Text: Illustrated articles on specific cars or bikes and their owners, plus features on other aspects of American-style youth culture such as clothing, music, sport, etc. 1,000–2,000 words. Always check with the editor before submitting.

Overall freelance potential: Car coverage welcome, but best scope in the field of lifestyle features.

Fees: Pictures by negotiation. £100 per 1,000 words for text.

CLASSIC AND SPORTSCAR

Haymarket Magazines Ltd, 60 Waldegrave Road, Teddington, Middlesex TW11 8LG. Tel: 081-943 5000.

Editor: Ian Bond.

Monthly magazine covering mainly post-1945 classic cars, generally of a sporting nature. Strong coverage of the owners scene.

Illustrations: B&W and colour. Mainly interested in coverage of club or historic car gatherings, unless staff photographer is present. Feature photography always commissioned.

Text: Articles of interest to the classic car enthusiast and collector, up to a maximum of 2,500 words.

Overall freelance potential: Small, as much material is staff produced.

Editor's tips: Always get in touch before submitting.

Fees: According to merit.

COMPANY CAR

Queensway House, 2 Queensway, Redhill, Surrey RH1 1QS. Tel: 0737 768611.

Editor: Curtis Hutchinson.

Monthly magazine for companies running in excess of ten cars. Aimed at main board directors and senior executives/managers.

Illustrations: B&W and colour. Exclusive and newsworthy pictures relating to fleet sales or fleet cars. Covers: topical colour pictures, including new car launches. 6x6cm minimum.

Text: Features on car management or cost. Exclusive material only. 1,000–1,500 words plus two to three pictures.

Overall freelance potential: Between 60 and 80 per cent comes from freelance sources.

Fees: Good; on a rising scale according to size of reproduction or length of feature.

DRIVING MAGAZINE

Safety House, Beddington Farm Road, Croydon, Surrey CR0 4XZ. Tel: 081-665 5151.

Editor: Graham Fryer.

Bi-monthly road safety publication for driving instructors and advanced drivers.

Illustrations: B&W and colour.Pictures of home or overseas motorists/driving school vehicles in unusual surroundings or circumstances. Humorous incidents, i.e. traffic accidents of an unusual nature, unusual road signs, humorous signs or those in extraordinary positions. Covers: colour, but generally from advertising agencies.

Text: Features on road safety, driver training and general driving articles. 500–2,000 words.

Overall freelance potential: Modest.

Fees: Photographs: £7.50–£15, variable, according to subject and quality.

FAST LANE

Perry-Motorpress Ltd, Compass House, 22 Redan Place, London W2 4SZ. Tel: 071-229 7799.

Executive Editor: David Raeside.

Monthly magazine devoted to performance road cars.

Illustrations: Colour. No scope for speculative submissions, but commissions available for experienced photographers. The editor will always discuss ideas before they have been put into action.

Text: Suggestions always welcome.

Overall freelance potential: Good for experienced contributors and the newcomer with exciting ideas.

Fees: By negotiation.

FLEET NEWS

EMAP Response Publishing Ltd, Wentworth House, Wentworth Street, Peterborough PE1 1DS. Tel: 0733 63100.

Editor: Mike Gunnell.

Weekly newspaper aimed at those responsible for running company car and light commercial vehicle fleets.

Illustrations: B&W and colour. Captioned news pictures concerning company car operations, handover of car fleets to companies, appointments in the trade, etc.

Text: News, articles on business car management and related subjects.

Overall freelance potential: Excellent.

Editor's tips: Always telephone first.

Fees: Negotiable.

4 x 4 MAGAZINE

Greenlight Publishing, The Publishing House, Hatfield Peverel, Chelmsford, Essex CM3 2HF. Tel: 0245 381011.

Editor: Iain Mackenzie.

Monthly magazine for four-wheel-drive owners, business users and enthusiasts, with the emphasis on off-road activities.

Illustrations: B&W and colour. Pictures of spectacular off-road action, special events, unusual or "one-off" vehicles, and club activities. Covers: spectacular colour shots of off-road action.

Text: Illustrated articles of 1,500–2,000 words, featuring unusual vehicles, events, off-road driving

(UK and abroad), overland expeditions, technical pieces, modifications, etc.
Overall freelance potential: Excellent – the editor is always open to suggestions.
Fees: £75 cover; £75 per 1,000 words; £15 internal colour; £5 B&W. Payment 14 days after publication.

GARAGE AND AUTOMOTIVE RETAILER
EMAP Response Publishing, Wentworth House, Wentworth Street, Peterborough PE1 1DS. Tel: 0733 63100.
Editor: Dave Thomas.
Monthly magazine serving motor dealers, accessory shops, and garages.
Illustrations: B&W and colour. Some scope for speculative submissions. Unusual or exclusive pictures relating to the motor trade always of interest.
Text: Mostly commissioned. However, anything directly related to the motor trade, with particular emphasis on how readers can improve the efficiency of their business, will be considered, as will technical articles. Up to 1,500 words.
Overall freelance potential: Always interested.
Fees: £100 per 1,000 words; photographs negotiable.

INTERNATIONAL OFF-ROADER
Milebrook Ltd, PO Box 237, Crawley, West Sussex RH10 5YH. Tel: 0293 525152.
Editor: Colin Dawson.
Monthly magazine for four-wheel-drive enthusiasts.
Illustrations: B&W and colour. Little scope for individual photographs unless accompanied by extended captions or background text.
Text: Well-illustrated articles on all aspects of the four-wheel-drive scene; travel/adventure stories, features on interesting individual vehicles and off-roading personalities, competition and club event reports. Limited scope for vehicle test reports.
Overall freelance potential: Excellent for those who can add words to their pictures.
Fees: By negotiation.

LAND ROVER OWNER
LRO Publications, PO Box 105, Bury St Edmunds, Suffolk IP33 1AD. Tel: 0284 750652.
Editor: Richard Thomas.
Monthly magazine for Land Rover owners and enthusiasts.
Illustrations: B&W and colour. Interesting or unusual pictures of Land Rovers and Range Rovers. Celebrities pictured with such vehicles.
Text: Illustrated articles on overland expeditions using Land Rovers. Length: 1,000 words, plus around six pictures.
Overall freelance potential: Good.
Fees: Text, £100 per 1,000 words; pictures by negotiation.

MOTOR TRADER
Quadrant House, The Quadrant, Sutton, Surrey SM2 5AS. Tel: 081-652 3276.
Editor: Leon Clifford.
Weekly trade newspaper, controlled circulation and subscription, read by dealers & manufacturers in the car and component industries, garage owners, body shop workers.
Illustrations: B&W and colour. News pictures on anything connected with the motor trade.
Text: News and features relevant to the motor trade and industry. 300–1,000 words.
Overall freelance potential: Call to discuss with editor or deputy before submitting material.
Editor's tips: This is the trade's only weekly newspaper; it is particularly interested in hard news.
Fees: Negotiable.

MOTORING AND LEISURE

CSMA Ltd, Britannia House, 95 Queens Road, Brighton, East Sussex BN1 3WY. Tel: 02733 21921.
Editor: David Arnold. **Picture Editor**: Lisa Pritchard.
Monthly journal of the Civil Service Motoring Association, covering motoring, travel and leisure activities.
Illustrations: B&W and colour. General car-related subjects and Continental travel.
Text: Illustrated articles on motoring, travel, camping and caravanning. 750–1,000 words.
Overall freelance potential: Limited.
Fees: By arrangement.

911 & PORSCHE WORLD

CH Publications Ltd, PO Box 75, Tadworth, Surrey KT20 7XF. Tel: 0737 814311.
Editor: Clive Househam.
Bi-monthly magazine devoted to Porsche or Porsche-derived cars.
Illustrations: B&W and colour. All commissioned, but good opportunities for those who have original ideas and can produce top quality car photography.
Text: Ideas for articles always of interest; write with details in the first instance.
Overall freelance potential: Very good for specialist coverage.
Fees: Photography by arrangement; around £100 per 1,000 words.

OFF ROAD AND FOUR WHEEL DRIVE

Link House Magazines Ltd, Link House, Dingwall Avenue, Croydon CR9 2TA. Tel: 081-686 2599.
Editor: Graham Scott.
Monthly magazine devoted to four-wheel-drive vehicles.
Illustrations: B&W and colour. Pictures of vehicles in action during club trials and other "off road" events. Must be captioned with full details of driver, event, and location.
Text: Illustrated articles concerning four-wheel-drive vehicles and off-road activities. 1,000–2,000 words.
Overall freelance potential: There is plenty of room for new contributors.
Fees: By negotiation.

PERFORMANCE FORD

PO Box 14, Hazel Grove, Stockport, Cheshire SK7 6HL. Tel: 061-480 2652.
Editor: Dennis Foy.
Monthly magazine devoted to Ford or Ford-based vehicles, and with the emphasis on high-performance road use.
Illustrations: B&W and colour. Pictures to illustrate features, or topical single pictures of particular quality. Medium format transparencies preferred in the case of colour.
Text: Illustrated articles on maintenance and modification of Ford-based cars. Personality profiles with a direct relevance to Ford Products.
Overall freelance potential: Fair.
Editor's tips: Always raise ideas with the editor before submitting material.
Fees: According to size of reproduction or length of text.

POPULAR CLASSICS

EMAP National Publications Ltd, Bushfield House, Orton Centre, Peterborough PE2 0UW. Tel: 0733 237111.
Editor: Martin Hodder.
Monthly magazine concentrating on "affordable" classic cars.
Illustrations: B&W and colour. Coverage of post-war classic cars of all types; pictures of interesting individual cars with a story behind them.
Text: Illustrated articles on any aspect of the classic car scene. 1,000–2,000 words.
Overall freelance potential: Very good. Best scope is for colour coverage.
Fees: By negotiation.

RALLY SPORT
A&S Publishing, Central House, 162 Southgate Street, Gloucester GL1 2EX. Tel: 0452 307181.
Editor: Simon Cooke.
Monthly magazine covering the sport of motor rallying and all matters of interest to rally enthusiasts.
Illustrations: B&W and colour. Pictures of, or connected with, rallying or high-performance road cars. Covers: dramatic colour shots of rallying.
Text: Articles, of varying lengths, about rallying or high-performance cars.
Overall freelance potential: About a third of the magazine is contributed by freelances.
Fees: (Minimum) B&W pictures £7.50; colour £20; covers £50. Articles up to £250 by negotiation.

STREET MACHINE
EMAP National Publications Ltd, Bushfield House, Orton Centre, Peterborough PE2 5UW. Tel: 0733 237111.
Editor: Russ Smith.
Monthly magazine mainly for young men with an interest in personalised cars which they can identify with and aspire to.
Illustrations: B&W and colour. Only as part of a story/picture package on subjects detailed below. Prefers British-sourced material.
Text: Well-illustrated features on completed cars, step-by-step illustrated material on how to do it subjects, track tests of modified cars and coverage of allied subjects.
Overall freelance potential: One or two features used per month.
Editor's tips: Totally unsolicited material is a waste of time. Freelances with something to offer should telephone or write first to discuss the idea.
Fees: £95 per 1,000 words, minimum £11 for colour photos.

TOP RACE & RALLY
Top Publications Ltd, Suite 2, Westcombe House, 7–9 Stafford Road, Wallington, Surrey SM6 9AN. Tel: 081-773 3404.
Editor-in-Chief: Rick Smith.
Monthly magazine covering rallying both in UK and internationally.
Illustrations: B&W and colour. Coverage of UK rallies, drivers and related subjects. An original, creative approach is preferred to straightforward shots.
Text: Well-illustrated features on rallying and rally-cross, including historical material and performance car features with relevance to motorsport. Ideas should be discussed with the editor in the first instance.
Overall freelance potential: Excellent.
Fees: From £6 upwards for B&W; £15 upwards for colour. £40 per published page for text.

VW MOTORING
RFWW Publications Ltd, PO Box 283, Cheltenham, Gloucestershire GL52 3BT. Tel: 0242 262723.
Editor: Robin Wager.
Monthly magazine for owners and enthusiasts, concerning Volkswagen and Audi vehicles.
Illustrations: B&W and colour. Self-contained picture stories or pictures as illustrations to features. Covers: colour pictures of VW, Audi, Porsche, NSU vehicles or derivatives, either interesting vehicles in their own right or more commonplace vehicles in interesting or picturesque settings.
Text: Features of VW and Audi interest, especially do-it-yourself, historical and technical subjects. No set length.
Overall freelance potential: Most of the material comes from freelances, but almost exclusively from regular contributors.
Editor's tips: An in-depth knowledge of the subject is needed. No articles unless illustrated with photographs and/or drawings.
Fees: By agreement.

Music

BLUES AND SOUL
Napfield Ltd, 153 Praed Street, London W2 1RL. Tel: 071-402 5051/6869.
Editor: Bob Kilbourn.
Fortnightly publication devoted to soul, R&B, funk, fusion, jazz, Afro, Soca, Salsa, Latin, Hip dance Hop/electro. All forms of black music *excepting* reggae.
Illustrations: Mostly B&W; colour used on front and back covers and centre spread. Original and exclusive pictures of black music performers.
Text: Small amount of scope for exclusive articles or interviews.
Overall freelance potential: Limited.
Editor's tips: Think of the readership, and the format, in order to produce something really striking and eye-catching.
Fees: By negotiation.

CLASSICAL MUSIC
Rhinegold Publishing Ltd, 241 Shaftesbury Avenue, London WC2H 8EH. Tel: 071-836 2383.
Editor: Keith Clarke. **Art Editor**: Sarah Davies.
Fortnightly news and feature magazine for classical music professionals and the interested general public.
Illustrations: B&W only. Very limited scope as most pictures are supplied by record companies, promoters, etc. Occasional urgent need for a musician or group in the news – most easily met if freelances can supply lists of photographs they hold.
Text: Short news items and news stories about events in the music/arts world, including politics and performance, up to 800 words. Longer background features about musicians, usually relating to a forthcoming event, up to 1,500 words. All work is commissioned.
Overall freelance potential: Limited for photographers, but some 65 per cent of text is from commissioned freelance sources.
Editor's tips: The art editor is always happy to look at portfolios, subject to appointment.
Fees: Pictures by negotiation; text from £75 per 1,000 words.

COUNTRY MUSIC PEOPLE
Music Farm Ltd, 225A Lewisham Way, London SE4 1UY. Tel: 081-692 1106.
Editor: Craig Baguley.
Glossy monthly magazine for country music fans. Covering substantially the American music scene and US artists visiting Britain.
Illustrations: B&W and colour. Outstanding photographs of country music performers. Covers: medium format colour transparencies, composed to fit the upright format of the magazine.
Text: Articles on all aspects of country music, but not superficial in approach.
Overall freelance potential: Good.
Editor's tips: Contributors should contact the editor before covering an event or preparing an article.
Fees: By negotiation.

ECHOES
Black Echoes Ltd, 15–16 Newman Street, London W1P 3HD. Tel: 071-436 4540/4550.
Editor: Chris Wells.
Weekly publication devoted to all aspects of black popular music.
Illustrations: Mostly colour. Outstanding photographs of popular black music performers, for immediate publication or for file.
Text: Little scope.
Overall freelance potential: Fair.
Fees: By negotiation.

FOLK ROOTS
Southern Rag Ltd, PO Box 337, London N4 1TW. Tel: 081-340 9651.
Editor: Ian Anderson.
Monthly publication concerned with folk music.
Illustrations: B&W only. Pictures to be used in conjunction with interviews, reviews of records or reports on events. Mostly commissioned. Covers: colour pictures of artists covered editorially.
Text: Interviews and reviews concerned with folk music.
Overall freelance potential: Very small for the contributor unknown in this field. The magazine favours its regular contributors.
Fees: By agreement.

FUTURE MUSIC
Future Publishing Ltd, Beauford Court, 30 Monmouth Street, Bath BA1 2BW. Tel: 0225 442244.
Editor: Karl Foster. **Art Editor**: Mark Nottley.
Monthly magazine covering developments in modern music technology, aimed at both amateur and professional rock musicians.
Illustrations: B&W and colour. Opportunities for commissions to cover shows, studio profiles, etc.
Text: Articles from writers who are fully familiar with the technology and can write in an entertaining and informative manner. Always query the editor in the first instance.
Overall freelance potential: Limited.
Fees: Photography negotiable. Text £80 per 1,000 words.

KERRANG!
EMAP Metro, 52/55 Carnaby Street, London W1V 1PF. Tel: 071-437 8050.
Editor: Phil Alexander.
Weekly magazine for "heavy metal" rock music fans.
Illustrations: B&W and colour. Pictures of relevant bands. On-stage performance shots preferred, with the emphasis on action. Some posed shots and portraits of popular performers also used.
Text: Little freelance market.
Overall freelance potential: Very good. The magazine is heavily illustrated and uses a lot of colour.
Fees: According to size of reproduction.

KEYBOARD PLAYER
Bookrose Ltd, 27 Russell Road, Enfield, Middlesex EN1 4TN. Tel: 081-367 2938.
Editor: Steve Miller.
Monthly magazine for players of all types of keyboard instrument. Covers pianos, organs, keyboards and synthesisers; and all forms of music, from pop to classical.
Illustrations: Mainly B&W; some colour. Photographs of keyboard instruments and their players, preferably accompanied by a newsy caption. Covers: colour pictures of keyboard instruments.
Text: Articles of around 1,000 words on any topic of interest to keyboard players.
Overall freelance potential: Fairly limited, but scope is there for the right type of material.
Editor's tips: Run-of-the-mill pictures of players seated at their instruments will not be met with much enthusiasm – a strikingly different approach is required.
Fees: By negotiation.

MELODY MAKER
IPC Magazines Ltd, 26th Floor, King's Reach Tower, Stamford Street, London SE1 9LS. Tel: 071-261 5502.
Editor: Allan Jones.
Weekly music paper for the 15–24 age group.
Illustrations: B&W and colour. Contemporary rock music subjects.
Text: Features, news and reviews relevant to pop and rock music. 300 words.
Overall freelance potential: Occasional use of outside contributors, but mostly staff-produced.

Fees: Text, £94.74 per 1,000 words. Pictures, from £21.78, according to size of reproduction.

NEW MUSICAL EXPRESS
IPC Magazines Ltd, 25th Floor, King's Reach Tower, Stamford Street, London SE1 9LS. Tel: 071-261 5715.
Editor: Steve Sutherland. **Art Editor**: Priscilla Watkins.
Weekly tabloid covering all aspects of popular music and allied youth culture.
Illustrations: B&W and colour. All aspects of contemporary popular music.
Text: Scope for exclusive interviews with rock musicians, film stars, or other personalities of interest to a young and aware readership.
Overall freelance potential: Good, but very dependent on subject matter.
Editor's tips: NME only covers those parts of the music scene considered worthwhile by the editorial team.
Fees: On a rising scale according to size of reproduction.

Q
EMAP Metro Publications Ltd, Mappin House, 4 Winsley Street, London W1N 1AR. Tel: 071-436 1515.
Editor: Danny Kelly.
Monthly rock music magazine aimed at the 18–35 age group.
Illustrations: B&W and colour. Most pictures staff-produced or commissioned from a pool of regular contributors, but suitable stock pictures of relevant personalities will always be considered.
Text: Top quality profiles, interviews and feature articles of interest to a rock-oriented readership, invariably by commission.
Overall freelance potential: Very limited for commissions; good for library/stock shots.
Fees: By negotiation.

RAW
EMAP Metro Publications Ltd, 52/55 Carnaby Street, London W1A 3AU. Tel: 071-437 8050.
Editor: Jon Hotton.
Fortnightly rock music magazine, concentrating on the "heavy metal" scene.
Illustrations: B&W and colour. Mostly by commission or from agency sources. Good live performance material, especially from overseas, will be considered on spec.
Text: Illustrated lifestyle features covering the wider context and cultural influence of the music. Length variable.
Overall freelance potential: Good for those with experience of the rock music scene.
Editor's tips: Always check with the editor before submitting.
Fees: On a rising scale according to size of reproduction or length of text.

RHYTHM
Rhythm Publications Ltd, Alexander House, Forehill, Ely, Cambridge CB7 4AF. Tel: 0353 665577.
Editor: Simon Braund.
Monthly magazine for drummers and percussionists in the rock and pop music field.
Illustrations: B&W and colour. Interesting photographs relating to contemporary percussion instruments and their players, including the use of electronic and computer-aided equipment. Covers: always related to a major article inside.
Text: Illustrated profiles, interviews and features about leading contemporary drummers and percussionists. Articles on technique and programming from knowledgeable contributors.
Overall freelance potential: Limited.
Fees: £50 per 1,000 words for text; photographs according to use.

RIFF RAFF – ROCKING ACROSS FRONTIERS
EG Publishing. Editorial: PO Box 1900, London N5 1EP. Tel: 071-226 4695.

Editor: Mark Crampton.
Monthly rock music magazine published throughout Europe; bias towards "heavy metal".
Illustrations: Mostly colour. Coverage of bands in performance and on tour, mainly by commission.
Text: Original ideas for features and profiles always of interest.
Overall freelance potential: Reasonable for those with experience of covering the scene.
Fees: Negotiable.

ROCK CD
Northern & Shell plc, PO Box 381, Mill Harbour, London E14 9TW. Tel: 071-987 5090.
Editor: Paul Trynka.
Alternate-monthly magazine covering the "adult rock" market.
Illustrations: Mainly colour. Good stock photographs of mainstream rock performers. Some commission available.
Text: Original, in-depth features on individual performers and bands, and aspects of the music business. Submit ideas only in the first instance.
Overall freelance potential: Good for those with some experience in this field.
Editor's tips: Prefer to hear from photographers who already have a strong body of work in their files, rather than from those seeking the odd commission.
Fees: Photographs according to use; Text £120 per 1,000 words.

SMASH HITS
EMAP Metro Publications Ltd, 3rd Floor, 52–55 Carnaby Street, London W1V 1PF. Tel: 071-437 8050.
Editor: Mike Soutar. **Art Editor**: Christa Dixon.
Fortnightly popular music magazine aimed at 11–19 year olds. Features complete song lyrics of current hits accompanied by interviews and pin-up style photographs of the performers.
Illustrations: Some B&W; mostly colour. Posed, pin-up style photographs of performers who currently have a record in the charts, usually studio shots. Faces should be clearly shown. Covers: usually commissioned.
Overall freelance potential: Very good for photographers in touch with the current pop music scene.
Fees: £35 to £60 for black and white pictures; £100 for full-page colour. Covers: £200.

VOX
Specialist Publishing Group, IPC Magazines Ltd, King's Reach Tower, Stamford Street, London SE1 9LS. Tel: 071-261 6312.
Editor: Paul Colbert. **Art Editor**: Paul Aarons.
Monthly magazine for adult rock fans in the 20–30 age group.
Illustrations: Mainly colour. Scope for experienced music photographers to undertake commissions. Few openings for speculative work unless of an exclusive and highly original nature.
Text: Mainly staff-produced but some scope for established music press contributors.
Overall freelance potential: Good for specialists.
Fees: By negotiation.

Photography & Video

AMATEUR PHOTOGRAPHER
IPC Specialist Group, King's Reach Tower, Stamford Street, London SE1 9LS. Tel: 071-261 5100.
Editor: Keith Wilson.
Weekly magazine for all photographers, from beginners to experienced enthusiasts.
Illustrations: B&W and colour. Pictures to illustrate specific photo techniques and general photo features. Series ideas welcomed. General portfolios in B&W and colour. Send no more than 20 pictures,

prints unmounted, slides in a plastic slide wallet. No glass mounts. Covers: colour pictures, mostly glamour, but occasionally other strong subjects. Sometimes linked with portfolio inside. Always leave space for logo and coverlines.

Text: Technique articles on all types of photography. Picture captions on a separate sheet. 1,000–1,500 words.

Overall freelance potential: Good. Around one-third of photography comes from freelance sources.

Fees: £100 per full page colour and pro rata; £100 per page black and white. Text: £90 per 1,000 words. Covers, £120–£150.

AUDIO VISUAL

EMAP Maclaren, PO Box 109, Scarbrook Road, Croydon, Surrey CR9 1QH. Tel: 081-688 7788.
Editor: Peter Lloyd.

Monthly magazine for managers in industry and commerce, public services, government etc. who use audio-visual communication techniques, e.g. slides, film, video, overhead projection and filmstrips, plus the new technologies of computer graphics and telecommunication.

Illustrations: B&W and colour. Pictures of programmes being shown to audiences, preferably supported by case history details; relevant news; new products or location shooting pictures. All must be backed with solid information. Covers: colour pictures of same, but check before submission.

Text: Case histories of either shows, conferences or studies of particular companies' use of AV techniques. Good location/conference stories always welcome. 1,000–2,500 words.

Overall freelance potential: Up to 25 per cent comes from freelance sources.

Editor's tips: This is a market where it is essential to check before submitting anything. Don't be afraid to telephone.

Fees: Text, £110–£130 per 1,000 words. Pictures by agreement.

THE BRITISH JOURNAL OF PHOTOGRAPHY

Bouverie Publishing Ltd, 186–187 Temple Chambers, Temple Avenue, London EC4Y 0DT. Tel: 071-583 3030.
Editor: Reuel Golden.

Weekly publication for professional and semi-professional photographers, technicians, etc., and all those engaged in professional photography.

Illustrations: B&W and colour. Portfolios along with some biographical notes about the photographer concerned.

Text: Interested in anything related to professional photography, particularly the more unusual aspects.

Overall freelance potential: Good for bringing freelances to the attention of potential clients.

Editor's tips: Remember the magazine is aimed at those engaged in professional and semi-professional photography, and does not use the type of how-to-do-it material used in photo magazines aimed at amateur photographers.

Fees: Portfolios not normally paid for; exposure in the magazine frequently leads to commissions elsewhere. Negotiable for text.

CAMCORDER USER

WV Publications, 57–59 Rochester Place, London NW1 9JU. Tel: 071-485 0011.
Editor: Robert Uhlig.

Monthly magazine for buyers and users of camcorders. Technique articles on producing better video movies, tests on machines and accessories, personality, application and action features. Also bi-monthly *Computer Video* supplement.

Illustrations: B&W and colour. General shots of camcorders in use, shots to illustrate technique and advice features. Spectacular locations. Good colour pictures of camcorders in use at various locations especially welcomed, e.g. on the beach, at sports events, at social occasions, on expeditions. Covers: colour pictures of similar.

Text: Technique, action and application features, equipment reviews and personality interviews.
Overall freelance potential: Excellent. Around 50 per cent from such sources.
Fees: By agreement.

PHOTO ANSWERS
EMAP Apex National Publications Ltd, Apex House, Oundle Road, Peterborough PE2 9NP. Tel: 0733 898100.
Editor: Steve Moore.
Monthly photographic magazine aimed at everyone interested in photography.
Illustrations: Mainly colour. Good quality photographs, slide or print, of any subject. Also portfolios.
Text: Mostly staff-produced.
Overall freelance potential: Very good opportunities for photographers.
Editor's tips: Study the magazine first.
Fees: Negotiable.

PHOTO PRO
Icon Publications Ltd, Maxwell Lane, Kelso, Roxburghshire TD5 7BB. Tel: 0573 226032.
Editor: David Kilpatrick.
Alternate-monthly magazine for all involved in professional or semi-professional photography.
Illustrations: B&W and colour. Mostly required to accompany and illustrate specific articles. Limited scope for outstanding single pictures and portfolios.
Text: Articles and features on all aspects of serious and professional photography.
Overall freelance potential: Most of the content is freelance produced.
Editor's tips: Always make contact before submitting.
Fees: Features £50–£75 per page. Covers: £70. Portfolios: £150 regardless of space used.

THE PHOTOGRAPHER
British Institute of Professional Photography. Editorial: Icon Publications Ltd, Maxwell Lane, Kelso, Roxburghshire TD5 7BB. Tel: 0573 226032.
Editor: David Kilpatrick.
Monthly official journal of the BIPP. Aimed at professional photographers in general practice.
Illustrations: B&W and colour. Photographs only required in conjunction with features as below.
Text: Photo-feature material describing specific professional techniques. Also interviews and profiles concerning individual BIPP members or companies with BIPP connections. Around 1,600 words.
Overall freelance potential: Good for material of genuine interest to the practising professional.
Editor's tips: There is definitely no scope here for amateur photo press type material (e.g. travel features), no matter how good the photographs.
Fees: From £25–£50 per page depending on quality and nature of the material.

PRACTICAL PHOTOGRAPHY
EMAP Apex Publications Ltd, Apex House, Oundle Road, Peterborough PE2 9NP. Tel: 0733 898100.
Editor: William Cheung FRPS.
Monthly magazine offering practical information to amateur photographers, plus news, interviews, equipment tests and general interest items on related topics.
Illustrations: B&W and colour. Pictures on any subject considered for the magazine's files – any shots showing some aspect of photographic technique. Colour and black & white portfolios are used regularly. Covers: glamour or portraits in colour. 35mm acceptable, but medium format preferred.
Text: Any feature on a practical aspect of photography will be considered, although most basic techniques are covered by staff writers. Contact with ideas only in the first instance.
Overall freelance potential: Relatively little scope for written material, but many published pictures are from freelances.
Fees: from a minimum of £10 per picture and at least £80 per 1,000 words. Negotiable for outstanding material.

PROFESSIONAL PHOTOGRAPHER
Market Link Publishing, Tye Green, Elsenham, Bishops Stortford, Hertfordshire CM22 6DY. Tel: 0279 647555.
Editor: Jon Tarrant.
Monthly magazine for professional photographers.
Illustrations: B&W and colour. Only with features.
Text: Techniques, equipment, business skills and general issues of interest to professional photographers.
Overall freelance potential: Good – for the right material appropriately written.
Editor's tips: The magazine is intended to appeal to readers who find other magazines too superficial. It is therefore more important than ever that potential contributors study recent issues of the magazine.
Fees: Based on £75 per page, for both words and pictures.

WHAT VIDEO
WV Publications Ltd, 57–59 Rochester Place, London NW1 9JU. Tel: 071-485 0011.
Editor: Steve May.
Monthly video magazine for newcomers and enthusiasts. Contains test reports, buyers' guide, general features and news of new films on video. Plus bi-annual *What Television* supplement.
Illustrations: B&W and colour. Pictures of video recorders, cameras and "ordinary people" using them. Covers: colour pictures of similar.
Text: Technical subjects easily explained, plus interviews and showbusiness pieces – stars with interest in video photography. 850–1,000 words.
Overall freelance potential: Around 70 per cent is from freelance sources.
Fees: By agreement.

WIDESCREEN INTERNATIONAL
The Widescreen Centre, 48 Dorset Street, London W1H 3FH. Tel: 071-935 2580.
Editor: Tony Shapps.
Alternate-monthly publication for audio-visual and cine photography with a bias towards all forms of panoramic presentation and three-dimensional photography.
Illustrations: B&W only. Pictures that relate to audio-visual, panoramic and three-dimensional photography.
Text: Features on audio-visual subjects, CinemaScope, widescreen filming and prints, plus other sound subjects.
Overall freelance potential: Most of the contents comes from freelances.
Fees: By agreement.

Politics & Current Affairs

CONSERVATIVE NEWSLINE
The Conservative and Unionist Party, Conservative Central Office, 32 Smith Square, London SW1P 3HH. Tel: 071-222 9000.
Editors: Keith Britto and John Desborough.
Monthly newspaper of the Conservative Party, aimed at Party members throughout the country.
Illustrations: B&W and colour. Photographs with political content will be considered. Also local constituency activities, local Party news, fund-raising drives, etc.
Text: Short articles and news items concerning any Party activities. A small amount of scope for brief personality pieces about political figures may be found in the diary column.
Overall freelance potential: Good scope for freelance contributions, on a wide range of

political matters.
Fees: According to size of reproduction.

THE DIPLOMAT and LADY DIPLOMAT

Diplomatist Associates Ltd, 58 Theobalds Road, London WC1X 8SF. Tel: 071-405 4874/4903.
Editor: Wendy Holden.
Controlled circulation house journals for the foreign diplomatic community in London. *The Diplomat* is published every two months and goes to husbands and wives; *Lady Diplomat* is published twice a year as a separate magazine within *The Diplomat*.
Illustrations: Mostly colour. Pictures required for illustrating forthcoming articles. *The Diplomat* uses illustrations for travel, social, political and diplomatic articles. *Lady Diplomat* uses pictures of shops, cookery, fashion and anything that might interest the wife of a foreign diplomat in London.
Text: Commissions are possible, but not often. They are always to a specific brief. 1,000–2,000 words.
Overall freelance potential: Limited.
Fees: Variable.

THE ECONOMIST

The Economist Newspaper Ltd, 25 St James's Street, London SW1A 1HG. Tel: 071-839 7000.
Editor: Bill Emmott. **Picture Editor**: Selina Dunlop.
Weekly publication covering world political, business and scientific affairs.
Illustrations: B&W only inside. Pictures of politicians, businessmen, social conditions (housing, health service, etc.), major industries (coal, steel, oil, motor, agriculture, etc.). Always prepared to keep pictures for stock. Covers: colour pictures of a topical and political nature.
Text: All staff-produced.
Overall freelance potential: Only for serious and experienced photojournalists.
Editor's tips: Telephone picture editor in the first instance.
Fees: On a rising scale according to size of reproduction inside; covers £400.

GPMU JOURNAL

Graphical, Paper & Media Union, Keys House, 63–67 Bromham Road, Bedford, Bedfordshire MK40 2AG. Tel: 0234 351521.
Editor: Tony Dubbins.
Published ten times per year for members of the union. Gives information on union policies and activities, plus personalities and sports news.
Illustrations: B&W and colour. Pictures involving the trade union and labour movement, printing and papermaking industries, plus some general pictures, i.e. sport, personalities, travel etc.
Text: Features on subjects mentioned above. 300–1,000 words.
Overall freelance potential: Limited.
Fees: By agreement.

JEWISH CHRONICLE

Jewish Chronicle Newspapers Ltd, 25 Furnival Street, London EC4A 1JT. Tel: 071-405 9252.
Editor: Edward J. Temko.
Weekly newspaper publishing news and features about, and of interest to, the Jewish community.
Illustrations: B&W and colour. Any topical pictures related to the purpose stated above. Also material for the paper's wide range of supplements that deal with subjects such as holidays, fashion, furniture, video, regional development, etc. Pictures also required for colour magazine published six times a year.
Text: Features on topics detailed above. 600–2,500 words.
Overall freelance potential: At least 40 per cent of the content comes from freelance sources.
Fees: By negotiation.

JOURNAL

National Union of Civil and Public Servants, 124–130 Southwark Street, London SE1 0TU. Tel: 071-928 9671.

Editor: Nick Wright.

Monthly publication for members of the NUCPS trade union in the Civil Service and related bodies, including the Post Office and British Telecom.

Illustrations: Mostly B&W. Trade union activity of any kind, but especially involving Civil Servants who are NUCPS members.

Text: No requirements.

Overall freelance potential: Good: 75 per cent of pictures come from outside contributors.

Fees: Good; on a rising scale according to size of reproduction.

LIBERAL DEMOCRAT NEWS

Liberal Democrats, 4 Cowley Street, London SW1P 3NB. Tel: 071-222 7999.

Editor: David Boyle.

Weekly tabloid newspaper of the Liberal Democrats.

Illustrations: B&W and colour. Prints only (no transparencies). Pictures of Liberal Democrat activities around the country and general political news pictures.

Text: News and features: politics, current affairs.

Overall freelance potential: Limited.

Fees: By negotiation.

THE MIDDLE EAST

7 Coldbath Square, London EC1R 4LQ. Tel: 071-404 4333.

Editor: Graham Benton.

Monthly publication directed at senior management, governmental personnel and universities. Covers current affairs of a political, cultural and economic nature.

Illustrations: B&W only inside. Pictures of all Middle Eastern subjects. Covers: colour pictures of Middle Eastern personalities and scenes.

Text: Features on Middle Eastern subjects or world subjects that relate to the area. 1,000–3,000 words.

Overall freelance potential: Most of the pictures come from freelances and around 50 per cent of the overall editorial.

Fees: Text, £70 per 1,000 words; B&W pictures, £15–£35; covers by agreement.

MILAP WEEKLY and NAVIN WEEKLY

59–61 Broughton Road, London SW6 2LA. Tel: 071-385 8966.

Editors: R. Soni and R. Kumar.

Weekly publications for Indian, Pakistani and Bangladeshi people. Published in Hindi (*Navin*) and Urdu (*Milap*).

Illustrations: B&W only for inside and cover use, concerning topical immigrant matters.

Text: All matters of interest to immigrant Asian communities.

Overall freelance potential: Good for those in touch with the immigrant community.

Fees: By negotiation.

NEW STATESMAN AND SOCIETY

The Statesman and Nation Publishing Co Ltd, Foundation House, Perseverance Works, 38 Kingsland Road, London E2 8DQ. Tel: 071-739 3211.

Editor; Steve Platt. **Art Editor**: Susan Head.

Independent political and current affairs weekly, with large arts review section.

Illustrations: B&W and colour. Major news pictures of all kinds – political events, politicians, marches, demonstrations, etc. Coverage of major foreign political events, wars, etc. Also social reportage coverage. Covers: colour shots of major politicians or hot news stories.

Text: Short captions with pictures, or short news stories up to 500 words. Original and well-researched features will be considered – around 1,200 words.
Overall freelance potential: Most contributions are from freelance sources.
Fees: Variable.

PEOPLE & THE PLANET
Planet 21, 60 Twisden Road, London NW5 1DN. Tel: 071-485 3136.
Editor: John Rowley.
Quarterly publication concerned with population, environment and development topics.
Illustrations: Mainly B&W inside. Pictures showing environment and family planning projects, family life, rural and urban living conditions, mothers and children. Covers: colour pictures related to features.
Text: Freelance material accepted, but usually only on commission.
Overall freelance potential: Good for quality material on Third World.
Fees: Full page pictures, £70; half page, £45.

SCOTS INDEPENDENT
Scots Independent (Newspapers) Ltd, 51 Cowane Street, Stirling FK8 1JW. Tel: 0786 473523.
Editor: Kenneth Fee.
Monthly publication bringing news, features and reviews to Scottish Nationalists. Political, industrial, economic, cultural and historical interests catered for.
Illustrations: B&W only. Pictures for stock: Scottish industrial subjects and townscapes. Pictures for features: anything of interest to patriotic Scots, e.g. Scots achievements worldwide, Scottish political/economic/industrial/artistic figures abroad. Factual captions imperative.
Text: Features on Scottish history, literature, economy, politics, Scots abroad, famous Scots etc. 400–800 words.
Overall freelance potential: Small; most material comes from Scottish sources and by prior arrangement.
Editor's tips: Would welcome details of freelances outside Scotland for potential commissions. "Do not send pictures of kilts, haggis or Billy Connolly!"
Fees: By negotiation.

Railways

INTERNATIONAL RAILWAY JOURNAL
Simmons-Boardman Publishing Corporation, PO Box 8, Falmouth, Cornwall TR11 4RJ. Tel: 0326 313945.
Editor: Mike Knutton.
Monthly publication for the principal officers of the railways of the world, ministers and commissioners of transport, railway equipment manufacturers and suppliers.
Illustrations: B&W and colour. Pictures of new line construction projects, electrification projects, track or signalling improvements, new locomotives, passenger coaches and freight wagons. Interesting pictures of railway operations from far-flung corners of the world. No steam or nostalgia material. Covers: colour shots tied in with the theme of a particular issue.
Text: Features on any sizeable contracts for railway equipment; plans for railway developments, i.e. new line construction, track or signalling improvements; almost anything which involves a railway spending money or making improvements and techniques. No padding or speculation.
Overall freelance potential: Quite good for the right business-oriented material; 15–20 per cent is bought.
Editor's tips: Accuracy is vital.
Fees: Rising scale according to size of pictures; text, £100 per 1,000 words.

RAIL

EMAP National Publications, Apex House, Oundle Road, Peterborough PE2 9NP. Tel: 0733 898100.
Editor: Murray Brown.
Fortnightly magazine dealing with modern railways.
Illustrations: Mostly black and white inside, some colour. Single photographs and up-to-date news pictures on any interesting railway topic, both in Britain and Europe.
Text: Illustrated articles of up to 1,500 words on any railway topic.
Overall freelance potential: Very good.
Editor's tips: Try to get away from straightforward pictures of trains; be imaginative.
Fees: Up to £35 for colour; up to £15 for B&W. Illustrated articles around £90–£150.

RAILNEWS

British Railways Board, Euston House, 24 Eversholt Street, London NW1 1DZ. Tel: 071-922 6977.
Editor: Stephen Knight.
Monthly newspaper of British Rail, giving latest news of technical and industrial developments on the system and news of staff.
Illustrations: B&W and colour prints. Railway news pictures, unusual pictures with good captions. shots of track working, BR engineering activities, etc. for stock. Pictures should always contain people and action. Covers: B&W or colour prints of topical railway news events.
Text: Difficult market for those outside the industry. Diary pieces, 100 words; features 1,000–1,250 words. short illustrated personality pieces always welcome.
Overall freelance potential: A frequent need for freelance coverage in certain areas for specific commissions. Contact the publication for details.
Editor's tips: Approach before submitting.
Fees: By negotiation.

STEAM CLASSIC

Argus Specialist Publications Ltd. Editorial Office: 46 Rydens Avenue, Walton-on-Thames, Surrey KT12 3JH. Tel: 0932 225330.
Editor: Peter Herring.
Monthly magazine for steam railway enthusiasts, inter-relating current activity with nostalgia.
Illustrations: B&W and colour. Top quality coverage of active steam trains, including close-up detail and atmospheric shots. Newsy pictures accepted on spec, but portfolio submissions should be discussed with the editor before submitting. Details of relevant collections/archive material always of interest.
Text: Well-illustrated articles on suitable subjects, which must follow the magazine's well-defined style.
Overall freelance potential: Excellent.
Fees: By negotiation.

STEAM RAILWAY

EMAP Apex Publications Ltd, Apex House, Oundle Road, Peterborough PE2 9NP. Tel: 0733 898100.
Editor: Nigel Harris.
Top-selling monthly magazine for the steam railway enthusiast. Closely concerned with railway preservation.
Illustrations: B&W and colour. Accurately captioned photographs depicting steam trains and railways past and present, preserved railway lines, and railway museums (topical subjects especially welcomed).
Text: Illustrated articles on relevant subjects.
Overall freelance potential: Most of the content is contributed by freelances.
Editor's tips: Material should be lively, topical and newsworthy, although some nostalgic or historic material is accepted.
Fees: By arrangement.

STEAM RAILWAY NEWS
Lancashire Publications Ltd, Martland Mill, Martland Mill Lane, Wigan WN5 0LX. Tel: 0942 228000.
Editor: John Huxley.
Weekly tabloid covering the contemporary steam railway scene.
Illustrations: Mostly B&W; colour used on the front page only. Newsy photographs of steam locomotives and steam-hauled trains operating on private railways or British Rail. No transparencies.
Text: Topical articles of 1,000–1,500 words on suitable subjects.
Overall freelance potential: By arrangement.
Fees: According to use and the nature of the material.

Religion

CATHOLIC GAZETTE
114 West Heath Road, London NW3 7TX. Tel: 081-458 3316.
Editor: Father Paul Billington.
Monthly publication concerned essentially with evangelisation.
Illustrations: B&W only. Pictures of nature or the countryside, plus people with natural or unusual expressions to illustrate points in articles, religious sculptures and architecture.
Text: Well researched articles on religious topics and human stories from personal experience. 2,000–3,000 words.
Overall freelance potential: Around 80 per cent is contributed by freelances.
Editor's tips: Articles should not be over-written and the human element should be kept to the forefront. Don't preach.
Fees: By agreement.

CATHOLIC HERALD
Herald House, Lamb's Passage, Bunhill Row, London EC1Y 8TQ. Tel: 071-588 3101.
Editor: Cristina Odone. **Picture Editor**: Murray White.
Weekly newspaper reflecting on Catholicism/Christianity and its place in the wider world.
Illustrations: B&W only. Principal need for news photographs of events involving churches, clerics or prominent Catholics.
Text: Articles of up to 1,200 words on the social, economic and political significance of the church domestically and internationally plus spiritual and reflective writings.
Overall freelance potential: Better for features than other material.
Fees: By arrangement but not high.

THE CHRISTIAN HERALD
Herald House Ltd, 96 Dominion Road, Worthing, West Sussex BN14 8JP. Tel: 0903 821082.
Editor: Bruce Hardy.
Weekly publication for Christians of all Protestant denominations.
Illustrations: B&W only. Stock pictures of family life, nature, scenic views, people in a variety of situations, holidays, jobs, festive occasions, news events, novelty and fun items.
Text: Some freelance market; contributors' notes available.
Overall freelance potential: Several freelance pictures and articles used every week.
Fees: Variable.

PARENTWISE
37 Elm Road, New Malden, Surrey KT3 3HB. Tel: 081-942 9761.
Editor: Clive Price.
Monthly Christian magazine for parents and partners with a concern for family issues.

Illustrations: B&W and colour. Pictures mainly for use with features. Colour transparencies used for covers.
Text: Articles on Christian living and family issues with a Christian viewpoint. Up to 1,400 words.
Overall freelance potential: Good; many contributed articles used each month.
Fees: Up to £70 for 1,400 words.

WOMAN ALIVE

Herald House Ltd, 96 Dominion Road, Worthing, West Sussex BN14 8JP. Tel: 0903 821082.
Editor: Elizabeth Round.
Monthly publication for women with church links.
Illustrations: B&W and colour. Stock pictures of family life, nature, scenic views, people in various situations (holidays, jobs, festive occasions), news events, novelty and fun items.
Text: Limited freelance market.
Overall freelance potential: Several freelance pictures used each month.
Fees: Variable.

Science & Technology

CHEMISTRY IN BRITAIN

The Royal Society of Chemistry, Burlington House, Piccadilly, London W1V 0BN. Tel: 071-437 8656.
Editor: Mr R. Stevenson.
Monthly publication for all members of the Royal Society of Chemistry. Aimed primarily at industrial chemists.
Illustrations: B&W inside. News pictures concerning research and manufacturing, and general pictures with a chemical connection. Covers: colour pictures of same. 35mm acceptable but medium format preferred.
Text: No freelance market.
Overall freelance potential: Variable.
Fees: By agreement.

CHEMISTRY AND INDUSTRY

Society of Chemical Industry, 15 Belgrave Square, London SW1X 8PS. Tel: 071-235 3681.
Editor: Andrew Miller.
Fortnightly science and trade magazine for chemists and the chemical industry.
Illustrations: B&W and colour. Photographs of chemical factories, chemistry research and environmental pollution.
Text: News stories and articles from contributors with the requisite technical background.
Overall freelance potential: Limited.
Editor's tips: Always contact the editor before preparing any submission.
Fees: £160 per 1,000 words for text; photographs by negotiation.

CLEAN AIR & ENVIRONMENTAL PROTECTION

National Society for Clean Air and Environmental Protection, 136 North Street, Brighton BN1 1RG. Tel: 0273 326313.
Editor: Ms Loveday Murley.
Quarterly publication for professionals in the field of air and noise pollution and environmental control; selected representatives of local authorities, researchers; and anyone generally interested in the subject.
Illustrations: B&W only. Pictures of air pollution, environment and conservation.

Text: Features on air pollution, noise, water pollution control, waste, open cast mining, conservation and energy issues. 4,000–8,000 words.
Overall freelance potential: Limited.
Fees: Be negotiation.

EDUCATION IN CHEMISTRY
The Royal Society of Chemistry, Burlington House, Piccadilly, London W1V 0BN. Tel: 071-437 8656.
Editor: Kathryn Roberts.
Bi-monthly publication for teachers, students, lecturers in schools, universities and polytechnics.
Illustrations: B&W only. Pictures that deal with the classroom, laboratories or the chemical industry. Covers: B&W pictures relating to specific articles inside.
Text: Features concerned with chemistry or the teaching of it. Under 2,500 words.
Overall freelance potential: Moderate.
Fees: By agreement.

THE GEOGRAPHICAL MAGAZINE
Centurion Publications Ltd, 52 George Street, London W1H 5RF. Tel: 071-487 4284.
Editor: Alexander Goldsmith. **Art Editor**: Alan Ashby.
Monthly magazine of the Royal Geographical Society. Covers topical geographical subjects from an academic and scientific point of view whilst still appealing to the general reader.
Illustrations: B&W and colour. Sets of pictures linked to geographical topics – human, political, economic and physical subjects. Interesting single pictures relevant to current geographical issues. Maps and/or graphs always needed.
Text: Well-illustrated articles on any geographical subject, written from a scientific perspective but with popular appeal. Length variable.
Overall freelance potential: Excellent for the right type of material.
Fees: Negotiable, but in the region of £70 per published page. Single pictures according to use.

NEW SCIENTIST
New Science Publications, King's Reach Tower, Stamford Street, London SE1 9LS. Tel: 071-261 5000.
Editor: Alun Anderson. **Picture Researcher**: Karen Gunnell.
Weekly magazine about science and technology for people with some scientific or technical education and also for the intelligent layman.
Illustrations: B&W and colour. Pictures on any topic that can be loosely allied to science and technology. Particularly interested in news photographs related to scientific phenomena and events. Covers: B&W and colour pictures, usually connected with a feature inside.
Text: News and features on scientific/technical subjects that might appeal to a wide audience.
Overall freelance potential: A lot of freelance work used, but best to consult the magazine before submitting.
Fees: On a rising scale according to the length of article or size of reproduction.

Sport

AIR GUNNER
Romsey Publishing Company, 4 The Courtyard, Denmark Street, Wokingham, Berkshire RG11 2AZ. Tel: 0734 771677.
Editor: Paul Dobson.
Monthly magazine for all airgun enthusiasts.
Illustrations: B&W only. Illustrated news items, and stock shots of small field animals (rats, rabbits) and pest species of birds (pigeons, magpies, crows). Covers: colour, usually commissioned, but a freelance picture might be used.

Text: Articles on any aspect of airgun use, 700–1,000 words, and accompanied by a good selection of B&W prints.
Overall freelance potential: Good for file photos and illustrated articles.
Fees: In the region of £50 per published page.

BOXING MONTHLY
24 Notting Hill Gate, London W11 3JE. Tel: 071-229 9944.
Editor: Glyn Leach.
Heavily illustrated monthly publication for boxing enthusiasts, covering both professional and amateur boxing.
Illustrations: B&W and colour. Coverage of boxing at all levels, including the amateur scene.
Text: Knowledgeable articles, features, interviews, etc. on any aspect of the boxing scene. Always contact the editor in the first instance.
Overall freelance potential: Excellent scope for boxing specialists, and for good amateur boxing coverage.
Fees: By negotiation.

CLIMBER AND HILL WALKER
The Plaza Tower, The Plaza, East Kilbride, Glasgow G74 1LW. Tel: 03552 46444.
Editor: Tom Prentice.
Monthly magazine dealing with world-wide mountain climbing from Lakeland fells to Everest. Highly literate readership. Contributors range from "unknowns" to top climbers like Chris Bonington.
Illustrations: B&W and colour. First ascents and newsworthy events but, in the main, used only with text. Covers: action shots of climbers or dramatic mountain pictures.
Text: Features on hill walking, trekking, rock climbing, Alpinism, high altitude climbing, cross-country and mountain skiing (*not* downhill racing). 1,500–2,000 words.
Overall freelance potential: Good; 90 per cent of articles and 100 per cent of pictures come from freelances, but many are regulars.
Editor's tips: This is a specialist field and is full of good writer/photographers. There is potential for the freelance to break in, but the magazine is usually well stocked with material.
Fees: Variable.

CRICKET WORLD
Cricket World Ltd, Mews House, 2a Chelverton Road, Putney, London SW15 1RH. Tel: 081-788 3230.
Editor: Michael Blumberg.
Monthly magazine with a strong emphasis on contemporary aspects of English cricket, and with some international coverage.
Illustrations: B&W and colour. News pictures. Action, general human interest and humorous pictures.
Text: Some scope for writers who know their subject.
Overall freelance potential: Good for knowledgeable contributors.
Fees: By negotiation.

THE CRICKETER INTERNATIONAL
The Cricketer Ltd, Third Street, Langton Green, Tunbridge Wells, Kent TN3 0EN. Tel: 0892 862551.
Editor: Peter Perchard.
Monthly publication for cricket enthusiasts of all ages. Covers all aspects of the sport.
Illustrations: B&W and colour. Pictures of less fashionable players needed, plus historical pictures. Covers: colour pictures of cricketing subjects, usually supplied by staff photographers, but occasionally bought from freelances.
Text: Features taking an original look at the subject. Up to 1,000 words.
Overall freelance potential: A high percentage comes from freelances, but usually by commissions.

Fees: Covers, £60; Inside pictures and text by agreement, but on average £5 per 100 words; £16 per B&W picture; £30 per colour picture.

DARTS WORLD
World Magazines Ltd, 241 High Street, Beckenham, Kent BR3 1BN. Tel: 081-650 6580.
Editor: A. J. Wood.
Monthly magazine for darts players and organisers.
Illustrations: B&W only inside. Pictures on any darts theme, action shots and portraits of leading players. Covers: colour pictures usually of star players. Good colour also required for the annual *Darts Player*.
Text: Features on all darts subjects.
Overall freelance potential: Most of the copy and pictures comes from freelances.
Editor's tips: The darts-playing environment is often dim and smoky, which can make it difficult to produce bright, interesting pictures. Photographers who can come up with colourful shots that catch the eye are welcomed.
Fees: Good, on a rising scale according to size of reproduction or length of feature.

FIGHTERS – THE MARTIAL ARTS MAGAZINE
Peterson Publications Ltd, Peterson House, Northbank, Berryhill Industrial Estate, Droitwich, Worcestershire WR9 9BL. Tel: 0905 795564.
Editor: Tim Ayling.
Monthly magazine for martial arts and similar disciplines.
Illustrations: B&W inside the magazine on events, clubs and individuals and any general martial arts interests. Covers: action shots in colour; 6x6cm minimum.
Text: Features on martial arts events, profiles of clubs and individuals and any other martial arts interests. 500–3,500 words.
Overall freelance potential: Quite good.
Fees: By negotiation.

FIRST DOWN
Mediawatch Ltd, Spendlove Centre, Charlbury, Chipping Norton, Oxfordshire OX7 3PQ. Tel: 0608 811266.
Editor: Stephen Anglesey.
Weekly magazine covering American football, in the UK, Europe and USA.
Illustrations: B&W and colour. Main requirement is for news pictures and personality portraits from the British scene.
Text: Short news items, match reports, and profiles or interview features.
Overall freelance potential: Quite good.
Fees: According to use.

FORE!
EMAP Pursuit Publishing Ltd, Bretton Court, Bretton, Peterborough PE3 8DZ. Tel: 0733 267454.
Editor: Bob Warters.
Monthly golfing magazine with an aspirational and youthful approach.
Illustrations: Colour only. Top quality photographs of golf courses around the country, not so much the well-known ones but the "hidden gems" that will spark interest amongst golfers looking for fresh courses to play. Off-beat shots always of interest. No tournament coverage required.
Text: Little scope.
Overall freelance potential: Very good for those who can provide suitable quality coverage.
Editor's tips: "The keyword is aspirational; we look for photographs of courses that make the reader think: 'I'd really like to play that course'. Most suitable shots are likely to be taken in either early morning or late afternoon, when courses are less busy and at their most attractive."
Fees: Negotiable, according to use.

FORMULA 1 NEWS

Formula 1 News Ltd, 116–118 Liscombe, Birch Hill, Bracknell, Berks RG12 7DE. Tel: 0344 427846.

Editor: Derek Wright. **Picture Editor**: Graham Bull.

News magazine devoted exclusively to Formula 1 motor racing. Published fortnightly only during the nine month racing season.

Illustrations: Mainly colour. Very up-to-date news pictures depicting anything relevant to the Formula 1 scene.

Text: Little freelance scope for non-specialists.

Overall freelance potential: Limited; most material is obtained from professional motor racing photographers and agencies.

Editor's tips: Always contact the picture editor to establish interest before submitting.

Fees: By negotiation.

GOLF MONTHLY

IPC Magazines, King's Reach Tower, Stamford Street, London SE1 9LS. Tel: 071-261 7237.

Editor: Colin Callander.

Monthly international consumer magazine for golfers.

Illustrations: B&W and colour. Mainly for use as illustrations to articles. Small market for one-off pictures from golf tournaments of golf-related events.

Text: Illustrated features on golf instruction, golf-related features and occasional fiction. Also in-depth profiles of leading world players. Around 2,000 words, but not critical.

Overall freelance potential: Most of the magazine is commissioned. Room for more material of the right type from freelances.

Editor's tips: This is an international magazine and so material must have a wide appeal. No features of a parochial nature.

Fees: By agreement.

GOLF WORLD

Golf World Ltd, Advance House, 37 Millharbour, Isle of Dogs, London E14 9TX. Tel: 071-538 1031/0941.

Editor: Robert Green.

Monthly publication for golfers, covering all aspects of the sport.

Illustrations: B&W and colour. Unusual golfing pictures always of interest.

Text: Profiles of leading golfers and general or instructional features. 1,500–2,000 words.

Overall freelance potential: Around 20 per cent comes from freelance sources.

Fees: By agreement.

THE GOLFER

Village Publishing Ltd, 10A London Mews, Paddington, London W2 1HY. Tel: 071-224 9242.

Editor: Derek Lawrenson. **Art Editor**: Sarah Snelling.

Monthly magazine aimed at the armchair golf fan. Concentrates on tournament coverage and player profiles.

Illustrations: Colour only. Portraits and action shots of well-known golfers for stock and general illustration of features. Commissions available for experienced golf photographers.

Text: Suitable illustrated articles and profiles welcome, but always raise ideas with the editor in the first instance. No instructional articles.

Overall freelance potential: Excellent for suitable coverage; all contributions are freelance.

Fees: Photography negotiable. Text around £200 per 1,000 words.

HARPERS SPORTS & LEISURE

47A High Street, Bushey, Watford, Herts WD2 1BD. Tel: 081-950 9522.

Editor: Martin Johnson.

Magazine aimed at the UK sports retail trade. 18 issues per year.

Illustrations: B&W and colour. Topical pictures concerning the retail trade, usually to illustrate specific news stories and features.
Text: Illustrated features and news stories on anything to do with the sports retail industry, including manufacturer and retailer profiles etc.
Overall freelance potential: Limited.
Fees: Text, £100 per 1,000 words; pictures by negotiation.

MARTIAL ARTS ILLUSTRATED
Martial Arts Ltd, 8 Revenue Chambers, St Peter Street, Huddersfield, West Yorkshire HD1 1EL. Tel: 0484 435011.
Editor: Bob Sykes.
Monthly magazine covering all forms of Oriental fighting and self-defence techniques.
Illustrations: B&W and colour. Single pictures or sets depicting well-known martial artists, club events, tournament action and aspects of technique.
Text: Well-illustrated articles on any relevant subject – profiles of leading figures and individual clubs, interviews, technique sequences and self-defence features.
Overall freelance potential: Excellent for those with access to the martial arts scene.
Editor's tips: Always write in the first instance with suggestions.
Fees: Should be negotiated before submission, as many contributions are supplied free of charge.

MARTIAL ARTS TODAY
HHL Publishing Ltd, Greater London House, Hampstead Road, London NW1 9QQ. Tel: 071-388 3171.
Editor: Steven Day.
Bi-monthly magazine covering all forms of martial arts.
Illustrations: Mainly colour. Stock pictures and good action coverage of any form of martial arts. Commissions available to cover tournaments and portraiture for profile features.
Text: Regional reports and tournaments coverage. Illustrated articles of up to 1,500 words on specific topics, profiles of leading figures, and related topics such as exercise, history and travel.
Overall freelance potential: Excellent.
Fees: By negotiation.

MATCH
EMAP Pursuit Publishing Ltd, Bretton Court, Bretton Centre, Bretton, Peterborough PE3 8DZ. Tel: 0733 260333.
Editor: Adrian Curtis.
Weekly publication, looking at the whole spectrum of soccer. Aimed at readers in the 9–15 age group.
Illustrations: Colour only. Good soccer action shots. Usually bought only after consultation with the editor. Covers: Top quality colour action.
Text: Profiles and interviews concerning personalities in the soccer field. Length by prior arrangement.
Overall freelance potential: Fair.
Fees: By agreement.

90 MINUTES
IPC Magazines, King's Reach Tower, Stamford Street, London SE1 9LS. Tel: 071-261 7450.
Editor: Paul Hawksbee.
Weekly football magazine covering the game at all levels.
Illustrations: All colour. Coverage of football at all levels, especially below The Premier League and including non-League games and European coverage.
Text: News items and short features always welcomed. Background stories and well-researched and perhaps controversial features, aimed at a teenage and adult readership.

Overall freelance potential: Excellent.
Editor's tips: Main interest is in "the news behind the news".
Fees: By negotiation.

NON-LEAGUE FOOTBALL

HHL Publishing Ltd. Editorial: PO Box 283, St Albans, Herts AL2 3JD. Tel: 0923 894355.
Editor: Bruce Smith.
Monthly magazine covering all levels of non-League football.
Illustrations: All colour. Always interested in up-to-date coverage of non-League games and person-alities.
Text: Will always consider ideas, especially for stories at local level. Also profiles of players currently in the news, around 700 words.
Overall freelance potential: Very good; the sports agencies rarely cover games at this level so there are always opportunities for freelances.
Editor's tips: Always pleased to hear from photographers who can produce really decent results – especially floodlit coverage that doesn't suffer from too much grain.
Fees: By negotiation.

ON THE LINE

On the Line, 24 Catterick Road, Didsbury, Manchester M20 0HJ. Tel: 061-445 4443.
Editor: Peter Brookes.
Regional tennis magazine for the North West, published eight times per year. Covers the tennis scene in Greater Manchester, Lancashire, Cheshire, Cumbria, Isle of Man and bordering regions.
Illustrations: B&W and colour, but colour submissions preferred. Coverage of local tennis tourna-ments and events in the region.
Text: Illustrated articles about tennis in the region. Submit ideas only in the first instance.
Overall freelance potential: Good for those based in the area.
Editor's tips: Always make contact before covering an event as coverage may already have been arranged.
Fees: By negotiation.

POT BLACK MAGAZINE

"Fairwinds", First Avenue, Hook End, Brentwood, Essex CM15 0HL. Tel: 0277 823263.
Editor: Terry Smith.
Monthly magazine for snooker enthusiasts, including coverage of billiards and pool.
Illustrations: B&W and colour. Top quality material depicting leading snooker players in action or at leisure, and any other pictures with a snooker connection.
Text: In-depth interviews with leading players, and humorous or offbeat items. However, opportuni-ties are limited as most articles come from regular contributors.
Overall freelance potential: Limited.
Editor's tips: The magazine takes an informal and colourful view of the game.
Fees: By negotiation.

RACING PIGEON PICTORIAL

The Racing Pigeon Publishing Co. Ltd, Unit 13, 21 Wren Street, London WC1X 0HF. Tel: 071-833 5959.
Editor: Tony Oates.
Monthly magazine for pigeon fanciers. Provides in-depth articles on methods, successful fanciers, sci-entific information, etc.
Illustrations: B&W and colour. Pictures used as illustrations for features, plus some one-off pictures of pigeons. Covers: colour pictures of pigeons, pigeon lofts, pigeon fanciers and related subjects.
Text: Features on pigeons, pigeon lofts, pigeon fanciers and related subjects. 1,500 words.
Overall freelance potential: Around 10–15 per cent of the pictures come from freelance photogra-

phers. Articles are mostly by specialist writers.
Editor's tips: Short, colourful, exotic articles with good illustrations stand a reasonable chance.
Fees: £35 per published page minimum.

RANGERS NEWS
Argyle House, Ibrox Stadium, Glasgow G51 2XD. Tel: 041-427 8844.
Editor: Derek Watson.
Weekly newspaper of Rangers Football Club. Aimed at Rangers supporters but also has substantial coverage of Scottish, European and world football.
Illustrations: Colour. General action pictures of Scottish, European and world football.
Text: Little freelance market.
Overall freelance potential: Around 20 per cent of the newspaper is supplied by freelance photographers.
Fees: By arrangement.

RUGBY LEAGUER
Lancashire Publications Ltd, Martland Mill, Martland Mill Lane, Wigan WN5 0LX. Tel: 0942 228000.
Editor: John Huxley.
Weekly paper covering rugby league football at home and abroad.
Illustrations: B&W and colour. Match coverage, stock pictures of individual players, and coverage of any other events relating to rugby league.
Text: Little scope.
Overall freelance potential: Limited.
Fees: By arrangement with editor.

RUGBY NEWS
Pyramid Publishing, 51a Coningham Road, London W12 8BS. Tel: 081-749 8991.
Editor: Richard Bath.
Monthly rugby magazine covering all levels of the sport.
Illustrations: Almost exclusively colour. Coverage at the top level is usually obtained from agency sources, so scope for the freelance is mostly at local and "grass roots" level, including school tournaments.
Text: Articles and local match reports may be considered, but always query the editor first.
Overall freelance potential: Fair.
Editor's tips: The different picture with really good action, at whatever level, will always be of interest.
Fees: By negotiation.

RUGBY WORLD & POST
Harmsworth Active, 10 Sheet Street, Windsor, Berks SL4 1BG. Tel: 0753 856061.
Editor: Duncan Mackay.
Monthly magazine giving general coverage of Rugby Union.
Illustrations: B&W and colour. Main scope is for regional/local coverage, since the top level matches are covered by regulars. Photographs of Cup matches, County championships, personalities, off-beat shots, etc. Covers: colour action shots of top players. Enclose s.a.e. for return of material.
Text: Little scope except for some regional news items.
Overall freelance potential: Limited, but good regional coverage is always of interest.
Fees: On a rising scale according to size of reproduction or length of text.

RUNNER'S WORLD
Rodale Press Ltd, 67–71 Goswell Road, London EC1V 7EN. Tel: 071-972 9119.
Editor: Nick Troop. **Art Director**: Robin Benson.
Monthly publication for running enthusiasts.

Illustrations: B&W and colour. Pictures relating to sports, recreational and fitness running. Consult art editor before submitting.
Text: Feature material considered, but only by prior consultation with the editor.
Overall freelance potential: Fair.
Fees: By agreement.

SCOTLAND'S RUNNER
ScotRun Publications Ltd, 113 St George's Road, Glasgow G3 6JA. Tel: 041-332 5738.
Editor: Kevin Ferrie.
Monthly magazine for Scottish running enthusiasts, with coverage ranging from general fitness running to top level athletics.
Illustrations: Mostly B&W. Good action shots or portraits of leading Scottish athletes, and news pictures of specific events involving a Scottish interest. Some colour is used, but is usually from agency sources.
Text: Illustrated articles on any aspect of running for sport, fitness or leisure. 500–1,500 words.
Overall freelance potential: Good.
Editor's tips: All contributions must relate to Scottish interests.
Fees: By negotiation.

THE SCOTTISH SPORTING GAZETTE
22 Market Brae, Inverness IV2 3AB. Tel: 0463 232104/222757.
Editor: John Ormiston.
Annual publication to market Scottish shooting, fishing, stalking and allied services. Aimed at the upper income bracket in the UK, Europe and America.
Illustrations: B&W and colour. Pictures of shooting, fishing, stalking; live game animals; subjects relating to whisky distilleries; antique Scottish weapons; tartans, castles and hunting lodges. Covers: exceptional colour pictures of game animals or action sporting shots.
Text: Features on shooting, fishing and stalking in Scotland or articles on other topics that are particularly Scottish, e.g. whisky, tartans, castles, antiques, etc. Also, Scottish fashions for women. 600–2,000 words.
Overall freelance potential: Good.
Editor's tips: Pictures and text must be unusual, not the normal anecdotes associated with this field. Material should have a good Scottish flavour. It does not have to be essentially sporting, but should be allied in some way.
Fees: Open to negotiation.

SHOOT!
IPC Magazines Ltd, King's Reach Tower, Stamford Street, London SE1 9LS. Tel: 071-261 6287.
Managing Editor: Peter Stewart. **Picture Editor**: Duncan Bond.
Weekly football magazine aimed primarily at the youth market.
Illustrations: All colour. Stock material covering all English divisions, Scottish cup matches, European and International games. Offbeat pictures of national teams. Team groups from The Premier League, First Division and leading Scottish clubs. International games featuring home countries and Republic of Ireland. All cup games and European matches. Covers: pictures of top players from The Premier League, and Internationals, particularly those from UK and Ireland.
Text: Topical newsworthy articles on and by players in the limelight. In-depth features on clubs and all aspects of the game. Usual length either one-page (450–500 words), or two-page (800–1,000 words).
Overall freelance potential: Excellent, virtually 100 per cent of photographic content comes from freelances.
Editor's tips: Picture choice is selective with only top quality material from the top levels of the game being used.
Fees: According to size of reproduction or length of text.

THE SHOOTING GAZETTE

BPG (Bourne) Ltd, 2 West Street, Bourne, Lincolnshire PE10 9NE. Tel: 0778 393747.
Editor: Mike Barnes.
Bi-monthly magazine for shotgun shooting enthusiasts. Britain's only magazine covering exclusively game and rough shooting.
Illustrations: B&W and colour. Pictures for general illustration and stock depicting any aspect of clay and game shooting.
Text: Well-illustrated articles from those with specialist knowledge, and profiles or interviews with leading shooters. Up to 1,000 words.
Overall freelance potential: Fair.
Fees: By negotiation.

SHOOTING TIMES & COUNTRY MAGAZINE

Harmsworth Active, 10 Sheet Street, Windsor, Berkshire SL4 1BG. Tel: 0753 856061.
Editor: Tim O'Nions.
Weekly magazine concentrating on all aspects of quarry shooting (game, pigeon, rough shooting, wildfowling and stalking). Also covers clay shooting, other fieldsports and general country topics.
Illustrations: Mostly colour. Good photographs of shooting subjects plus gundogs, wildlife, rural crafts, country food. Some scope for good generic photographs of British counties, showing known landmarks. B&W news pictures. Covers: shots should be vertical in shape with room for title at the top – medium format preferred but *sharp* 35mm acceptable.
Text: Illustrated features on all aspects of quarry shooting and general country topics as above. In the region of 900 words.
Overall freelance potential: Excellent; plenty of scope for new contributors.
Editor's tips: The magazine likes to keep pictures on file as it is not always possible to know in advance when a picture can be used. For features, remember that the readers are real country people.
Fees: Colour inside £15–£60 according to size; covers £70. Features £40 per 500 words.

SKI SURVEY

The Ski Club of Great Britain, 118 Eaton Square, London SW1W 9AF. Tel: 071-245 1033.
Editor: Roland White.
Published five times a year. Official journal of the Ski Club of Great Britain, covering the sport at all levels.
Illustrations: B&W and colour. Pictures of holiday skiing, ski-touring, racing, and equipment. Shots illustrating snowcraft and particular techniques. Good, attractive pictures of ski resorts and ski slopes in season. Covers: good colour action with the skier taking up at least two-thirds of the pictures. 35mm acceptable but larger formats preferred.
Text: Some scope for general articles about skiing, and on techniques.
Overall freelance potential: Quite good.
Fees: Covers £80; all other fees by arrangement.

THE SKIER

48 London Road, Sevenoaks, Kent TN13 1AS. Tel: 0723 743644.
Editor: Frank Baldwin.
Published six times a year during September–April. Covers all aspects of skiing.
Illustrations: B&W and colour. Good action pictures and anything spectacular, odd or humorous.
Text: Original ideas for illustrated features always welcome. Possible scope for resort reports and news items.
Overall freelance potential: Good.
Fees: By negotiation.

SNOOKER SCENE

Cavalier House, 202 Hagley Road, Edgbaston, Birmingham B16 9PQ. Tel: 021-454 2931.

Editor: Clive Everton.
Monthly publication for snooker players and enthusiasts.
Illustrations: B&W only inside. Snooker action pictures and coverage related to actual tournaments.
Covers: Colour pictures on similar themes.
Text: Features on snooker and billiards. 250–1,000 words.
Overall freelance potential: Limited.
Fees: By arrangement.

SNOWBOARD UK

Air Publications Ltd, Unit 1A, Franchise Street, Kidderminster, Worcs DY11 6RE. Tel: 0562 827744.
Editor: Mark Sturgeon.
Magazine covering the sport of snowboarding. Published six times a year, during the winter sports season.
Illustrations: Mainly colour. Good action coverage of the sport always required; should be colourful and stylish. Mainly UK coverage but material from Europe and North America also of interest.
Text: Short, heavily-illustrated articles on any aspect of the sport.
Overall freelance potential: Excellent; the magazine is very photo-based.
Editor's tips: The magazine is keen to build up a pool of photographers who can be relied upon to produce quality coverage of the sport.
Fees: Variable; according to use and nature of material.

SPORTS QUARTERLY

Sports Quarterly Ltd, The Vinegar Factory, Bowden Street, Kennington, London SE11 4DS. Tel: 071-582 6161.
Editor: Peter Bills. **Art Director**: Gareth Walters.
Alternate-monthly glossy magazine concentrating on major sports and aimed at an up-market male readership.
Illustrations: Mainly colour, but exceptional B&W work also of interest. Most photography obtained through picture agencies, but top quality pictures of major sporting activity always considered.
Text: No scope.
Overall freelance potential: Limited.
Editor's tips: Do not submit run-of-the-mill photographs; only top quality material is of interest.
Fees: Negotiable.

SPORTS TRADER

Bouverie Publishing Company Ltd, 244–249 Temple Chambers, London EC4Y 0BP. Tel: 071-583 3030.
Editor: Derek Steel.
Monthly publication for retailers, manufacturers, importers and exporters in the sports clothing and equipment trade.
Illustrations: B&W and colour. General sporting pictures, sporting events linked to sponsorship by manufacturers, sponsorships, sports product pictures.
Text: General news stories linked to the sports industry, usually concerning manufacturers, retailers, importers and exporters. General features concerning the sports industry. In-depth features on trends, legal articles on legislation. News stories, 250 words; features 750–1,000 words.
Overall freelance potential: Good market for the right type of material.
Editor's tips: Always telephone first.
Fees: Pictures £10–£20. Text, £100 per 1,000 words.

SWIMMING TIMES

Harold Fern House, Derby Square, Loughborough, Leicestershire LE11 0AL. Tel: 0509 234433.
Editor: Karren Glendenning.
Official magazine of the Amateur Swimming Association and Institute of Swimming Teachers and Coaches. Covers all aspects including diving, synchro-swimming, water polo, etc.

Illustrations: B&W only inside. News pictures of swimmers at major events and any off-beat or particularly interesting shots of swimming related activity. Covers: colour pictures of swimming-related subjects.
Text: Human interest stories about individual swimmers.
Overall freelance potential: Limited.
Editor's tips: Photographers should avoid ordinary "swimming along" type pictures or straightforward "mug shots". Text should be tight and non-technical. Ensure that statistics quoted are accurate.
Fees: Negotiable.

TARGET GUN

Peterson Publications Ltd, Peterson House, Northbank, Berryhill Industrial Estate, Droitwich, Worcestershire WR9 9BL. Tel: 0905 795564.
Editor: Richard Atkins.
Monthly publication for target shooters (fullbore and smallbore, pistols and rifles, airweapons).
Illustrations: B&W and colour. Pictures of weapons, events, technical/engineering matters and pictures of general interest in the sport. Some opportunities for colour covers.
Text: General and technical instructional articles; reports of meetings. 500–2,500 words.
Overall freelance potential: Quite good.
Fees: By negotiation.

TENNIS WORLD

Presswatch Ltd, The Spendlove Centre, Enstone Road, Charlbury, Oxon OX7 3PQ. Tel: 0608 811446.
Editor: Alastair McIver.
Monthly for tennis enthusiasts, covering both the British and international scene.
Illustrations: B&W and colour. Top quality tournament coverage always considered. Also action shots and portraits of leading individual players.
Text: Tournament reports, profiles of individual players and technique features, 500–1,500 words.
Overall freelance potential: Fair.
Fees: By negotiation.

TODAY'S GOLFER

EMAP Pursuit Publishing Ltd, Bretton Court, Bretton, Peterborough PE3 8DZ. Tel: 0733 264666.
Editor: Martin Vousden.
Monthly for golfing enthusiasts.
Illustrations: B&W and colour. Stock shots of leading players and courses, and anything off-beat.
Text: Instructional material; features on challenging non-championship courses to play; player profiles.
Overall freelance potential: Good.
Fees: By negotiation.

TODAY'S RUNNER

EMAP Pursuit Publishing Ltd, Bretton Court, Bretton, Peterborough PE3 8DZ. Tel: 0733 264666.
Editor: Allan Haines.
Monthly magazine aimed at the average runner who wants to improve.
Illustrations: Colour. Coverage of competitions and running events at local or regional level, off-beat pictures, and general stock shots of runners showing "effort and strain". Runners' training pictures also welcome. Covers: good action pictures.
Text: Illustrated articles of a practical and non-technical nature, giving advice on training, diet, etc. 1,000–1,500 words.
Overall freelance potential: Good.
Fees: By negotiation.

WATFORD

Watford Football Club, Vicarage Road Stadium, Watford, Herts WD1 8ER. Tel: 0923 230933.
Editor: Ed Coan.
Published on match days during August to May, and read by supporters of Watford Football Club.
Illustrations: B&W and colour. Watford players in action at home or at away matches. Covers: colour pictures of same.
Text: Use some freelance material on general subjects agreed with the editor.
Overall freelance potential: This is an outlet for professional or very good amateur sports photographers.
Fees: By negotiation.

WISDEN CRICKET MONTHLY

Wisden Cricket Magazines Ltd, 6 Beech Lane, Guildford, Surrey GU2 5ES. Tel: 0483 32573.
Editor: David Frith.
Monthly publication aimed at all cricket lovers. Concentrates on the game at first-class level.
Illustrations: B&W and colour. Pictures of first-class cricket. Demand for topical county cricket matches, especially away from the major grounds such as Lord's and The Oval. Covers usually provided by a retained photographer.
Text: Scope for features about first-class cricket, but check first before submitting. Up to 800 words.
Overall freelance potential: Limited; only around 5 per cent comes from freelance sources.
Fees: On a rising scale according to size of pictures or length of article.

Trade

THE BOOKSELLER

J. Whitaker and Sons Ltd, 12 Dyott Street, London WC1A 1DF. Tel: 071-836 8911.
Editor: Louis Baum.
Weekly trade paper aimed at librarians, booksellers, publishers, agents, authors and anyone interested in the book industry. Covers financial news, government affairs, trade trends and events, authors, etc.
Illustrations: B&W only. Pictures of bookshops and book-related activities outside London. Busy book fairs, busy book shops, etc.
Text: Serious, humorous, analytical, descriptive articles connected with the book trade, plus author interviews.
Overall freelance potential: Only for those freelances who have good access to the book trade.
Fees: Variable; depends on material.

BRITISH BAKER

EMAP Maclaren Ltd, Maclaren House, Scarbrook Road, Croydon CR9 1QH. Tel: 081-688 7788.
Editor: Martin Roebuck.
Weekly news journal covering the whole baking industry.
Illustrations: Mainly B&W. Interesting photographs relating to working bakeries, especially news items such as shop openings, promotions, charity events, etc. Also good stock shots of bakery products, B&W or colour.
Text: Short news stories (300 words) or features (500–1,000 words) on any baking industry topic.
Overall freelance potential: Fair, for those who can supply relevant material.
Fees: £110 per 1,000 words for text; photographs by negotiation.

CABINET MAKER

Benn Publications Ltd, Sovereign Way, Tonbridge, Kent TN9 1RW. Tel: 0732 364422.
Editor: Sandra Danby.

Weekly publication for all those in the furniture and furnishing trade and industry.
Illustrations: B&W and colour. Freelances commissioned to cover news assignments in the trade. Some scope for pictures to illustrate features.
Text: Features about companies starting to make furniture for sale to retailers and interior designers. Length from one to four pages (1,000 words plus three pictures makes two pages).
Overall freelance potential: Around 10 per cent contributed, including news coverage.
Editor's tips: It is best to approach the editor, features editor or news editor for a brief before submitting.
Fees: By agreement.

CATERER & HOTELKEEPER
Reed Business Publishing, Quadrant House, The Quadrant, Sutton, Surrey SM2 5AS. Tel: 081-652 8680/3485.
Editor: *To be appointed.*
Weekly magazine for the hotel and catering trade.
Illustrations: B&W and colour. News pictures relevant to hotel and catering establishments – openings, extensions, refurbishments, people, etc. Special interest in regional material. Commissions possible to cover establishments, equipment and food.
Text: Specialist articles of interest to the trade, by commission only.
Overall freelance potential: Growing.
Fees: On a rising scale according to size of reproduction or length of text.

CHEMIST AND DRUGGIST
Benn Publications Ltd, Benn House, Soverign Way, Tonbridge, Kent TN9 1RW. Tel: 0732 364422.
Editor: John Skelton.
Weekly news publication for retail pharmacists; the pharmaceutical, toiletries and cosmetics industries; pharmaceutical wholesalers, etc.
Illustrations: B&W and colour. News pictures concerning individual retailers, such as shops involved in flooding etc.
Text: Little scope.
Overall freelance potential: Limited.
Fees: On a rising scale, according to contribution.

CONVENIENCE STORE
William Reed Ltd, Broadfield Park, Crawley, West Sussex RH11 9RT. Tel: 0293 613400.
Editor: Tony Hurren.
Fortnightly magazine for independent retailers and convenience stores, and their wholesale suppliers.
Illustrations: B&W and colour. Photographs usually to illustrate specific features; little scope for pictures on their own.
Text: Illustrated features or stories concerning late night, local, food-based shops. Such material should feature a retailer who is doing something a bit different, or who has been highly successful in some way.
Overall freelance potential: Modest, but the editor will be pleased to hear from freelances who can produce an interesting illustrated feature in this field.
Fees: By negotiation.

DRAPERS RECORD
EMAP Maclaren, Maclaren House, 19 Scarbook Road, Croydon, Surrey CR9 1QH. Tel: 081-688 7788.
Editor: Juliet Warkentin.
Weekly news publication for clothing and textile retailers.
Illustrations: B&W and colour. News pictures of interest to the trade. Commissioned coverage for fashion and major trade stories.
Text: Features and news items of relevance to retailers in the fashion and textile fields.

Overall freelance potential: Limited for news; fair for commissioned work.
Editor's tips: Please do not send unsolicited material – call the editor first.
Fees: Good; on a rising scale according to size of illustration or length of feature.

EUROFRUIT MAGAZINE

Market Intelligence Ltd, 4th Floor, Market Towers, New Covent Garden Market, One Nine Elms Lane, London SW8 5NQ. Tel: 071-498 6711.
Editor: Linda Bloomfield.
Monthly magazine of the fresh fruit and vegetable trade, published in French, German, Italian, English and Spanish. Aimed at leading producers, exporters, importers, merchants and buyers of fruit and vegetables.
Illustrations: B&W and colour. Subjects such as harvesting fruit, loading on to ships or lorries, quality checks on fruit, packing etc. Photographs mostly for magazine's own picture library.
Text: Features on fruit and vegetables, e.g. Chilean apples in Europe, French Iceberg lettuce, Egypt's expanding export range, Norway as an alternative market etc. 1,250–2,000 words.
Overall freelance potential: Quite good. Some regular contributors, but scope for the freelance writer who can also supply pictures.
Editor's tips: It is best to work in close contact with the editorial department to get names of people who would be of interest to the publication.
Fees: Negotiable

FX

ETP Partnership, 87 Brewer Street, London W1R 3PG. Tel: 071-287 3063.
Editor: Janine Furness.
Quarterly interior design magazine for the retail, hotel and commercial sectors. Aimed at designers, architects and their clients.
Illustrations: Mainly colour. By commission only; experienced architectural and interiors photographers with fresh ideas always welcome.
Text: Articles on commercial design matters and related business issues, only from those with real expertise in these areas.
Overall freelance potential: Good for the experienced worker.
Editor's tips: We are very receptive to original ideas. Articles should be hard-hitting and possibly contentious.
Fees: Photography around £200–£250 per day. £160 per 1,000 words.

FASHION EXTRAS

Reflex Publishing Ltd, 86 Clarendon Road, West Croydon, Surrey CR0 3SG. Tel: 081-681 3056/7.
Editor: Chris McCarthy.
Monthly trade publication dealing with fashion accessories such as gloves, scarves, jewellery, hosiery and shoes, and including leathergoods, i.e. handbags, luggage.
Illustrations: B&W and colour. Interested in stock fashion pictures or fashion show coverage.
Text: Features on the legal, insurance and cash side of the business. Specialist articles on all aspects of selling to the consumer. Retail trends. Fashion articles. Up to 1,000 words.
Overall freelance potential: Small but regular income possible for outside contributors. About 20 per cent is contributed.
Editor's tips: New approaches and thoughts on still-life photography always welcome.
Fees: Negotiable.

FASHION WEEKLY

EMAP Maclaren, Maclaren House, 19 Scarbook Road, Croydon, Surrey CR9 1QH. Tel: 081-688 7788.
Editor: Martin Raymond.
Weekly retail trade paper, covering women's, men's and children's fashion.
Illustrations: B&W and colour. Fashion coverage, always commissioned. Covers: B&W and colour

news pictures concerning the fashion, textile and related trades.
Text: Little scope.
Overall freelance potential: Good for the specialist freelance.
Fees: Negotiable.

THE FLORIST TRADE MAGAZINE
Lonsdale Publications Ltd, 120 Lower Ham Road, Kingston-upon-Thames, Surrey KT2 5BD. Tel: 081-546 1535.
Editor: Caroline Marshall-Foster.
Monthly publication for retail florists.
Illustrations: B&W and colour. News pictures about the trade and other interesting pictures of floristry in the retail context, i.e. special displays, promotions, etc.
Text: Features on anything relating to floristry and retailing, shop profiles, practical aspects, advertising and promotion, etc.
Overall freelance potential: Limited.
Fees: Text, £60 per 1,000 words published; pictures by agreement.

FORECOURT TRADER
William Reed Ltd, Broadfield Park, Crawley, West Sussex RH11 9RT. Tel: 0293 613400.
Editor: Merril Boulton.
Monthly magazine for petrol station operators.
Illustrations: B&W and colour. News pictures relating to petrol stations and the petrol sales business generally.
Text: News and features relating to all areas of petrol retailing.
Overall freelance potential: Fair.
Fees: Text, £120 per 1,000 words; pictures according to use.

HARDWARE & GARDEN REVIEW
Faversham House Group Ltd, Faversham House, 111 St James's Road, Croydon, Surrey CR9 2TH. Tel: 081-684 9659.
Editor: Sue Norris.
Monthly magazine for the hardware, housewares, garden centre and DIY trade.
Illustrations: B&W and colour. Picture stories concerning particular stores and outlets. Trade news pictures.
Text: Illustrated articles on store redesign, and retailer profiles. Around 1,000 words.
Overall freelance potential: Fair.
Editor's tips: Articles should be exclusive in this field. Always send an outline in the first instance.
Fees: On a rising scale according to size of reproduction or length of text.

INDEPENDENT GROCER
Reed Business Publishing, Quadrant House, The Quadrant, Sutton, Surrey SM2 5AS. Tel: 081-652 8754.
Editor: Jim Muttram.
Fortnightly publication for independent, convenience and licensed grocers. Assists them in being more profitable and aware of new products and campaigns.
Illustrations: Colour only. News pictures and picture stories of interest to independent grocery and convenience store traders. Medium format preferred.
Text: Articles and stories about successful grocers, small grocers fighting off the giants, unfair trading, warnings of unscrupulous dealings and novelty ideas. Price surveys and comparisons. 650 words minimum.
Overall freelance potential: Obtain 50 per cent of news pictures from freelances and about 20 per

cent of stories either from freelance writers or from freelance tip-offs.

Editor's tips: A sample copy of the magazine is available to potential contributors. Always ring first with ideas.

Fees: Photographs according to size of reproduction, but around £35–40. £75 per 1,000 words for commissioned features; 20p per line for news stories.

INTERNATIONAL TAX-FREE TRADER

International Trade Publications Ltd, Queensway House, 2 Queensway, Redhill, Surrey RH1 1QS. Tel: 0737 768611.

Editor: Peter Tipthorp.

Monthly publication for executives in duty-free trade worldwide, on airlines, cruise ships, ferry services etc., and suppliers of duty-free goods in all fields, e.g. alcohol, tobacco, cosmetics, toiletries, watches, luxury gifts.

Illustrations: B&W and colour. Specially interested in pictures which illustrate locations and displays at duty-free shops – general views, and especially close-ups of customers, individual displays and individual products. Covers: colourful and attractive pictures of duty-free shops.

Text: Features on products, shops and personalities in the international duty-free trade. 2,000–2,500 words.

Overall freelance potential: Around 40 per cent comes from freelances.

Editor's tips: Send an outline of ideas in the first instance.

Fees: £130 per 1,000 words; pictures by agreement.

MEAT & POULTRY NEWS

Yandell Publishing Ltd, 9 Vermont Place, Tongwell, Milton Keynes, Buckinghamshire MK15 6JA. Tel: 0908 613323.

Editor: Pam Brook.

Monthly journal for the whole meat and poultry trade.

Illustrations: B&W and colour. Pictures relating to any current meat trade issue, including legislation, food scares, court cases, etc.

Text: Stories on current issues as above. Illustrated features of around 1,000 words on current food issues, research, technology, and profiles of individual businesses.

Overall freelance potential: Very good for those in a position to cover this industry.

Editor's tips: It is much preferred if material offered is exclusive.

Fees: £15 for B&W reproductions; £25 for colour. £100 per 1,000 words for text. Higher rates may be payable for material of special interest.

MEAT TRADER

Apple Communications Ltd, Press House, 130a Godinton Road, Ashford, Kent TN23 1LJ. Tel: 0233 643574.

Editor: Gordon Tucker.

10 issues a year. The official magazine of the National Federation of Meat Traders.

Illustrations: B&W and colour. Topical pictures related to the meat trade.

Text: Topical features on the meat and livestock trade. Up to 2,000 words.

Overall freelance potential: Fair for those in close contact with the trade.

Editor's tips: To be considered, material must be exclusive.

Fees: By negotiation.

MENSWEAR

EMAP Maclaren, Maclaren House, 19 Scarbook Road, Croydon, Surrey CR9 1QH. Tel: 081-688 7788.

Editor: Chris Scott-Gray.

Fortnightly publication for retailers and buyers of men's and boys' clothing.

Illustrations: Mostly B&W. News pictures concerning the trade. Pictures to illustrate merchandise features, usually comissioned.

Text: Illustrated news and features on the industry.
Overall freelance potential: Limited, but best market for news pictures from photographers out of London.
Fees: On a rising scale according to size of reproduction or length of article.

PROFESSIONAL INTERIORS
(Three separate titles covering **CORPORATE, HIGH STREET**, and **HOTEL AND RESTAURANT** interiors)
Scroll Communications Ltd, PO Box 45, Dorking, Surrey RH5 5YZ. Tel: 0306 712712.
Editor: Tony Ellis.
Alternate-monthly publications covering interior design in the three commercial sectors specified above. Aimed at managers concerned with large-scale interiors in the fields of office administration, retail and catering, and the designers serving them.
Illustrations: Colour only. News pictures or good stock shots of interesting new interiors and developments, especially striking examples of good (or bad) design and decor, lighting, and specific problems encountered.
Text: News stories, and profiles of relevant individual companies or projects, but always contact the editor with suggestions first.
Overall freelance potential: Fair.
Editor's tips: Remember that these are professional publications for the businessman and interior designer, specifically those dealing with larger environments.
Fees: By negotiation.

SCOTTISH FISHING WEEKLY
PO Box 1, Oban, Argyll PA34 5PY. Tel: 0631 63058.
Editor: Alison Chadwick.
Weekly tabloid for the the Scottish fishing industry, but with coverage extending to the rest of Britain and Europe.
Illustrations: B&W only. Captioned news pictures covering any subject relating to the Scottish fishing industry, including fish farming, processing, etc.
Text: Short illustrated news items, and longer features from contributors with suitable knowledge of the industry.
Overall freelance potential: Good, especially for those with connections in the fishing industry.
Fees: By negotiation.

SHOE AND LEATHER NEWS
EMAP Maclaren, Maclaren House, 19 Scarbook Road, Croydon, Surrey CR9 1QH. Tel: 081-688 7788.
Editor: Alan Cork.
Monthly trade publication for specialist footwear retailers, plus repairers, shoemakers and suppliers to the footwear trade and leather industry.
Illustrations: B&W and colour. News pictures relating to the market and items of interest to the trade in general. Portraits of trade personalities.
Text: Features on all aspects of the trade, especially on footwear retailing, fashion, as well as repairing. Manufacturing of footwear or allied products also of interest. 500–1,500 words.
Overall freelance potential: Variable.
Fees: By agreement.

SHOPPING CENTRE
William Reed Ltd, Broadfield Park, Crawley, West Sussex RH11 9RT. Tel: 0293 613400.
Editor: Eric Williams.
Monthly publication for managers in the shopping centre and retail parks business, with a strong emphasis on news.
Illustrations: Mainly colour. News pictures depicting any events in the shopping centre field: open-

ings, refurbishments, special promotions, awards, etc.
Text: News items always of interest. For features, possible scope for those with specialist knowledge.
Overall freelance potential: Good for relevant coverage.
Fees: By negotiation.

THE SUBPOSTMASTER

National Federation of Subpostmasters, Mansfield Woodhouse Post Office, 52 Station Street, Mansfield Woodhouse, Mansfield, Notts NG19 8AB. Tel: 0623 23610.
Editor: Pam Jervis.
Monthly journal of the Federation, with strong news content concerning subpostmasters.
Illustrations: B&W, or colour prints. Pictures of any subpostmaster in the news for any reason, with captions.
Text: No freelance market.
Overall freelance potential: Small, but possible growth.
Editor's tips: More interested in subjects with unusual hobbies, histories, etc. than in attack stories.
Fees: On a rising scale, according to the size of reproduction.

WORLD FISHING

The Oban Times Ltd, Royston House, Caroline Park, Edinburgh EH5 1QJ. Tel: 031-551 2942.
Editor: Martin Gill.
Monthly journal for the commercial fishing industry. Covers fishing, fish farming and fish processing from an international perspective.
Illustrations: B&W and colour. Mainly to accompany specific articles, but some scope for scene-setting shots of commercial fishing activity in specific locations worldwide.
Text: Illustrated articles on any commercial fishing topic. should always contain some international interest. Maximum 1,800 words.
Overall freelance potential: Good for those with connections in the industry.
Fees: Photographs by negotiation.Text £75 per 1,000 words.

Transport

COACH AND BUS WEEK

EMAP Response Publishing Ltd, Wentworth House, Wentworth Street, Peterborough PE1 1DS. Tel: 0733 63100.
Editor: Mike Morgan.
Weekly magazine covering bus and coach operations. Aimed at licensed bus, coach and tour operators.
Illustrations: B&W only. Pictures as illustrations to features mentioned below; coach and bus related news items. Places of interest to coach parties.
Text: Features on bus and coach operators, hotels, ferry operations, resorts and venues, anything that would be of interest to a coach party or its operator, articles on subjects that an operator might find useful in his day to day business. Up to 2,000 words.
Overall freelance potential: Always interested in seeing work from freelances.
Fees: By negotiation.

COACHING JOURNAL AND BUS REVIEW

Yandell Publishing Ltd, 9 Vermont Place, Tongwell, Milton Keynes, Buckinghamshire MK15 8JA. Tel: 0908 613323.
Editor: Pam Brook.
Published 10 times per year, covering the road passenger transport industry with the accent on luxury touring and express coaches.
Illustrations: B&W and colour. Pictures with captions for use on news pages.

Text: Operating articles on bus and coach companies and vehicles with specific reference to a point of particular interest, as opposed to general history. 1,000–1,500 words. Also articles on suppliers to the industry.
Overall freelance potential: Limited; the magazine usually works with its own contacts on a regular or occasional basis. However, please ring the editor and check if prospective contributions could be considered.
Fees: By negotiation.

CONTAINERISATION INTERNATIONAL
National Magazine Co Ltd, 72 Broadwick Street, London W1V 2BP. Tel: 071-439 5000.
Editor: Jane R. C. Boyes.
Monthly business-oriented magazine on issues facing the international container transport industry.
Illustrations: Colour. Unusual pictures of container shipping activities, especially in exotic locations overseas, or interesting uses for containers inland.
Text: Well-researched and *exclusive* articles, preferably on some aspect of the container transport business not covered by staff writers. Around 2,000 words.
Overall freelance potential: Limited; about 5 per cent comes from freelance sources.
Fees: By agreement.

OLD GLORY
CMS Publishing, Knowle Lane, Cranleigh, Surrey GU6 8JP. Tel: 0483 274855.
Editor: Brian Gooding.
Monthly devoted to industrial heritage and vintage restoration, including traction engines etc.
Illustrations: B&W and colour. Pictures of all forms of traction engines, tractors, buses, commercial vehicles, fairground machinery and maritime subjects such as old steamboats. News pictures of individual machines, restoration projects, etc. Detailed captions necessary including where and when picture taken. Covers: colour pictures of traction engines etc. in attractive settings.
Text: Illustrated articles on subjects as above.
Overall freelance potential: Excellent. A lot of scope for good colour material.
Fees: Generally £10–£15 for B&W; £10–£25 for colour.

ROADWAY
Road Haulage Association Ltd, Roadway House, 35 Monument Hill, Weybridge, Surrey KT13 8RN. Tel: 0932 841515.
Editor: Steve Gray.
Monthly news magazine for the road haulage industry.
Illustrations: B&W only. Pictures of trucks on motorways; at depots; involved in accidents; etc. Should be newsworthy or of unusual interest.
Text: Articles on any aspect of the road haulage industry. Length by prior arrangement with the editor.
Overall freelance potential: Limited.
Fees: By arrangement.

TRUCK
Village Publishing Ltd, 24A Brook Mews North, Paddington, London W2 3BW. Tel: 071-224 9242.
Editor: George Bennett.
Monthly magazine for truck operators and lorry drivers.
Illustrations: B&W and colour. Pictures of interesting individual trucks, unusual situations involving trucks and their drivers, humorous situations, and news items.
Text: Commissioned features on any topic of relevance to truck drivers. The editor is always interested in hearing from freelances with ideas.
Overall freelance potential: Good.
Fees: By negotiation.

Travel

ACTION HOLIDAYS
Activity Magazines Ltd, 27 Belsize Lane, London NW3 5AS. Tel: 071-435 5472.
Editor: Chris Thomas.
Annual review of activity holidays worldwide.
Illustrations: Mainly colour. Good action shots of activities such as ballooning, hang-gliding, sailing, windsurfing, cycling, etc. Also coverage of specific locations and facilities for such activities.
Text: Illustrated articles on any form of activity holiday. 750–1,000 words. Query features editor before submitting.
Overall freelance potential: Good.
Fees: By negotiation.

BBC HOLIDAYS
Redwood Publishing Ltd, 101 Bayham Street, London NW1 0AG. Tel: 071-331 8000.
Editor: Alison Rice. **Art Director**: Norma Martin. **Picture Editor**: Angela Steele.
Monthly magazine covering all types of holidays, from weekend breaks in Britain to long-haul destinations.
Illustrations: Colour only. Speculative submissions not required, but lists detailing good travel collections can be sent to the picture editor. Some commissions available.
Text: Good scope for experienced travel writers. Send details of experience and examples of previous work in the first instance.
Overall freelance potential: Limited.
Fees: By negotiation.

BUSINESS TRAVELLER
Perry Motorpress Ltd, Compass House, 22 Redan Place, London W2 4SZ. Tel: 071-229 7799.
Editor: Gillian Upton.
Monthly consumer journal aimed at the frequently travelling international business executive.
Illustrations: B&W and colour. Pictures to illustrate destination report articles on a wide variety of cities around the world. No photo features.
Text: Features on business travel, but only by consultation with the editor.
Overall freelance potential: Around 65 per cent of the magazine is contributed by freelances.
Fees: Text, £150 per 1,000 words; pictures on a similar scale to London photo agencies.

EXECUTIVE TRAVEL
6 Chesterfield Gardens, London W1Y 8DN. Tel: 071-355 1600.
Editor: Mike Toynbee. **Picture Editor**: Catherine Chetwynd.
Monthly magazine for the frequent traveller.
Illustrations: Colour only. High quality photographs of destinations worldwide. The emphasis is on business rather than pleasure, although some leisure pursuits are covered.
Text: Only by commission, but ideas are always welcome.
Overall freelance potential: Good, for genuinely suitable material.
Fees: by negotiation.

FRANCE
France Magazine Ltd, Dormer House, Digbeth Street, Stow-on-the-Wold, Gloucestershire GL54 1BN. Tel: 0451 831398.
Editor: Philip Faiers.
Quarterly magazine for Francophiles, with the emphasis on leisure and pleasure.
Illustrations: Colour only. Picture stories, and top quality individual pictures to illustrate articles, on French regions, annual events, cuisine, travel, arts, history, shopping, fashion and sport. Especially

interested in character and human interest shots, and mood pictures. Covers: pictures that capture the essence of France.

Text: Lively and colourful features of around 700–1,000 words, factual accuracy important.

Overall freelance potential: Excellent for top quality material.

Fees: £100 per thousand words for text; photographs by negotiation.

TRAVELLER

WEXAS International Ltd, 45 Brompton Road, London SW3 1DE. Tel: 071-581 4130.

Editor: Caroline Brandenburger.

Quarterly publication containing informative and entertaining articles on travel, and travel-related subjects of an "ethnographic" nature, in the developing countries of the world. Aimed at the independent traveller who prefers to travel off the beaten track and with minimal cultural impact.

Illustrations: Mainly colour. Travel pictures, especially close-ups of local people, shot in developing countries, rarely Europe or North America. No "tourist brochure" shots.

Text: Well-illustrated travel articles with the angles specified above. Up to 2,000 words. Contact editor for full specification sheet.

Overall freelance potential: The magazine uses a lot of freelance contributions, but excellent photographic work is essential.

Fees: Photographs, £25; £50 for cover. Text, £12.50 per 100 words.

Women's Interest

BELLA

H. Bauer Publishing Ltd, Shirley House, 25–27 Camden Road, London NW1 9LL. Tel: 071-284 0909.

Editor: Jackie Highe. **Picture Editor**: Geoffrey Palmer.

Weekly magazine for women, covering human interest stories, fashion, cookery, shopping and celebrities.

Illustrations: B&W and colour. Pictures of celebrities, Royalty, off-beat pictures and curiosities. Fashion and food, mostly commissioned.

Text: Some scope for exclusive human interest features and celebrity interviews. Always check with the editor first.

Overall freelance potential: Limited for speculative work.

Fees: By negotiation.

BEST

G&J of the UK, Portland House, Stag Place, London SW1E 5AU. Tel: 071-245 8700.

Editor: Sue James. **Art Editor**: Wendy Hawley.

Weekly magazine for women, covering affordable fashion, health matters, cookery, home improvements, etc.

Illustrations: B&W and colour. Scope for off-beat, general human interest and curiosity shots. Commissioned coverage of fashion, food, etc.

Text: Articles with a practical slant, aimed at working women.

Overall freelance potential: Quite good.

Fees: Commissioned photography by negotiation; other material according to use.

CHAT

IPC Magazines, King's Reach Tower, Stamford Street, London SE1 9LS. Tel: 071-261 6565.

Editor: Terry Tavner. **Picture Editor**: John Kilpatrick.

Weekly magazine of general interest to 25–45 year old women.

Illustrations: B&W and colour. Fashion, beauty, food, celebrities, etc. Coverage all produced by freelances on commission.

Text: Short, chatty features written in a high-calibre style. Must be human interest and of appeal to the average women.

Overall freelance potential: Very good for experienced contributors to the women's press. Always keen to hear from photographers with fresh ideas.

Editor's tips: The magazine uses a huge amount of material each week, so always keen to receive fresh ideas.

Fees: By negotiation.

COMPANY

National Magazine Company Ltd, 72 Broadwick Street, London W1V 2BP. Tel: 071-439 5000.

Editor: Mandi Norwood. **Art Editor**: Sabine Pick.

Monthly magazine aimed at up-market young women in their twenties.

Illustrations: B&W and colour. Photographs to illustrate features on fashion, beauty, careers, travel, personalities, etc., invariably by commission.

Text: Articles on the above topics, of varying lengths. Also, more topical and "newsy" features.

Overall freelance potential: Fair scope for experienced contributors.

Fees: By negotiation.

COSMOPOLITAN

National Magazine Company Ltd, 72 Broadwick Street, London W1V 2BP. Tel: 071-439 5000.

Editor: Marcelle d'Argy Smith. **Art Editor**: Suzie Lane.

Monthly magazine for women in the 18–34 age group.

Illustrations: Colour. Photographs to illustrate features on fashion, style and beauty, by commission only. Some top quality stock situation pictures may be used to illustrate more general features.

Text: Articles of interest to sophisticated young women. Always query the editor in the first instance.

Overall freelance potential: Only for the experienced contributor to the women's press.

Fees: By negotiation.

ELLE

Hachette-EMAP Magazines Ltd, 20 Orange Street, London WC2H 7ED. Tel: 071-957 8383.

Editor: *To be appointed*. **Picture Editor**: June Stanier.

Up-market monthly magazine with the emphasis on fashion.

Illustrations: Mainly colour. Top quality coverage of fashion and style subjects, portraiture and still life, always by commission.

Text: Some scope for top quality feature articles and photojournalism, usually by commission and from established contributors.

Overall freelance potential: Good for contributors experienced at the top level of magazine journalism.

Fees: By negotiation.

ESSENTIALS

GE Publishing (for IPC Magazines), Elme House, 133 Long Acre, London WC2E 9AD. Tel: 071-836 0519.

Editor: Gilly Cubitt. **Art Editor**: Simon Hilton.

Monthly mass-market magazine for women with the emphasis on practical matters.

Illustrations: B&W and colour. Health, interior decoration, travel, food, etc. Some commissioned work available.

Text: Practical articles, health, features, short stories of interest to women. Synopsis essential in the first instance.

Overall freelance potential: Good for those experienced in contributing to quality women's magazines.

Fees: By negotiation.

EVERYWOMAN
Everywoman Publishing Ltd, 34 Islington Green, London N1 8DU. Tel: 071-359 5496.
Editor: Barbara Rogers.
Curent affairs monthly with a feminist perspective.
Illustrations: B&W only. News pictures relating to women's issues and "what women are doing".
Covers: colour pictures relating to major news stories.
Text: Articles about current women's issues.
Overall freelance potential: Fair.
Fees: £30 for pictures inside; covers by negotiation.

FIRST CHOICE
HHL Publishing Ltd, Greater London House, Hampstead Road, London NW1 7QQ. Tel: 071-388 3171.
Editor: Dorothy Stefanczyk.
Quarterly magazine for shoppers in Co-op superstores. Aimed at women, 25–40 years.
Illustrations: Colour only. Pictures of general interest to women, e.g. holidays, gardening, cookery, etc.
Text: Features on general women's interests, 1,000 words.
Overall freelance potential: Most of the written material comes from freelance contributors.
Fees: Negotiable.

GOOD HOUSEKEEPING
National Magazine Company Ltd, National Magazine House, 72 Broadwick Street, London W1V 2BP.
Tel: 071-439 5000.
Editor: Sally O'Sullivan. **Art Editor**: Lorraine Alder.
General interest magazine for up-market women. Concentrates on home and family life.
Illustrations: B&W and colour. Interiors, gardening, food, fashion, travel and reportage. Usually by commission to illustrate specific articles.
Text: Articles of interest to up-market women – interesting homes (with photos), gardening, personality profiles, emotional features, humorous articles, etc.
Overall freelance potential: Good scope for the highest quality material.
Fees: By negotiation.

HARPERS AND QUEEN
National Magazine Company Ltd, 72 Broadwick Street, London W1V 2BP. Tel: 071-439 7144.
Editor: Vicki Woods. **Art Editor**: Mike McCafferty.
Monthly glossy magazine featuring fashion, design, travel, beauty and health.
Illustrations: B&W and colour. Photography to illustrate subjects as above, only by commission.
Text: General interest features of very high quality. 1,500–3,000 words.
Overall freelance potential: Good for those who can produce the right material.
Fees: Good; on a rising scale according to length of feature.

HELLO!
Wellington House, 69/71 Upper Ground, London SE1 9PQ. Tel: 071-334 7404.
Editor: Maggie Koumi. **Picture Editor**: Eve George.
Weekly magazine for women covering people and current events. Some coverage of more traditional topics such as cookery, fashion, beauty and travel.
Illustrations: Mainly colour. Pictures and picture stories on personalities and celebrities of all kinds. People in the news and current news events. Off-beat pictures. Dramatic picture stories of bravery, courage or rescue.
Text: Little scope.
Overall freelance potential: Excellent for quality material.
Editor's tips: "We have short lead times and this is something we wish to exploit to the full. We can include late stories in colour up the the Thursday of the week before publication."
Fees: By negotiation.

HOME COOKING
Argus Consumer Publications, 2–4 Leigham Court Road, Streatham, London SW16 2PD. Tel: 081-677 7538.
Editor: Sue Marks.
Monthly magazine aimed at women with young families. Concentrates on on cookery, but also covers home, health, parenting, etc.
Illustrations: Mostly colour. Most food pictures are commissioned from regulars. There is some market, however, for non-food pictures to illustrate health and general features.
Text: Personal experience features relating to women's interests. 1,000 words.
Overall freelance potential: Limited.
Editor's tips: Always interested in female humour, practical hints.
Fees: By negotiation.

HOME AND COUNTRY
NFWI, 104 New Kings Road, Fulham, London SW6 4LY. Tel: 071-731 5777.
Editor: Penny Kitchen.
Monthly publication for Women's Institute members. Includes WI news and features, plus general articles of interest to women.
Illustrations: B&W and colour. Pictures of WI events, etc.
Text: Features of general women's interest, commissioned in advance. 800–1,200 words.
Overall freelance potential: A small, but regular amount bought each month.
Editor's tips: Always consult the editor before submitting.
Fees: By agreement.

THE LADY
The Lady, 39–40 Bedford Street, Strand, London WC2E 9ER. Tel: 071-379 4717.
Editor: Arline Usden.
Weekly general interest magazine for women.
Illustrations: B&W only inside. Pictures only to accompany particular articles. Covers: colour pictures depicting traditional British scenes.
Text: Illustrated articles on British and foreign travel, the countryside, human interest, wildlife, pets, cookery, gardening, fashion, beauty, British history and commemorative subjects. 800–1,000 words.
Overall freelance potential: Excellent for complete illustrated articles.
Fees: B&W reproductions, £14–£18. Text £60 per 1,000 words.

LOOKS
EMAP Women's Group Ltd, 5th Floor, 20 Orange Street, London WC2H 7ED. Tel: 071-957 8400.
Editor: Jenny Tucker. **Art Editor**: Isabella Brodou.
Monthly magazine aimed at 16–25 year old girls, covering every subject relating to their appearance.
Illustrations: Mainly colour. Comissioned coverage of fashion and beauty subjects.
Text: Little scope.
Overall freelance potential: Excellent scope for experienced photographers to obtain commissions.
Fees: By negotiation.

MARIE CLAIRE
European Magazines Ltd, 2 Hatfields, London SE1 9PG. Tel: 071-261 5240.
Editor: Glenda Bailey. **Art Editor**: Suzanne Sykes.
Fashion and general interest monthly for sophisticated women in the 20–35 age group.
Illustrations: Mainly colour. Top quality fashion, beauty, portraits, interiors, still life, etc., always be commission.
Text: In-depth articles, features and profiles aimed at an intelligent readership. Up to 4,000 words.
Overall freelance potential: Very good for experienced contributors in this field.
Fees: By negotiation.

MORE!
EMAP Women's Group Ltd, 20 Orange Street, London WC2H 7ED. Tel: 071-957 8383.
Editor: Fiona Gibson. **Art Editor**: Naomi Lowe.
Fortnightly magazine for young women in the 18–24 age group.
Illustrations: Mainly colour. Up-to-date news pictures featuring celebrities. Fashion, beauty, health and pictures to illustrate specific articles, invariably by commission.
Text: Articles and features, often with a practical slant, of general interest to young women. Length variable.
Overall freelance potential: Quite good for quality material.
Fees: By negotiation.

MOTHER & BABY
EMAP Elan, Victory House, 14 Leicester Place, London WC2H 7BP. Tel: 071-437 9011.
Editor: Stephanie Neuman. **Art Editor**: Jennifer Bayliss.
Monthly aimed at pregnant women and mothers of young children.
Illustrations: Mostly colour. High quality photographs of mothers with babies, or babies (under one year) on their own. Medium format preferred.
Text: Articles on all subjects related to pregnancy, birth, baby care and the early years.
Overall freelance potential: Limited, since the magazine is frequently overstocked.
Editor's tips: Only top quality pictures will be considered.
Fees: From £30 upwards for single pictures.

MRS BEETON TRADITIONAL HOUSEKEEPING TODAY
EMP Plc, EMP House, Pembroke Road, London N10 2HR. Tel: 081-444 3401.
Editor: Susan Wolk. **Art Editor**: Nick McKay.
Quarterly magazine mainly concerned with household and cookery matters. Stresses the continuing relevance of Victorian values and lifestyles for women today.
Illustrations: Colour only. Will consider stock pictures of traditionally presented food in a Victorian setting or with Victorian props (dishes, glassware, etc). Some commissions available for experienced food photographers.
Text: Articles from professional food writers only. Submit only ideas in the first instance with cuttings of published work.
Overall freelance potential: Good.
Editor's tips: Study the magazine carefully. "Writers unfamiliar with Victorian history and customs, and Mrs Beeton's book, should not apply."
Fees: £175–£200 per 1,000 words for text; pictures by negotiation.

MS LONDON WEEKLY
Employment Publications Ltd, 7–9 Rathbone Street, London W1P 1AF. Tel: 071-636 6651.
Editor: Bill Williamson. **Art Editor**: Tony Baldwin.
Weekly magazine for young, independent women working in London.
Illustrations: B&W and colour. Mostly fashion and portraits, some still life and reportage work. Covers: colour fashion and general interest subjects; medium format preferred.
Text: Off-beat, sharply-written features of interest to young, aware, working Londoners. 800–1,000 words.
Overall freelance potential: Around 90 per cent of the magazine comes from freelances.
Editor's tips: Best to send copies of recently-published work plus list of ideas before actual submission.
Fees: Approximately £120 per 1,000 words; pictures by agreement.

19
IPC Magazines Ltd, King's Reach Tower, Stamford Street, London SE1 9LS. Tel: 071-261 6360.
Editor: April Joyce. **Art Editor**: Jo Sams.

Popular young women's magazine aimed at the 17–24 age group, covering topical issues, fashion and beauty.
Illustrations: B&W and colour. Pictures to illustrate fashion and beauty features, always by commission. Some scope for still-life, celebrity or reportage material.
Text: Articles on general topics of interest to young women, ranging from the amusing and entertaining to more serious social matters. Length variable according to importance of subject, up to around 3,000 words.
Overall freelance potential: Good.
Fees: By arrangement.

NURSERY WORLD

Nursery World Ltd, Unit A, The Schoolhouse Workshop, 51 Calthorpe Street, London WC1X 0HH. Tel: 071-837 7224.
Editor: Lindsay Blythe.
Weekly child care publication.. Aimed at professional baby and child care workers as well as mothers.
Illustrations: B&W and colour. Pictures of babies and young children (0–5) involved in various activities, also photographs of babies in general. Covers: colour pictures of nursery workers, children in work situations, playing, etc.
Text: Features on child care, education, health, and any aspect of bringing up children, e.g. physical, intellectual, emotional etc. Ideas for nurseries and playgroups.
Overall freelance potential: Many features come from freelance contributors.
Editor's tips: Material must have authority.
Fees: By arrangement.

OPTIONS

Southbank Publishing Group, IPC Magazines, King's Reach Tower, Stamford Street, London SE1 9LS. Tel: 071-261 5000.
Editor: Maureen Rice. **Art Editor**: Jackie Hempsey.
Monthly magazine for women in the 25–40 age group, those who have grown out of the younger magazines and want a magazine relevant to their lifestyle now. Modern "thirty-something" attitude.
Illustrations: B&W and colour. Small B&W shots required for "Update" and "Leisure" features. Colour travel, health and beauty, personalities, etc. Mostly commissioned. Covers: good quality head-shots.
Text: Features of interest to readership mainly composed of modern career women in a settled relationship, with or without children. Fashion, health, cookery, entertaining articles, plus strong individual general features – personality profiles, investigative, sociological.
Overall freelance potential: Very good; a lot of outside contributors are used.
Fees: By negotiation.

PARENTS

EMAP Elan, Victory House, Leicester Place, London WC2H 7BP. Tel: 071-437 9011.
Editor: Sarah Kilby. **Art Director**: Dominic Healey.
Monthly magazine for parents with children up to around 5 years old. Covers pregnancy, birth, babies, children, health, education, home ideas, food, relationships, nutrition, medicine and fashion.
Illustrations: Mainly colour. Mostly used as illustrations for features on above topics. Covers: Appealing colour shots of children; medium format preferred.
Text: Features on the above subjects.
Overall freelance potential: Approximately 75 per cent of the magazine is contributed from outside.
Fees: £65 per half-page, £90 per page. Covers, £200.

PRIMA

G+J of the UK, Portland House, Stag Place, London SW1E 5AU. Tel: 071-245 8700.
Editor: Sue James. **Art Editor**: Christine Gilliatt.

General interest women's monthly with a strong emphasis on practical subjects. Major topics covered include cookery, gardening, crafts, health, pets, fashion and homecare.
Illustrations: B&W and colour. Top quality work in the fields of food, fashion, still-life, interiors and portraiture, usually by commission. Some scope for good stock shots of family and domestic situations, food, pets, etc., that could be used for general illustration purposes.
Text: Short, illustrated practical features with a "how-to-do-it" approach.
Overall freelance potential: The magazine relies heavily on freelances.
Fees: Commissioned photography in the region of £410 per day. Other fees by negotiation.

SHE

National Magazine Company Ltd, National Magazine House, 72 Broadwick Street, London W1V 2BP. Tel: 071-439 5000.
Editor: Linda Kelsey. **Art Editor**: Andrea Hewison.
Monthly magazine for women who "juggle home, partner, career and children".
Illustrations: B&W and colour. Most material by commission for specific articles; anything else only considered by appointment.
Text: Top quality features of interest to intelligent women; always query the editor first.
Overall freelance potential: Litttle unsolicited material used, but quite good for commissions.
Editor's tips: Please study the format before contacting magazine.
Fees: By arrangement.

WOMAN

IPC Magazines Ltd, King's Reach Tower, Stamford Street, London SE1 9LS. Tel: 071-261 6421.
Editor: David Durman. **Picture Editor**: Alison Thurston.
Weekly magazine devoted to all women's interests.
Illustrations: B&W and colour. Most pictures commissioned to illustrate specific features. Some scope for human interest shots which are dramatic, off-beat or unusual.
Text: Interviews with leading personalities, human interest stories, campaigns. Features on beauty, fashion, cookery, knitting, home, etc. mostly staff-produced. Submit a synopsis in the first instance.
Overall freelance potential: Only for experienced contributors in the field.
Fees: Good; on a rising scale according to size of reproduction or length of articles.

WOMAN AND HOME

IPC Magazines Ltd, King's Reach Tower, Stamford Street, London SE1 9LS. Tel: 071-261 5423.
Editor: Sue Dobson. **Art Editor**: Peter Davies.
Monthly magazine of interest to all women concerned with family and home. Subjects covered include cookery, knitting, fashion, beauty, home features, DIY, gardening, travel, financial advice, topical issues and personality articles.
Illustrations: B&W and colour. All photography on above subjects commissioned from experienced freelances.
Text: Articles on personalities, either well-known or who lead interesting lives. 1,500 words.
Overall freelance potential: Including regular contributors, about 50 per cent of the magazine is contributed by freelances.
Fees: £120 per 1,000 words. Pictures by negotiation.

WOMAN'S JOURNAL

IPC Magazines Ltd, King's Reach Tower, Stamford Street, London SE1 9LS. Tel: 071-261 6622.
Editor: Deirdre Vine. **Art Editor**: John Tennant.
Monthly glossy magazine for women.

Illustrations: B&W and colour. Commissioned coverage for home, beauty, cookery, fashion, portraits, travel and general features.

Text: Features of general interest to women and on subjects detailed above. 2,000 words maximum.

Overall freelance potential: Good for commissioned work.

Fees: Negotiable.

WOMAN'S OWN

IPC Magazines Ltd, King's Reach Tower, Stamford Street, London SE1 9LS. Tel: 071-261 5000.

Editor: Keith McNeill. **Picture Editor**: Mike Hardy.

Weekly publishing articles and practical features of interest to women.

Illustrations: B&W and colour. Mostly commissioned to illustrate articles and features. Not a great deal of scope for single pictures, although the occasional unusual or off-beat shot may be used.

Text: Features on beauty, fashion, cookery and other women's interests are used, but tend to be staff-produced. Send a brief outline of any proposed feature in the first instance.

Overall freelance potential: Fair for commissioned work, but much is produced by regulars.

Fees: Good; on a rising scale according to size of reproduction or length of article.

WOMAN'S REALM

IPC Magazines Ltd, King's Reach Tower, Stamford Street, London SE1 9LS. Tel: 071-261 5000.

Editor: Sue Reid. **Picture Editor**: Brian Mumford

Weekly general interest women's magazine, with the emphasis on short features and human interest stories.

Illustrations: B&W and colour. Some opportunities for commissioned work in the usual women's interest fields – fashion, beauty, cookery, home and garden, personalities, travel, etc.

Text: Some scope for short features on subjects of general women's interest as above, and illustrated (B&W) romantic or dramatic true-life stories.

Overall freelance potential: Limited; much is staff-produced.

Fees: According to use and nature of material.

NEWSPAPERS

In this section we list the national daily and Sunday newspapers, and their associated magazine supplements. While the supplements may publish a wide range of general interest subject matter, the parent papers are obviously only likely to be interested in hard news pictures and stories of genuine interest to a nationwide readership.

News pictures

Despite the heavy presence of newspaper staff and agency photographers at major events, it is still perfectly possible for an independent freelance to get the shot that makes the front page. And when it comes to the unexpected, the freelance is often only one on the spot to capture the drama.

If you think you have obtained a "hot" news picture or story, don't wait to get the film processed and see the results; the best procedure is to telephone the papers most likely to be interested as soon as possible and let them know what you have to offer. If interested, they will either make arrangements to have the pictures or undeveloped film collected, or will ask you to send it by the fastest convenient method.

In the listings that follow you will find direct line telephone numbers which bypass the main switchboard and take you directly through to the picture desk of the paper concerned, except in a few cases where such lines are not available.

Fax numbers are also listed here due to the occasional need to send an urgent message or story by this method, but a word of warning should be sounded. It is advisable to always check the correct number for the department you want before sending anything by fax. Most newspapers offices have numerous fax machines; the numbers listed here are necessarily general editorial numbers and if used without checking might delay your message getting through to the specific department you need.

Other material

There is some scope for other material apart from hard news in most of the papers. Some use the occasional oddity or human interest item as a "filler", and in most there is always a good market for celebrity pictures for the gossip pages.

Finally, of course, there is a market for top quality glamour material of the "Page 3" variety in several of the tabloids.

The supplements operate much like any other general interest magazine. Most of their content is commissioned from well-established photographers and writers, though some will accept exceptional photojournalistic features or exclusives on spec. A couple also have regular single picture slots which offer excellent opportunities for the freelance.

Fees

Fees paid by newspapers can vary tremendously according to what is offered and how it is used. However, it can be taken for granted that rates paid by the leading papers listed here are good. Generally, picture fees are calculated on standard rates based on the size of the reproduction.

However, for material that is exclusive or exceptional the sky is almost literally the limit. If you think you have something very special and are prepared to offer it as an exclusive, make sure you negotiate a fee, and perhaps get several offers, before committing the material to anyone.

National Daily Newspapers

DAILY EXPRESS
Express Newspapers, Ludgate House, 245 Blackfriars Road, London SE1 9UX. Tel: 071-928 8000. Picture desk: 071-922 7171. Fax: 071-922 7976.
Editor: Sir Nicholas Lloyd. **Picture Editor:** Chris Djukanovic.

DAILY MAIL
The Daily Mail Ltd, Northcliffe House, Derry Street, London W8 5TT. Tel: 071-938 6000. Picture desk: 071-938 6373. Fax: 071-937 5560.
Editor: Paul Dacre. **Picture Editor:** Andy Kyle.

DAILY MIRROR
Mirror Group Newspapers Ltd, Holborn Circus, London EC1P 1DQ. Tel: 071-353 0246. Picture desk: 071-822 3851. Fax: 071-822 2248.
Editor: David Banks. **Picture Editor:** Ron Morgans.

DAILY RECORD
The Scottish Daily Record and Sunday Mail Ltd, Anderston Quay, Glasgow G3 8DA. Tel: 041-248 7000. Picture desk: 041-242 3245. Fax: 041-242 3340.
Editor: Endell Laird. **Picture Editor:** Andrew Allan.

DAILY SPORT
19 Great Ancoats Street, Manchester M60 4BT. Tel: 061-236 4466. Fax: 061-236 4535.
Editor: Andy Carson. **Picture Editor:** Barry Williamson.

DAILY STAR
Express Newspapers, Ludgate House, 245 Blackfriars Road, London SE1 9UX. Tel: 071-928 8000. Picture desk: 071-922 7353. Fax: 071-922 7960.
Editor: Brian Hitchin. **Picture Editor:** James Sutherland.

THE DAILY TELEGRAPH
The Daily Telegraph Plc, 1 Canada Square, Canary Wharf, London E14 5DT. Tel: 071-538 5000. Picture desk: 071-922 7356. Fax: 071-922 7960.
Editor: Max Hastings. **Picture Editor:** Robert Bodman.
TELEGRAPH MAGAZINE
Editor: Nigel Horne. **Picture Editor:** Michael Collins.

FINANCIAL TIMES
The Financial Times Ltd, 1 Southwark Bridge, London SE1 9HL. Tel: 071-873 3000. Picture desk: 071-873 3466. Fax: 071-873 3073.
Editor: Richard Lambert. **Picture Editor:** Glyn Genin.

THE GUARDIAN
119 Farringdon Road, London EC1R 3ER. Tel: 071-278 2332. Picture desk: 071-239 9585. Fax: 071-239 9951.
Editor: Peter Preston. **Picture Editor:** Eamonn McCabe.

THE HERALD
The Herald, Glasgow Ltd, 195 Albion Street, Glasgow, Scotland G1 1QP. Tel: 041-552 6255. Fax: 041-552 2288.
Editor: Arnold Kemp. **Picture Editor:** James Connor.

THE INDEPENDENT
Newspaper Publishing Plc, 40 City Road, London EC1Y 2DE. Tel: 071-253 1222. Picture desk: 071-956 1829. Fax: 071-608 1149.
Editor: Andreas Whittam-Smith. **Picture Editor:** Andy Bull.
THE INDEPENDENT MAGAZINE
Editor: John Walsh. **Picture Editor:** Colin Jacobson.

MORNING STAR
Morning Star Co-operative Society Ltd, 1/3 Ardleigh Road, London N1 4HS. Tel: 071-254 0033. Fax: 071-254 5950.
Editor: Tony Chater.

THE SCOTSMAN
The Scotsman Publications Ltd, 20 North Bridge, Edinburgh EH1 1YT. Tel: 031-225 2468. Picture desk: 031-243 3389. Fax: 031-226 7420.
Editor: Magnus Linklater. **Picture Editor:** Patricia Hutchinson.

THE SUN
News Group Newspapers Ltd, Virginia Street, London E1 9XJ. Tel: 071-782 4000. Picture desk: 071-782 4112/3/4. Fax: 071-488 3253.
Editor: Kelvin MacKenzie. **Picture Editor:** Paul Buttle.

THE TIMES
Times Newspapers Ltd, Virginia Street, London E1 9XT. Tel: 071-782 7000. Picture desk: 071-782 5877. Fax: 071-782 5014.
Editor: Peter Stothard. **Picture Editor:** Andrew Moger.

TODAY
News International, 1 Virginia Street, London E1 9BS. Tel: 071-782 4600. Picture desk: 071-782 4622/3/4/5. Fax: 071-782 4822.
Editor: Richard Stott. **Picture Editor:** Geoff Webster.

National Sunday Newspapers

THE MAIL ON SUNDAY
Northcliffe House, 2 Derry Street, Kensington, London W8 5TS. Tel: 071-938 6000. Picture desk: 071-938 7016. Fax: 071-937 3829.
Editor: Jonathan Holborow. **Picture Editor:** Gary Woodhouse.
YOU MAGAZINE
Editor: Dee Nolan. **Picture Editor:** Harvey Mann.

NEWS OF THE WORLD
News Group Newspapers Ltd, Virginia Street, London E1 9XR. Tel: 071-782 4000. Picture desk: 071-782 4421/4422. Fax: 071-583 9504.
Editor: Patsy Chapman. **Picture Editor:** Ian Bradley.
SUNDAY MAGAZINE
Editor: Tony Harris. **Picture Editor:** Lili Gooch.

THE OBSERVER
The Observer Ltd, Chelsea Bridge House, Queenstown Road, London SW8 4NN. Tel: 071-627 0700. Picture desk: 071-350 3402. Fax: 071-627 5570.
Editor: Jonathan Fenby. **Picture Editor:** Tony McGrath.
THE OBSERVER MAGAZINE
Editor: Rebecca Nicholson. **Picture Editor:** Tony McGrath.

THE PEOPLE
Mirror Group Newspapers Ltd, Holborn Circus, London EC1P 1DQ. Tel: 071-353 0246. Picture desk: 071-822 3901. Fax: 071-822 3810.
Editor: Bridget Rowe. **Picture Editor:** Paul Bennett.
THE PEOPLE MAGAZINE
Editor: Frank Walker. **Picture Editor:** Paula Dale.

SCOTLAND ON SUNDAY
The Scotsman Publications Ltd, 20 North Bridge, Edinburgh EH1 1YT. Tel: 031-225 2468. Fax: 031-220 2443.
Editor: Andrew Jaspan. **Picture Editor:** Alexandra Aikman.

SUNDAY EXPRESS
Express Newspapers, Ludgate House, 245 Blackfriars Road, London SE1 9UX. Tel: 071-928 8000. Picture desk: 071-922 7635. Fax: 071-922 7964.
Editor: Eve Pollard. **Picture Editor:** Les Wilson.
SUNDAY EXPRESS MAGAZINE
Editor: Jean Carr. **Picture Editor:** John Lyth.

THE SUNDAY MAIL
The Scottish Daily Record and Sunday Mail Ltd, Anderston Quay, Glasgow G3 8DA. Tel: 041-248 7000. Picture desk: 041-242 3434. Fax: 041-242 3145/6.
Editor: Jim Cassidy. **Picture Editor:** David McNeil.

SUNDAY MIRROR
Mirror Group Newspapers Ltd, Holborn Circus, London EC1P 1DQ. Tel: 071-353 0246. Picture desk: 071-822 3335/6. Fax: 071-822 2160.
Editor: Colin Myler. **Picture Editor:** Russell Cox.
SUNDAY MIRROR MAGAZINE
Editor: Colin Myler. **Picture Editor:** Isobel Prime.

SUNDAY POST
D. C. Thomson & Co Ltd, Courier Place, Dundee DD1 9QJ. Tel: 0382 23131. Fax: 0382 201064.
Editor: Russell Reid. **Picture Editor:** Iain MacKinnon.

SUNDAY SPORT
Sport Newspapers Ltd, 3rd Floor, Marten House, 39-47 East Road, London N1 6AH. Tel: 071-251 2544. Fax: 071-608 1979.
Editor: Gary Thompson. **Picture Editor:** Barrie Williamson.

THE SUNDAY TELEGRAPH
The Telegraph Plc, 1 Canada Square, Canary Wharf, London E14 5DT. Tel: 071-538 5000. Picture desk: 071-538 5000. Fax: 071-513 2504.
Editor: Charles Moore. **Picture Editor:** Nigel Skelsey.

THE SUNDAY TIMES
Times Newspapers Ltd, 1 Pennington Street, London E1 9XW. Tel: 071-782 5000. Picture desk: 071-782 5666. Fax: 071-782 5658.
Editor: Andrew Neil. **Picture Editor:** Ray Wells.

THE SUNDAY TIMES MAGAZINE
Editor: Kate Carr. **Picture Editor:** Vincent Page.

WALES ON SUNDAY
Western Mail & Echo Ltd, Thomson House, Havelock Street, Cardiff CF1 1WR. Tel: 0222 223333. Fax: 0222 342462.
Editor: Peter Hollinson. **Picture Editor:** Lynne McEwan.

BOOKS

Books represent a substantial and growing market for the photographer. In an increasingly visual age the market for heavily illustrated books continues to expand, with hundreds of new titles being published every year.

In this section we list major book publishers, and specifically those companies that make considerable use of photographic material.

As well as publishers, also listed here are book packagers, marked (P). These are companies that offer a complete editorial production service and specialise in producing books that can be sold as finished packages to publishers internationally. The majority of their products are of the heavily illustrated type, and thus these companies often present a greater potential market for photographic material than do individual publishers.

Making an approach

In this field the difficulty for the individual freelance is that there is no easy way of knowing who wants what and when. Obviously book publishers only require pictures of specific subjects when they are currently working on a project requiring such material. Much of the time they will rely heavily on known sources such as picture libraries, but this does not mean that there is not good scope for the individual photographer who has a good collection of material on particular subjects, or who can produce suitable work to order. The solution for the photographer, therefore, is to get details of what he or she has to offer in front of all those companies that might conceivably require material of that type.

The initial approach is simply to send an introductory letter outlining the sort of material that you can supply. A detailed list of subjects can be attached where appropriate. There is little point however, in sending any photographs at this stage, unless it be one or two samples to indicate a particular style. And one should not expect an immediate response requesting that work be submitted; most likely the publisher will simply keep your details on file for future reference.

In the listings that follow, the major areas of activity for each publisher are detailed under "Subjects". Of course, the larger companies publish on the widest range of subjects and therefore their coverage may be listed as "general", but in most entries you will find a list of specific subject areas. These are by no means a complete list of all the subjects handled by each publisher, but indicate those areas where the company is most active and therefore most likely to be in need of photographic material.

In some entries a "Contact" name is given. However in most cases it is not possible to give a specific name as book publishers usually have large numbers of editorial personnel with constantly shifting responsibilities for individual projects. In addition, many companies frequently use the services of freelance picture researchers. A general approach should therefore simply be addressed to the editorial director.

Rights and fees

Whereas the rights sold in the magazine world are invariably for UK use only, book publishers – and especially packagers – make a good deal of their profit from selling their products to other publishers in overseas markets. It is therefore quite likely that when work is chosen for use in a particular book the publisher may at some stage request, in addition to British publishing rights, rights for other areas such as "Commonwealth", "US", "French language", etc. These differing rights will, of course, affect the fees that the photographer receives – the more areas the book sells into, the higher the fees.

Other major factors affecting fees are the size of reproduction on the page, and the quantity of the print-run. Thus there is no easy way to generalise about the sort of fees paid in this field. On the whole, however, fees in books publishing are quite good and comparable with good magazine rates. For packages destined for the international co-edition market they can be substantially higher.

A word about names and imprints

The use by large publishers of a multiplicity of names for different divisions can be quite confusing.

Imprints are the names used by publishers for specific sections of their list. Only relevant, illustrated imprints are listed here, and are generally cross-referenced to their parent company. Note, however, that in many cases an "imprint" may be run as a completely separate company.

Also, following a wave of takeovers and mergers in the late 1980s, many well-known publishing names are now concentrated under major umbrella groupings, and these too are cross-referenced in the list that follows.

AA PUBLISHING
Automobile Association, Fanum House, Basingstoke, Hampshire RG21 2EA. Tel: 0256 20123.
Contact: M D Buttler, Editorial Manager.
Subjects: Guide books, travel and leisure.

ACADEMY EDITIONS
42 Leinster Gardens, London W2 3AN. Tel: 071-402 2141.
Subjects: Art, architecture, crafts, design, photography, fashion.

AIRLIFE PUBLISHING LTD
101 Longden Road, Shrewsbury, Shropshire SY3 9EB. Tel: 0743 235651.
Imprints: Swan Hill Press.
Contact: John Beaton, Managing Editor.
Subjects: Aviation, country pursuits, military, natural history, photography.

ALBION PRESS LTD (P)
Spring Hill, Idbury, Oxfordshire OX7 6RU. Tel: 0993 831094.
Subjects: Children's, cookery, fine arts, social history.

IAN ALLAN PUBLISHING
Terminal House, Station Approach, Shepperton, Middx TW17 8AS. Tel: 0932 228950.
Subjects: Aviation, military, motoring, railways.

ALPHABET & IMAGE LTD (P)
Alpha House, South Street, Sherbourne, Dorset DT9 3LU. Tel: 0935 814944.
Subjects: Architecture, crafts, gardening, etc.

ANAYA PUBLISHERS LTD
3rd Floor, Strode House, 44-50 Osnaburgh Street, London NW1 3ND. Tel: 071-383 2997.
Subjects: Arts and crafts, cookery, gardening, health, interiors, biographies, sport.

ANTIQUE COLLECTORS' CLUB LTD
5 Church Street, Woodbridge, Suffolk IP12 1DS. Tel: 0394 385501.
Contact: Diana Steel, Managing Director (by letter only).
Subjects: Antiques, architecture, art, gardening.

THE APPLE PRESS
The Old Brewery, 6 Blundell Street, London N7 9BH. Tel: 071-700 6700.
Subjects: General; cookery, crafts, decorative arts, gardening, health and fitness, leisure.

AQUARIAN PRESS
Imprint of HarperCollins Publishers, 77-85 Fulham Palace Road, Hammersmith, London W6 8JB. Tel: 081-741 7070.
Contact: Rosamund Saunders.
Subjects: All New Age subjects – astrology, magic and occultism, paranormal, tarot and divination, mythology, etc.

ARGUS BOOKS LTD
Argus House, Boundary Way, Hemel Hempstead, Hertfordshire HP2 7ST. Tel: 0442 66551.
Subjects: Aviation, crafts, electronics, hobbies, home brewing and winemaking, maritime, military, model engineering and modelling, railways, woodworking.

ARMS & ARMOUR – see CASSELL

AURUM PRESS LTD
25 Bedford Avenue, London WC1B 3AT. Tel: 071-637 3225.
Subjects: General; art, design, film, travel.

BLA PUBLISHING LTD/THAMES HEAD (P)
1 Christopher Road, East Grinstead, West Sussex RH19 3BT. Tel: 0342 318980.
Subjects: General; for encyclopedias and reference books. Crafts, military, travel.

BANTAM PRESS
61-63 Uxbridge Road, London W5 5SA. Tel: 081-579 2652.
Subjects: General; biography, cookery, crafts, health, history, military, music, photography, politics and economics, science, travel.

BARRIE & JENKINS LTD
Random Century House, 20 Vauxhall Bridge Road, London SW1V 2SA. Tel: 071-973 9710.
Subjects: Antiques, art, design, history, photography.

B. T. BATSFORD LTD
4 Fitzhardinge Street, London W1H 0AH. Tel: 071-486 8484.
Subjects: Archaeology, architecture and design, art, building, cinema, costume, crafts, equestrian, gardening and horticulture, social work.

BELITHA PRESS LTD
31 Newington Green, London N16 9PU. Tel: 071-241 5566.
Subjects: Children's illustrated.

BISON BOOKS LTD (P)
Kimbolton House, 117a Fulham Road, London SW3 6RL. Tel: 071-823 9222.
Contact: Ian Westwell, Editorial Director.
Subjects: General; art and architecture, cars, film, history, pop music, railways, sport, travel.

A & C BLACK (PUBLISHERS) LTD
35 Bedford Row, London WC1R 4JH. Tel: 071-242 0946.
Subjects: Arts and crafts, children's educational and reference, drama, nautical, reference, sport, theatre, travel, ornithology.

BLACKWELL PUBLISHERS
108 Cowley Road, Oxford OX4 1JF. Tel: 0865 791100.
Subjects: Business, geography, history, medicine, politics, science.

BLANDFORD – see CASSELL

BLOOMSBURY PUBLISHING LTD
2 Soho Square, London W1V 5DE. Tel: 071-494 2111.
Subjects: General; biography, current affairs, reference, travel.

BOUNTY BOOKS – see REED ILLUSTRATED BOOKS

BOXTREE LTD
Broadwall House, 21 Broadwall, London SE1 9PL. Tel: 071-928 9696.
Subjects: General illustrated, popular music and sport.

BRESLICH & FOSS (P)
Golden House, 28-31 Great Pulteney Street, London W1R 3DD. Tel: 071-734 0706.
Subjects: Arts, children's, crafts, gardening, health.

JOHN CALMANN & KING LTD (P)
71 Great Russell Street, London WC1B 3BN. Tel: 071-831 6351.
Subjects: Arts and architecture, design, natural history.

CAMBRIDGE UNIVERSITY PRESS
The Edinburgh Building, Shaftesbury Road, Cambridge CB2 2RU. Tel: 0223 312393.
Subjects: Archaeology, architecture, drama, history, medicine, music, reference, religion, science, sociology.

CAMERON BOOKS (PRODUCTION) LTD (P)
P O Box 1, Moffat, Dumfriesshire DG10 9SU. Tel: 0683 20808.
Subjects: General; architecture, arts, crafts, collecting, cookery, natural history.

CASSELL PLC
Villiers House, 41-47 Strand, London WC2N 5JE. Tel: 071-839 4900.
Imprints: Arms & Armour, Blandford, Geoffrey Chapman, Mansell, Mowbray, Studio Vista, Ward Lock.
Subjects: General; art, crafts, cookery, education, equestrian, fishing, gardening, history, military, natural history, popular music, reference, religion, sport.

CENTURY BUSINESS
Random Century House, 20 Vauxhall Bridge Road, London SW1V 2SA. Tel: 071-973 9670.
Contact: Elizabeth Hennessy.
Subjects: Business, finance, management, marketing.

CHAMBERS HARRAP LTD
43-45 Annandale Street, Edinburgh EH7 4AZ. Tel: 031-557 4571.
Contact: J. S. Osborne, Production Director.
Subjects: General reference, educational, Scotland.

GEOFFREY CHAPMAN – see CASSELL

CHATTO & WINDUS LTD
20 Vauxhall Bridge Road, London SW1V 2SA. Tel: 071-973 9740.
Subjects: General; art, biography and memoirs, cookery, current affairs, history, politics, travel.

CLARENDON PRESS – see OXFORD UNIVERSITY PRESS

COLLINS – see HARPERCOLLINS PUBLISHERS

COLLINS & BROWN
Letts of London House, Great Eastern Wharf, Parkgate Road, London SW11 4NQ. Tel: 071-924 2575.
Subjects: General; biography, history, photography, travel.

CONRAN OCTOPUS LTD
37 Shelton Street, London WC2H 9HN. Tel: 071-240 6961.
Subjects: Antiques, cinema, cookery, crafts and hobbies, gardening, health and beauty, interior design, photography, travel.

CONSTABLE & CO LTD
3 The Lanchesters, 162 Fulham Palace Road, London W6 9ER. Tel: 081-741 3663.
Subjects: General; biography, current affairs, food, guide books, history, social sciences, travel.

DAVID & CHARLES PUBLISHING PLC
Brunel House, Newton Abbot, Devon TQ12 4PU. Tel: 0626 61121.
Subjects: Crafts, fine art, art techniques, gardening, equestrian, natural history, railways, sailing.

J. M. DENT & SONS LTD
Orion House, 5 Upper St Martin's Lane, London WC2H 9EA. Tel: 071-240 3444.
Subjects: Cookery, gardening, heritage and history, music, reference, science.

EDDISON SADD EDITIONS LTD (P)
St Chad's Court, 146B Kings Cross Road, London WC1X 9DH. Tel: 071-837 1968.
Contact: Elaine Partington, Art Director.
Subjects: General.

ELM TREE BOOKS – see HAMISH HAMILTON

FABER & FABER LTD
3 Queen Square, London WC1N 3AU. Tel: 071-465 0045.
Subjects: Archaeology, architecture, art, biography, film, music, politics, theatre, travel.

FARMING PRESS BOOKS
Wharfedale Road, Ipswich IP1 4LG. Tel: 0473 241122.
Contact: Roger Smith, Manager.
Subjects: Agriculture.

FONTANA – see HARPERCOLLINS PUBLISHERS

G. T. FOULIS & CO – see HAYNES PUBLISHING GROUP

W. FOULSHAM & CO LTD
837 Yeovil Road, Slough, Berkshire SL1 4JH. Tel: 0753 526769.
Subjects: Collecting, DIY, educational, hobbies, sport, travel.

GARDENHOUSE EDITIONS LTD (P)
15 Grafton Square, London SW4 0DQ. Tel: 071-622 1720.
Subjects: Architecture, cookery, fashion, gardening, interior design.

VICTOR GOLLANCZ
Villers House, 41-47 Strand, London WC2N 5JE. Tel: 071-839 4900.
Imprints: H. F. & G. Witherby.
Subjects: General; biography and memoirs, children's books, cookery, current affairs, history, music, natural history, sociology, travel.

GRISEWOOD & DEMPSEY LTD
Elsley House, 24-30 Great Titchfield Street, London W1P 7AD. Tel: 071-631 0878.
Imprint: Kingfisher Books.
Contact: Elaine Willis, Picture Research.
Subjects: Children's non-fiction, natural history, reference.

GRUB STREET (P)
The Basement, 10 Chivalry Road, London SW11 1HT. Tel: 071-924 3966.
Subjects: Aviation, cookery, humour.

GUINNESS PUBLISHING LTD
33 London Road, Enfield, Middlesex EN2 6DJ. Tel: 081-367 4567.
Subjects: General reference, sport and popular music.

ROBERT HALE LTD
Clerkenwell House, 45-47 Clerkenwell Green, London EC1R 0HT. Tel: 071-251 2661.
Subjects: General; biography, cookery, crafts, natural history, travel.

HAMISH HAMILTON LTD
27 Wrights Lane, London W8 5TZ. Tel: 071-416 3200.
Imprint: Elm Tree Books.
Subjects: General; children's non-fiction, current affairs, entertainment, history, music, natural history, politics, theatre and ballet, travel.

HAMLYN – see REED ILLUSTRATED BOOKS

HARPERCOLLINS COLLEGE DIVISION
77-85 Fulham Palace Road, London W6 8JB. Tel: 081-307 4114.
Contact: John Parsons, Marketing Director.
Subjects: Anthropology, business, cultural, economics, engineering, geography, history, life science, politics, psychology, sociology.

HARPERCOLLINS PUBLISHERS
77-85 Fulham Palace Road, London W6 8JB. Tel: 081-741 7070.
Imprints: Collins, Fontana, Harvill, Marshall Pickering.
Subjects: General.

HARVILL – see HARPERCOLLINS PUBLISHERS

HAYNES PUBLISHING GROUP
Sparkford, Yeovil, Somerset BA22 7JJ. Tel: 0963 40635.
Imprints: G. T. Foulis & Co, Oxford Publishing Company, Patrick Stephens.
Contact: Alison Roelich.
Subjects: Aircraft, boats, cars, DIY, military, motorcycles, railways, shipping.

HEADLINE BOOK PUBLISHING PLC
Headline House, 79 Great Titchfield Street, London W1P 7FN. Tel: 071-631 1687.
Contact: Alan Brooke, Publishing Director Non-Fiction.
Subjects: Biography, countryside, design, food and wine, gardening, music.

HEADWAY – see HODDER & STOUGHTON

WILLIAM HEINEMANN LTD
Michelin House, 81 Fulham Road, London SW3 6RB. Tel: 071-581 9393.
Subjects: Arts, biography, history, travel.

CHRISTOPHER HELM PUBLISHERS LTD
35 Bedford Row, London WC1R 4JH. Tel: 071-242 0946.
Subjects: Cricket, natural history, ornithology, travel.

HERBERT PRESS LTD
46 Northchurch Road, London N1 4EJ. Tel: 071-254 4379.
Subjects: General; art, archaeology, architecture, biography, design, crafts, fashion and costume, natural history.

HODDER & STOUGHTON LTD
47 Bedford Square, London WC1B 3DP. Tel: 071-636 9851.
Imprints: Headway.
Subjects: General; cookery, history, music, sport, travel.

JARROLD PUBLISHING
Whitefriars, Norwich NR3 1TR. Tel: 0603 763300.
Contact: Vivienne Buckingham, Picture Researcher.
Subjects: Guide books and travel (Britain only), natural history.

MICHAEL JOSEPH LTD
27 Wrights Lane, London W8 5TZ. Tel: 071-416 3200.
Subjects: General.

THE KENILWORTH PRESS LTD
Addington, Buckingham MK18 2JR. Tel: 0296 715101.
Subjects: Equestrian.

KINGFISHER BOOKS – see GRISEWOOD & DEMPSEY

CHARLES LETTS & CO LTD
Letts of London House, Parkgate Road, London SW11 4NQ. Tel: 071-407 8891.
Subjects: Cookery, crafts, gardening, needlecraft.

FRANCES LINCOLN LTD (P)
4 Torriano Mews, Torriano Avenue, London NW5 2RZ. Tel: 071-284 4009.
Subjects: General; crafts, gardening, health, interior design.

LITTLE, BROWN AND COMPANY (UK) LTD
165 Great Dover Street, London SE1 4YA. Tel: 071-334 4800.
Subjects: General.

LONGMAN GROUP UK LTD
5 Bentinck Street, London W1M 5RN. Tel: 071-935 0121.
Subjects: General academic and professional; agriculture, building, engineering, geography, history, politics, science and technology.

THE LUTTERWORTH PRESS
P O Box 60, Cambridge CB1 2NT. Tel: 0223 350865.
Subjects: Arts, biography, children's non-fiction, crafts, educational, environment, history, leisure, science, sociology, religion.

MACMILLAN LONDON – see PAN MACMILLAN

MANSELL – see CASSELL

MARSHALL CAVENDISH BOOKS
119 Wardour Street, London W1V 3TD. Tel: 071-734 6710.
Subjects: General; art, cookery, crafts, DIY, gardening, sport & leisure, social history,

MARSHALL EDITIONS LTD (P)
170 Piccadilly, London W1V 9DD. Tel: 071-629 0079.
Contact: Zilda Tandy, Picture Editor.
Subjects: General; crafts and hobbies, food and wine, gardening, natural history, photography, science, transport.

MARSHALL PICKERING – see HARPERCOLLINS PUBLISHERS

MITCHELL BEAZLEY – see REED ILLUSTRATED BOOKS

MOWBRAY – see CASSELL

JOHN MURRAY (PUBLISHERS) LTD
50 Albemarle Street, London W1X 4BD. Tel: 071-493 4361.
Subjects: General; art and architecture, biography, crafts, educational, health, history, travel.

NEW HOLLAND PUBLISHERS
37 Connaught Street, London W2 2AZ. Tel: 071-258 0204.
Subjects: Crafts, cookery, gardening, interior design, natural history, travel.

NEW LEAF BOOKS LTD (P)
BCM-New Leaf, London WC1N 3XX. Tel: 071-435 3056.
Subjects: General; mainly practical and instructional.

OMNIBUS PRESS/BOOK SALES LTD
8/9 Frith Street, London W1V 5TZ. Tel: 071-434 0066.
Contact: Chris Charlesworth, editor; David Brolan, picture researcher.
Subjects: Rock, pop and classical music.

OSPREY PUBLISHING LTD
1 Michelin House, 81 Fulham Road, London SW3 6RB. Tel: 071-581 9393.
Subjects: Aircraft, cars, military.

OXFORD PAPERBACKS – see OXFORD UNIVERSITY PRESS

OXFORD PUBLISHING COMPANY – see HAYNES PUBLISHING GROUP

OXFORD UNIVERSITY PRESS
Walton Street, Oxford OX2 6DP. Tel: 0865 56767.
Imprints: Clarendon Press, Oxford Paperbacks.
Subjects: General; academic, reference, educational.

PAN BOOKS – see PAN MACMILLAN

PAN MACMILLAN LTD
Cavaye Place, London SW10 9PG. Tel: 071-373 6070.
Imprints: Macmillan London, Pan Books, Sidgwick & Jackson.
Subjects: General; biography, children's, cookery, crafts, current affairs, practical, reference, travel, picture and novelty books.

PARKE SUTTON PUBLISHING LTD (P)
The Old Tannery, Barrack Street, Norwich, Norfolk NR3 1TS. Tel: 0603 667021.
Contact: Anne Priestley, Editor.
Subjects: General.

PARTRIDGE PRESS
Transworld Publishers, 61-63 Uxbridge Road, London W5 5SA. Tel: 081-579 2652.
Subjects: Sports and leisure.

PAVILION BOOKS
26 Upper Ground, London SE1 9PD. Tel: 071-620 1666.
Subjects: Food and wine, gardening, interior design, music, sport, travel.

PELHAM BOOKS LTD
27 Wrights Lane, London W8 5TZ. Tel: 071-416 3200.
Subjects: Dogs, countryside, crafts, sport and leisure.

PELICAN – see PENGUIN BOOKS

PENGUIN BOOKS LTD
27 Wrights Lane, London W8 5TZ. Tel: 071-416 3000.
Imprints: Pelican,Viking.
Contact: Ms Josine Meijer, Picture Research Manager.
Subjects: General.

PIATKUS BOOKS
5 Windmill Street, London W1P 1HF. Tel: 071-631 0710.
Subjects: Business, cookery, fashion, health, leisure, women's interests.

PLAYNE BOOKS (P)
New Inn Lane, Avening, Tetbury, Gloucestershire GL8 8NB. Tel: 0453 835155.
Contact: Gill Davies, Editor.
Subjects: General.

PLEXUS PUBLISHING LTD
26 Dafforne Road, London SW17 8TZ. Tel: 081-672 6067.
Subjects: Biography, fashion, film, music, popular culture.

MATHEW PRICE LTD (P)
Old Rectory House, Marston Magna, Yeovil, Somerset BA22 8DT. Tel: 0935 851158.
Contact: Elinor Bagenal.
Subjects: General children's books.

PRION – MULTIMEDIA BOOKS LTD
32-34 Gordon House Road, London NW5 1LP. Tel: 071-482 4248.
Subjects: General; cookery, travel, wildlife.

PUFFIN – see PENGUIN BOOKS

QUARTET BOOKS
27-29 Goodge Street, London W1P 1FD. Tel: 071-636 3992.
Imprints: Robin Clark.
Subjects: Biography, history, music.

QUARTO PUBLISHING PLC/QUINTET PUBLISHING LTD (P)
The Old Brewery, 6 Blundell Street, London N7 9BH. Tel: 071-700 6700.
Subjects: General.

THE READER'S DIGEST ASSOCIATION LTD
Berkeley Square House, London W1X 6AB. Tel: 071-629 8144.
Subjects: General illustrated; cookery, crafts, DIY, encyclopaedias, folklore, gardening, guide books, history, natural history.

REED ILLUSTRATED BOOKS
Michelin House, 81 Fulham Road, London SW3 6RB. Tel: 071-581 9393.
Imprints: Bounty, Hamlyn, Miller's, Mitchell Beazley, Philip's, Osprey.
Subjects: Illustrated reference, general reference and special interest.

WILLIAM REED DIRECTORIES (P)
The Old Bakehouse, High Street, Goring-on-Thames, Reading, Berks RG8 9AR. Tel: 0491 875800.
Contact: Ray Hurst, Publishing Director.
Subjects: General; food and drink.

REED'S NAUTICAL BOOKS
Barnacle Marine Ltd, PO Box 1539, Corsham, Wiltshire SN14 9HX. Tel: 0225 812024.
Subjects: Sailing and nautical.

ROUTLEDGE
11 New Fetter Lane, London EC4P 4EE. Tel: 071-583 9855.
Subjects: Academic, professional and reference.

SALAMANDER BOOKS LTD
129/137 York Way, London N7 9LG. Tel: 071-267 4447.
Subjects: Cookery, crafts, gardening, hobbies, military, music, natural history, pets.

SAVITRI BOOKS LTD (P)
115j Cleveland Street, London W1P 5PN. Tel: 071-436 9932.
Contact: M. S. Srivastava.
Subjects: General; especially crafts, ecology, natural history.

SECKER & WARBURG LTD
Michelin House, 81 Fulham Road, London SW3 6RB. Tel: 071-581 9393.
Subjects: Art, biography, cinema, history, jazz, politics, theatre, travel.

SHELDRAKE PRESS LTD (P)
188 Cavendish Road, London SW12 0DA. Tel: 081-675 1767.
Subjects: General; architecture, cookery, design, history, music, travel.

SIDGWICK & JACKSON LTD
18-21 Cavaye Place, London SW10 9PG. Tel: 071-373 6070.
Subjects: Biography, cinema, current affairs, food and wine, gardening, history, music, politics, showbusiness, sport, travel.

SINCLAIR-STEVENSON LTD
Michelin House, 81 Fulham Road, London SW3 6RB. Tel: 071-581 9393.
Subjects: General; biography, current affairs, history.

SOUVENIR PRESS LTD
43 Great Russell Street, London WC1B 3PA. Tel: 071-580 9307.
Subjects: General; childcare, cookery, gardening, health, hobbies, practical, sociology.

SPELLMOUNT LTD
12 Dene Way, Speldhurst, Tunbridge Wells, Kent TN3 0NX. Tel: 0892 862860.
Contact: Ian Morley-Clarke, Managing Director.
Subjects: Militaria, cricket and music biographies.

PATRICK STEPHENS LTD
Haynes Publishing Group, Sparkford, Nr Yeovil, Somerset BA22 7JJ. Tel: 0963 40635.
Subjects: Aviation, biography, maritime, military, modelling, motoring and motorcycling, motor racing, railways.

STUDIO VISTA – see CASSELL

ALAN SUTTON PUBLISHING LTD
Phoenix Mill, Far Thrupp, Stroud, Gloucestershire GL5 2BU. Tel: 0453 731114.
Subjects: General; academic, archaeology, biography, photography, railways, topography and travel.

SWAN HILL PRESS – see AIRLIFE PUBLISHING

THE TEMPLAR COMPANY PLC (P)
Pippbrook Mill, London Road, Dorking, Surrey RH4 1JE. Tel: 0306 876361.
Subjects: Mainly children's reference; geography, natural history, science.

THAMES AND HUDSON LTD
30-34 Bloomsbury Street, London WC1B 3QP. Tel: 071-636 5488.
Contact: Jamie Camplin, Editorial Head.
Subjects: Archaeology, anthropology, art and architecture, cinema, fashion, music, photography, practical guides, religion and mythology, theatre, travel.

THORSONS
Imprint of HarperCollins, 77-85 Fulham Palace Road, Hammersmith, London W6 8JB. Tel: 081-741 7070.

Contact: Rosamund Saunders.
Subjects: Complementary medicine, health, environmental issues, exercise and nutrition, parenting and childcare.

TOUCAN BOOKS LTD (P)
Albion Courtyard, Greenhill Rents, London EC1M 6BN. Tel: 071-251 3921.
Subjects: General.

UNICORN BOOKS
16 Laxton Gardens, Paddock Wood, Tonbridge, Kent TN12 6BB. Tel: 0892 833648.
Contact: Ray Green, Managing Director.
Subjects: Railways.

USBORNE PUBLISHING
83-85 Saffron Hill, London EC1N 8RT. Tel: 071-430 2800.
Contacts: Amanda Barlow or Steve Wright.
Subjects: Children's books, crafts, natural history, practical, reference.

VIKING – see PENGUIN BOOKS

VIRGIN PUBLISHING LTD
332 Ladbroke Grove, London W10 5AH. Tel: 081-968 7554.
Contact: Paul Forty.
Subjects: Arts, biography, current affairs, film, leisure, lifestyle, rock music, popular science, practical, theatre, true crime.

WARD LOCK – see CASSELL

WARD LOCK EDUCATIONAL COMPANY LTD
1 Christopher Road, East Grinstead, West Sussex, RH19 3BT. Tel: 0342 318980.
Subjects: General educational; science, music, geography, history.

WEBB & BOWER (PUBLISHERS) LTD
3 Cathedral Close, Exeter, Devon EX1 1EZ. Tel: 0392 435362.
Subjects: General; arts, biography, crafts, design, food and wine, gardening, nostalgia, reference, travel.

WEIDENFELD & NICOLSON LTD
Orion House, 5 Upper St Martin's Lane, London WC2H 9EA. Tel: 071-240 3444.
Subjects: General; biography, cookery, history, travel.

PHILIP WILSON PUBLISHERS LTD
26 Litchfield Street, London WC2H 9NJ. Tel: 071-379 7886.
Contact: J. A. Speers.
Subjects: Applied and decorative arts, architecture, fine art, wine.

H. F. & G. WITHERBY – see VICTOR GOLLANCZ

CARDS & CALENDARS

This section lists publishers of postcards, greetings cards and calendars, along with their requirements. Additionally, companies producing allied material, such as posters and prints have been included for convenience.

With the exception of traditional viewcard producers, who have always offered rather meagre rates for freelance material, fees in this area are generally quite good. However, only those who can produce precisely what is required as far as subject matter, quality and format are concerned, are likely to succeed.

Market requirements

Traditionally, greetings card and calendar publishers have required large format transparencies of the highest quality. While they still demand optimum quality material, the requirement for the really large format has eased up in recent years. Few now insist on 5x4in or larger formats. Nearly all of the companies listed here are happy to accept medium format, and many of them will even consider 35mm.

The need for material of the highest quality cannot be too strongly emphasised. The greetings card market, in particular, is highly specialised with very specific requirements. If you aim to break into this market, you must be very sure of your photographic technique. You must be able to produce professional quality material that is pin sharp and has excellent colour saturation. You must also know *exactly* what the market requires. The listings will help you, but you should also carry out your own field study by examining the photographic greetings cards on general sale. Unfortunately, there are fewer of them around than was once the case, many publishers employing only art or graphics nowadays. This means that there is greater competition than ever to supply material for those photographic cards that are produced.

None of this is to suggest that the calendar market is necessarily easier to supply. It is equally demanding, though fortunately there are still large numbers of calendars using photographs being produced every year. Many calendar producers obtain the material they need from picture agencies, but this is not say that individual photographers cannot successfully break into this field. Once again, though, you must be sure of your photographic technique and be able to produce really top quality work.

Before submitting material, make sure you know *exactly* what the market requires. Read carefully *all* of the listings that follow; they all contain information likely to help you. And again, make a point of studying the calendars that you see on general sale or hanging up in offices and in other places you visit. don't rely solely on what *you* think would make a good calendar picture; familiarise yourself with the type of pictures actually being used by calendar publishers.

Rights and fees

Where given to us by the company concerned, fees have been quoted. Some companies prefer to negotiate fees individually, depending upon the type of material you offer. If you are new to this field, the best plan is to submit your transparencies (preferably after making an initial enquiry, outlining the material you have available), and let the company concerned make you an offer. Generally speaking, you should not accept less than about £75 for Greetings Card or Calendar Rights.

Remember, you are not selling your copyright in the transparency for this fee; you are free to submit the same transparency to any *non-competitive* market (for example, a magazine), at a later date. But you should not attempt to sell a transparency to another greetings card publisher once you have sold Greetings Card Rights to a competing firm.

ATHENA INTERNATIONAL
PO Box 918, Harlow, Essex CM20 2DU. Tel: 0279 641125.
Contacts: Roger Watt, Trevor Jones, Martin Powderly; Art Directors. Requires material for posters, greetings cards, prints and postcards. All types of subjects considered, landscape, figurative, situation, fashion, humour, etc. Prefers 6x6cm or larger formats, but will consider 35mm if of the highest quality.
Fees: Greetings cards, around £150; Prints and posters on a royalties basis.

BERKSWELL PUBLISHING CO LTD
PO Box 420, Warminster, Wiltshire BA12 9XB. Tel: 0985 40189.
Contact: John Stidolph, Managing Director.
Calendars, diaries, posters and books featuring Royalty. Good colour and B&W photographs of members of the Royal Family and Royal events always required. Also organisers of the annual Martini Royal Photographic Competition; entry forms and details obtainable for the above address.
Fees: By negotiation.

CALENDAR CONCEPTS AND DESIGN
33 Albury Avenue, Isleworth, Middlesex TW7 5HY. Tel: 081-847 3777.
Contact: Brigitte Arora, Picture Editor.
Top-quality work suitable for up-market corporate calendars for a range of business clients. Subjects most in demand are: British landscapes (preferably large-format originals), world wildlife, small British mammals, cats, horses, glamour.
Fees: According to use and by negotiation.

JARROLD PUBLISHING
Whitefriars, Norwich, Norfolk NR3 1TR. Tel: 0603 763300 Ext. 333.
Contact: Ms Vivienne Buckingham, Picture Researcher.
Calendars. Will consider picturesque scenes within the British Isles, flora, fauna, pet animals, etc. Top quality 35mm and medium format transparencies only.
Fees: £35–£50 outright purchase.

THE MEDICI SOCIETY LTD
34-42 Pentonville Road, London N1 9HG. Tel: 071-837 7099.
Greetings cards. Limited requirement for transparencies of flowers, animals and birds in their natural surroundings, snow scenes, etc. 35mm transparencies can be accepted if of a high professional quality, but larger formats are preferred. Submissions should not consist of more than six transparencies. Please enclose a s.a.e.
Fees: From £140.

SANTORO GRAPHICS
63 Maltings Place, Bagleys Lane, London SW6 2BY. Tel: 071-610 6166
Contact: Lucy Price.
Posters, postcards and notecards. Requires striking and attractive images to the typical young poster/postcard buyer: atmospheric, romantic, humorous. B&W a speciality, but colour images in contemporary styles also of interest.
Fees: By negotiation.

SCANDECOR LTD
3 The Ermine Centre, Hurricane Close, Huntingdon, Cambridgeshire PE18 6XX. Tel: 0480 456395.
Contact: Marianne Cope, Product Manager.
Posters, prints, postcards and calendars. Will consider contributions mainly for poster/postcard

use on a wide range of subjects: animals, cars, tasteful glamour, romance, humour, etc. Most interested in dramatic, powerful images or humorous shots likely to appeal to the youth market.
Fees: Depends on material, how it is used, and on whether international distribution rights may be required.

W. N. SHARPE LTD
Bingley Road, Bradford, West Yorkshire BD9 6SD. Tel: 0274 542244.
Contact: R Hutchings, Director.
Greetings cards. Subjects: scenic and action shots, preferably using photographic techniques to enhance the subject. All require an element of human interest but not portraiture. Also poster style modern images such as still life florals etc., shots of painting out of copyright, especially winter scenes and views of London. Large format transparencies preferred.
Fees: "Negotiable for World Greetings Card Rights for all time."

VALENTINES OF DUNDEE LTD
PO Box 74, Dundee DD1 9NQ. Tel: 0382 833338.
Contact: Director of Product Management.
Greetings cards and calendars. Florals, animals, views, outdoor scenes, sporting activities, winter landscapes. Minimum transparency size: 6x6cm.
Fees: Negotiable.

AGENCIES

Picture libraries and agencies are in the business of selling pictures. They are not in the business of teaching photography or advising photographers how to produce saleable work – although they can sometimes prove remarkably helpful in the latter respect to those who show promise. Their purpose is strictly a business one: to meet the demand for stock pictures from such markets as magazine and book publishers, advertising agencies, travel operators, greetings card and calendar publishers, and many more. A typical agency has many thousands of pictures in its files, each one of which is carefully categorised and filed so that it can be easily located when an editor or picture buyer wants to see a selection of pictures of a particular subject.

Many photographers look upon an agent as a last resort; they have been unable to sell their photographs themselves, so they think they might as well try unloading them on an agent. This is the wrong attitude. No agent will succeed in placing pictures which are quite simply unmarketable. In any event, the photographer who has had at least some success in selling pictures is in a far better position to approach an agent.

Agency requirements

If you hope to interest an agency in your work, you must be able to produce pictures which the agency feels are likely to sell to one of their markets. Although the acceptance of your work by an agent is no guarantee that it will sell, an efficient agency certainly will not clutter up its files with pictures which do not stand a reasonably good chance of finding a market.

Agents handle pictures of virtually every subject under the sun. Some specialise in particular subjects – sport, natural history, etc. – while others act as general agencies, covering the whole spectrum of subject matter. Any photograph that could be published in one form or another is a suitable picture for an agency.

Even if you eventually decide that you want to place all your potentially saleable material with an agency, you cannot expect to leave every aspect of the business to them. You must continue to study the market, watching for trends; you must continue to study published pictures. For example, if your speciality is travel material, you should use every opportunity to study the type of pictures published in current travel brochures and other markets using such material. Only by doing this – by being aware of the market – can you hope to continue to provide your agent with marketable pictures.

Commission and copyright

Agencies generally work on a commission basis, 50 per cent being the most usual rate – if they receive £100 for reproduction rights in a particular picture, the photographer will get £50 of this.

A 50 per cent commission rate may seem high, but it should be remembered that a picture agency, like any other business, has substantial overheads to account for. There can also be high costs involved in making prospective buyers aware of the pictures that are available – the larger agencies produce lavish colour catalogues featuring selections of their best pictures. Nevertheless, agencies are sometimes willing to negotiate a lower rate of commission with their more prized contributors.

Agents do not normally sell pictures outright; indeed, they should never do so without the permission of the photographer concerned, who would normally always retain copyright in all pictures placed with the agent. As would the individual photographer, they merely sell "reproduction rights", the transparency being loaned to the buyer for a specified period of time while printing plates are produced.

However a few agencies do sometimes offer to buy pictures outright from a photographer, instead of working on the normal commission basis. The price in these cases will be a matter for negotiation between photographer and agent, but it should be remembered that once a picture is sold outright, the photographer has effectively disposed of the copyright and has no further rights in the picture.

A long-term investment

When dealing with a photographer for the first time, most agencies require a minimum initial submission – which can consist of anything from 50–500 pictures. Most also stipulate that you must leave your material with them for a minimum period of anything from one to five years.

When an agency takes on the work of a new photographer, they are involved in a lot of work – categorising, filing, cross-indexing and, in most cases, re-mounting the transparencies in the agency's own standard mounts (or, at least, adding the agency's name to the existing mounts). The next step will often be to make it known to picture buyers that these new pictures are available, sometimes including reproductions of them in any new catalogues or publicity material currently being prepared. Having been involved in all this work and expense, it is not unreasonable for them to want to be given a fair chance to market the pictures. If the photographer were able to demand the return of the work after only a few months, the agent will have been involved in a lot of work and expense for nothing.

Dealing with an agent must therefore be considered a long-term investment. Having initially placed, say, a few hundred pictures with an agent, it could be at least several months before any are selected by a picture buyer, and even longer before any monies are seen by the photographer.

Normally, the photographer will also be expected to regularly submit new material to the library. Indeed, only when you have several hundred pictures lodged with the library can you hope for regular sales – and a reasonable return on your investment.

Making an approach

Many agents prefer to meet new photographers personally to see and discuss their work. It is not a good idea, however, to turn up on their doorstep without an appointment. The best plan is to write to, or telephone, the agency of your choice, outlining the material you have available. It may also be worth mentioning details of any sales you have made yourself. If the agency is interested, they will suggest a mutually convenient appointment when you can bring your material along, or they may suggest that you initially post some samples to them.

But remember that there is little point in approaching an agency until you have a sizeable collection of potentially saleable material. Most agents will not feel it worth their while dealing with a photographer who has only a dozen or so marketable pictures to offer – it just wouldn't be worth all the work and expense involved. And the chance of the photographer seeing a worthwhile return on just a dozen pictures placed with an agent are remote indeed; you'd be lucky to see more than one cheque in ten years!

In the listings that follow, you'll find full information on over 70 agencies: the subjects they handle, the markets they supply, the formats they stock, their terms of business (including any minimum initial submission and retention period), and their standard commission charged on sales. Prefacing the listings you'll find an Agency Subject Index; this can be used to find the names of agents handling subjects you can supply.

Remember: simply placing material with an agency doesn't guarantee sales. And no agency can sell material for which there is no market. On the other hand, if you are able to produce good quality, marketable work, and can team up with the right agent, you could see a very worthwhile return from this association.

Agency Subject Index

Abstracts

Ace Photo Agency
BMV Picturebank
S&I Williams Power Pix

Aerial

Aerofilms Ltd
Geo Aerial Photography

Architecture & Archaeology

Ancient Art & Architecture Collection
Bruce Coleman Ltd
Houses & Interiors
The Hutchison Library

Art & Antiques

Ancient Art & Architecture Collection
The Bridgeman Art Library

Botany

A-Z Botanical Collection Ltd
NHPA
Natural Science Photos
Planet Earth Pictures

Business & Industry

Ace Photo Agency
Colorific Photo Library Ltd
Greg Evans Photo Library
International Stock Exchange Photo Library
The Telegraph Colour Library

Fashion & Beauty

Camera Press Ltd

General (all subjects)

Ace Photo Agency
Adams Picture Library

BMV Picturebank
Barnaby's Picture Library
J. Allan Cash Ltd
Cephas Picture Library
Colorific Photo Library Ltd
Euroart Photo Agency
Eye Ubiquitous Picture Library
Fotoccompli
The Robert Harding Picture Library
The Hutchison Library
The Northern Picture Library
The Telegraph Colour Library
Photo Library International
Pictor International Ltd
Picturepoint Ltd
Popperfoto
Spectrum Colour Library
Tony Stone Images
Visionbank & England Scene
S&I Williams Power Pix
Woodmansterne Publications Ltd
ZEFA (UK) Ltd

Geography & World Environment

J. Allan Cash Ltd
Bruce Coleman Ltd
Ecoscene
Geo Aerial Photography
Holt Studios International
Interfoto Picture Library Ltd
NHPA
Natural Science Photos
Oxford Scientific Films Ltd
Panos Pictures
Picturepoint Ltd
Swift Picture Library
Tropix Photographic Library

Glamour

Barnaby's Picture Library
The Northern Picture Library
Rex Features Ltd
Spectrum Colour Library
S&I Williams Power Pix

Historical

Barnaby's Picture Library
The Bridgeman Art Library
Popperfoto

Landscapes

Northern Picture Library
Oxford Scientific Films Ltd
Planet Earth Pictures
Swift Picture Library
Visionbank & England Scene

Natural History

Aquila Photographics
Bruce Coleman Ltd
Ecoscene
Frank Lane Picture Agency Ltd
NHPA
Natural Image
Natural Science Photos
Oxford Scientific Films Ltd
Planet Earth Pictures
Swift Picture Library

News & Current Affairs

Camera Press Ltd
Empics Ltd
Euro-Parly Services
Popperfoto
Rex Features Ltd

People/Human Behaviour

Bubbles Photo Library
Cephas Picture Library
Interfoto Picture Library Ltd
The Telegraph Colour Library

Personalities

Aquarius Literary Agency & Picture Library
Camera Press Ltd
Euro-Parly Services
Monitor Syndication
Popperfoto
Retna Pictures Ltd
Rex Features Ltd

Photojournalism

Camera Press Ltd
Euro-Parly Services
Popperfoto
Rex Features Ltd

Science & Technology

International Stock Exchange Photo Library
Oxford Scientific Films Ltd
Rex Features Ltd
Science Photo Library
The Telegraph Colour Library

Sport

Action Images Ltd
Empics Ltd
Greg Evans Photo Library
Retna Pictures Ltd
Sporting Pictures
The Telegraph Colour Library

Travel/Tourist

BMV Picturebank
Cephas Picture Library
Dagnall Worldwide Photo Library
James Davis Travel Photography
Greg Evans Photo Library
Footprints Colour Picture Library
Jayawardene Travel Photo Library
Pickthall Picture Library Ltd
Pictor International Ltd
Picturepoint Ltd
Spectrum Colour Library
The Still Moving Picture Company
Travel Photo International
Travel Trade Photography
S&I Williams Power Pix
World Pictures (Feature-Pix Colour Library)

Underwater

Bruce Coleman Ltd
Footprints Colour Picture Library
Frank Lane Picture Agency Ltd
Natural Science Photos
Oxford Scientific Films Ltd
Planet Earth Pictures

A-Z BOTANICAL COLLECTION LTD*
Bedwell Lodge, Cucumber Lane, Essendon, Hatfield, Herts AL9 6JB. Tel: 0707 649091.
Contacts: J. D. L. Finlay, M. A. Finlay (Directors).
Specialist subjects/requirements: All aspects of plant life, not just flowers.
Markets supplied: Publishers and advertising agencies etc.
Stock: Colour only. 5x4in, medium format, 35mm.
Usual terms of business: No minimum submission, but contributors expected to continue supplying pictures on a regular basis. Minimum retention period: 3 years.
Commission: 50 per cent.
Additional information: Except for "scenic" shots, all plants should be captioned with Latin botanic name. Write in first before submitting. Wants lists supplied.

ACE PHOTO AGENCY*
22 Maddox Street, Mayfair, London W1R 9PG. Tel: 071-629 0303.
Contact: John Panton (Managing Director).
Specialist subjects/requirements: Abstracts, animals, beaches, business, celebrities, couples, families, glamour, industry, leisure, music & arts, natural history, people, skies/sunsets, sports, still-lifes, technology, transport, UK travel, world travel.
Markets supplied: Audio visual; design consultants; advertising; publishing – books and magazines.
Stock: Colour only. All formats acceptable, 35mm to 10x8in.
Usual terms of business: Minimum initial submission: 200 accepted images. Minimum retention period: 3 years.
Commission: 50 per cent.
Additional information: "We look for high quality work with good composition and precise captions."

ACTION IMAGES LTD*
74 Willoughby Lane, London N17 0SP. Tel: 081-885 3000.
Contact: David Jacobs (Director).
Specialist subjects/requirements: High quality "pretty" sports pictures, or stock material of sportsmen/women.
Stock: Colour only. 35mm or medium formats.
Usual terms of business: No minimum initial submission, but please telephone first to discuss possible submissions.
Commission: 50 per cent.

ADAMS PICTURE LIBRARY*
156 New Cavendish Street, London W1M 7FJ. Tel: 071-636 1468.
Contact: Carol White (Director).
Specialist subjects/requirements: All subjects except hot news.
Markets supplied: All markets including advertising, publishing, calendars and posters.
Stock: Colour only. All formats.
Usual terms of business: Minimum initial submission: 200 transparencies. Minimum retention period: 5 years; one year's notice required for withdrawal. required. Return postage must be included with all submissions.
Commission: 50 per cent.

AEROFILMS LTD
Gate Studios, Station Road, Borehamwood, Hertfordshire WD6 1EJ. Tel: 081-207 0666.
Contact: R. C. A. Cox, BSc ARICS (Director).
Specialist subjects/requirements: Air-to-ground and air-to-air only. "We are prepared to consider for inclusion in our library, any aerial photography that may be submitted if not already

included from the work of our own photographers."
Stock: B&W and colour. Minimum 6x6cm colour transparencies.
Usual terms of business: Negotiable: "Our prime business is not that of an agency."
Commission: Negotiable.
Additional information: The exact location of every photograph must be specified. "We will not look at 35mm transparencies, nor any photographs that have been taken through the window of an aircraft."

ANCIENT ART & ARCHITECTURE COLLECTION*
6 Kenton Road, Harrow, Middlesex HA1 2BL. Tel: 081-422 1214.
Contact: Ronald Sheridan (Proprietor).
Specialist subjects/requirements: Historical art and artefacts mainly from pre-history up to the Middle Ages; everything which illustrates the civilisations of the ancient world, its cultures and technologies, religion, ideas, beliefs and development. Also warfare, weapons, fortifications and military historical movements. Statues, portraits and contemporary illustrations of histori-cally important people – kings and other rulers.
Markets supplied: Mainly book publishers, but including magazines and TV.
Stock: B&W and colour. 6x6cm or larger formats preferred, (though some 35mm accepted from remote overseas locations.)
Usual terms of business: 3 years minimum retention of material; 24 months notice of return.
Commission: 50 per cent.
Additional information: All submissions must be accompanied by return s.a.e. Only material of the highest quality can be considered.

AQUARIUS LITERARY AGENCY & PICTURE LIBRARY*
PO Box 5, Hastings, East Sussex TN34 1HR. Tel: 0424 721196.
Contacts: Gilbert Gibson, David Corkill (Directors).
Specialist subjects/requirements: All aspects of showbusiness and the performing arts – vin-tage and current films, both stills and film star portraits; TV personalities and performers; pop stars; opera, stage and ballet artists.
Markets supplied: Television, newspapers, book publishers, magazines and advertising.
Stock: B&W and colour. 35mm upwards for colour.
Usual terms of business: No minimum submission or retention period.
Commission: 50 per cent.
Additional information: "Most of our photographers operate in Hollywood, but we also have a constant demand for British material – old stock pictures as well as new. We welcome photogra-phers' lists or catalogues of available subjects."

AQUILA PHOTOGRAPHICS*
PO Box 1, Haydon House, Alcester Road, Studley, Warwickshire B80 7AN. Tel: 0527 852357.
Contact: Alan J. Richards (Director).
Specialist subjects/requirements: All natural history. Birds a speciality.
Markets supplied: Books and magazine publishers, calendars, greetings cards, TV, video, etc.
Stock: Colour only. All formats.
Usual terms of business: Minimum initial submission of 200 transparencies.
Commission: 50 per cent.
Additional information: Phone or write for *modus operandi* before submission of material. All submissions must include return postage.

BMV PICTUREBANK*
79 Farringdon Road, London EC1M 3JY. Tel: 071-405 5021.
Contact: Nigel Messett (Partner).
Specialist subjects/requirements: World travel a speciality, but also general subjects:

abstracts, agriculture, industry, people, natural history, sport, science, etc.
Markets supplied: Advertising, design, publishing, travel operators, AV and record companies.
Stock: Colour only. 35mm upwards.
Usual terms of business: Prefer to see 500 pictures initially, plus regular submissions.
Minimum retention period: 3 years.
Commission: 50 per cent.

BARNABY'S PICTURE LIBRARY*
19 Rathbone Street, London W1P 1AF. Tel: 071-636 6128.
Contacts: John and Mary Buckland (Directors).
Specialist subjects/requirements: All subjects, including large historic collection.
Markets supplied: Books, magazines, television, advertising, audio visual.
Stock: B&W and colour. All formats.
Usual terms of business: Minimum initial submission: 200 pictures. Minimum retention period: 4 years.
Commission: 50 per cent.

THE BRIDGEMAN ART LIBRARY*
19 Chepstow Road, London W2 5BP. Tel: 071-727 4065.
Contact: David Hopwood (Marketing Manager).
Specialist subjects/requirements: European and Oriental paintings and prints, antiques, antiquities, arms and armour, botanical subjects, ethnography, general historical subjects and personalities, maps and manuscripts, natural history, topography, transport, etc.
Markets supplied: Publishing, advertising, television, greetings cards, calendars, etc.
Stock: Mainly colour but some B&W. Minimum 5x4in transparencies.
Usual terms of business: No minimum initial submission. Retention period negotiable.
Commission: 50 per cent.

BUBBLES PHOTO LIBRARY*
23a Benwell Road, London N7 7BL. Tel: 071-609 4547.
Contacts: Sarah Robinson, Loisjoy Thurstun (Directors).
Specialist subjects/requirements: Babies, children, pregnancy, mothercare, child development, old age, family life, women's health and medical.
Markets supplied: Books, magazines and advertising.
Stock: Colour only. 35mm upwards.
Usual terms of business: Minimum submission: 100 transparencies. Regular contributions expected. Minimum retention period: 3 years.
Commission: 50 per cent.
Additional information: "Attractive women and children sell best. Photographers must pay close attention to selecting models that are healthy-looking and make sure that backgrounds are uncluttered. Best clothes to wear are light coloured and neutral fashion."

CAMERA PRESS LTD*
21 Queen Elizabeth Street, London SE1 2PD. Tel: 071-378 1300.
Contact: Jacqui Ann Wald (Managing Editor).
Specialist subjects/requirements: Mainly photo reportage. Also portraits of newsworthy personalities. Material suitable for women's magazines: general interest features, humour, science, pop, travel and stock.
Stock: B&W and colour. All formats.
Usual terms of business: "By mutual agreement."
Commission: 50 per cent.
Additional information: "Please submit only material that is excellent artistically, technically and, ideally, also journalistically."

J. ALLAN CASH LTD*
74 South Ealing Road, London W5 4QB. Tel: 081-840 4141.
Contact: Alan Denny (Manager).
Specialist subjects/requirements: All subjects reflecting the world and its people.
Markets supplied: General and educational publishing, travel, advertising, design.
Stock: B&W and colour. 35mm transparencies accepted if of top quality; prefer medium format and 5x4in.
Usual terms of business: Minimum initial submission: 100 pictures. Minimum retention period: 3 years; 12 months notice of withdrawal.
Commission: 50 per cent.
Additional information: "Please write for further details first."

CEPHAS PICTURE LIBRARY*
20 Bedster Gardens, West Molesey, Surrey KT8 1SZ. Tel: 081-979 8647.
Contacts: Michael and Annie Rock (Proprietors).
Specialist subjects/requirements: All aspects of all countries: people, family life, landscapes, festivals and ceremonies, agriculture, industry, buildings, tourism, food, religion, etc. Vineyards and the wine industry a major speciality. Good pictures of people always required: individuals, couples, families, groups, etc; all ages in all situations.
Markets supplied: Advertising, publishing, etc.
Stock: Colour. 35mm and medium format.
Usual terms of business: "To enable us to judge quality we ask to see your 40 best transparencies not more than two years old. Write first with stamp for Contributors' Information Sheet. Photographers with quality material and a professional attitude are always required."
Commission: 50 per cent.

BRUCE COLEMAN LTD
16 Chiltern Business Village, Arundel Road, Uxbridge, Middlesex UB8 2SN. Tel: 0895 257094.
Contact: Ian Thraves (Picture Editor).
Specialist subjects/requirements: Natural history, geographical, travel, scenics, archaeology, medical, science, anthropology, geological, horticulture, marine.
Markets supplied: Book publishers, magazines, advertising agencies, calendar publishers.
Stock: Colour only. 35mm, medium format and 5x4in.
Usual terms of business: Minimum submission: 250 transparencies. Minimum retention period: 5 years.
Commission: 50 per cent.
Additional information: Contributors are asked to write for library literature first.

COLLECTIONS*
13 Woodberry Crescent, London N10 1PJ. Tel: 081-883 0083.
Contacts: Brian Shuel (Director), Laura Boswell (Manager).
Specialist subjects: The British Isles only; subjects or areas covered in depth by individual photographers.
Markets supplied: All, but particularly books and magazines.
Stock: B&W and colour. All colour formats but not prints except in exceptional circumstances. B&W, 10x8in preferred.
Usual terms of business: By arrangement.
Commission: 50 per cent.
Additional information: "Most of our contributors are considerable experts on their subjects but we insist that they are good photographers too. We impose no conditions on our photographers except that their subject must be *thoroughly covered*. Obviously some subjects are 'bigger' than others, but we like to think that when clients ask for *anything* from one of our stated collections we will have it. Some photographers are building collections with our advice."

COLORIFIC PHOTO LIBRARY LTD*

Visual House, 1 Mastmaker Road, London E14 9WT. Tel: 071-515 3000.

Contacts: Christopher Angeloglou (General Manager), Maggie Gowan (Library Manager).

Specialist subjects/requirements: General top quality photography: industry, agriculture, beaches, couples, generic, life style, travel, skies, high tech.

Markets supplied: Advertising, books, brochures, calendars, and the whole editorial market.

Stock: Mainly colour. 35mm.

Usual terms of business: Minimum initial submission: 500 transparencies. Minimum retention period: 3 years.

Commission: 50 per cent.

Additional information: Material must be fully captioned and carry photographer's name. Introductory letters must include s.a.e.

DAGNALL WORLDWIDE PHOTO LIBRARY*

Far Mount Farm, Intake Lane, Upper Cumberworth, Huddersfield, W.Yorkshire HD8 8YE. Tel: 0484 689509.

Contact: Ian Dagnall (Proprietor).

Specialist subjects/requirements: Any travel-related subjects worldwide, including UK. Particularly interested in quality pictures of people in a holiday environment.

Markets supplied: All markets but particularly travel brochures and magazines.

Stock: Colour only. Medium or larger format, but 35mm considered if of exceptional quality.

Usual terms of business: Minimum initial submission: 100 transparencies. Minimum retention period: 2 years.

Commission: 50 per cent.

Additional information: Only the highest-quality material will be considered and all pictures must be accurately captioned.

JAMES DAVIS TRAVEL PHOTOGRAPHY*

30 Hengistbury Road, New Milton, Hampshire BH25 7LU. Tel: 0425 610328.

Contact: James Davis (Proprietor).

Specialist subjects/requirements: Worldwide travel coverage – people, places, emotive and tourism.

Markets supplied: Travel brochures, publishing, designers and advertising agencies.

Stock: Colour. 6x6cm or larger preferred, on Fujichrome or Ektachrome, usually 50 or 100 ASA. 35mm only acceptable where it is impracticable or impossible to use larger format.

Usual terms of business: Minimum initial submission not less than 300 transparencies.

Commission: 50 per cent.

DEFENCE PICTURE LIBRARY (PHOTO PRESS DEFENCE)

Glider House, 14 Addison Road, Plymouth, Devon PL4 8LL. Tel: 0752 251271.

Contact: David Reynolds (Director).

Specialist subjects/requirements: Military images covering all areas of the armed forces worldwide.

Markets supplied: Publishers etc.

Stock: Colour only. 35mm and medium format.

Usual terms of business: Minimum initial submission: 50 quality transparencies. Minimum retention period: 1 year.

Commission: 50 per cent.

Additional information: Always keen to hear from photographers who attend military airshows and tattoos. Welcomes submissions from retired servicemen who have collections of particular interest, such as the Falklands or Gulf War.

ECOSCENE*
The Oasts, Headley Lane, Passfield, Liphook, Hampshire GU30 7RX. Tel: 0428 751056.
Contact: Sally Morgan (Proprietor).
Specialist subjects/requirements: Ecology and the environment, natural history with special emphasis on ecology and environmental issues worldwide.
Markets supplied: Books, magazines, organisations, etc.
Stock: Colour only. All formats.
Usual terms of business: Minimum retention period: 2 years.
Commission: 55 per cent to photographer.
Additional information: Contributors' guidelines available on request.

EMPICS LTD*
26 Musters Road, West Bridgford, Nottinghamshire NG2 7PL. Tel: 0602 455885.
Contact: Colin Panter (Librarian).
Specialist subjects/requirements: Sport; most interested in the unusual, not run-of-the-mill coverage. Some scope for general hard news and topical features; the agency has an electronic picture desk and wire service for extensive syndication.
Markets supplied: Newspapers, magazines, etc.
Stock: Colour only. 35mm and colour neg.
Usual terms of business: No minimum terms.
Commission: 50 per cent.
Additional information: Always happy to consider unusual and exclusive material.

EURO-PARLY SERVICES
2 Denbigh Place, Westminster, London SW1V 2HB. Tel: 071-834 2889/071-730 8976 (24 hr).
Contact: Myles Sweeney (Director).
Specialist subjects/requirements: News pictures; current affairs; head and shoulders shots of hard news personalities (politicians etc). Specialist stock of London from unusual angles and street furnishings (statues, street lamps, etc).
Markets supplied: National and provincial press; general publishers.
Stock: B&W and colour. All formats.
Usual terms of business: Minimum initial submission: 250. Minimum retention period: 1 year.
Commission: 50 per cent.
Additional information: Picture wire facility for sending to provincial evening press from London. Darkroom also available for use (within walking distance of Whitehall). Cuttings service, mainly on European Parliament.

EUROART AGENCY AND LIBRARY
PO Box 533, London SE24 0QJ. 369 Shakespeare Road, London SE24 0QE. Tel: 071-733 7241.
Contact: Mr P. M. Minyo (Proprietor).
Specialist subjects/requirements: General stock material to illustrate particular subjects; fine art photography in limited editions; creative and artistic images to suit postcards and greetings cards. Also "green" issues in Europe, including Eastern Europe.
Markets supplied: Publishers, advertising, museums, calendars and cards, etc.
Stock: B&W and colour. B&W minimum size 10x8in, prefer A4. Colour, medium format and 5x4in transparencies preferred, but high quality 35mm (Kodachrome or Fujichrome/Velvia) is acceptable.
Usual terms of business: No minimum submission but regular contributions expected. Minimum retention period: 3 years. 1 year notice of withdrawal.
Commission: 50 per cent.
Additional information: Pictures sent must be captioned with name, year and place. "We would like to hear from photographers who are able to produce high quality business portrait, product shot and advertising photography on commission. Further details of particular requirements will be sent on request."

GREG EVANS PHOTO LIBRARY*

91 Charlotte Street, London W1P 1LB. Tel: 071-636 8238.

Contacts: Greg Evans (Director), Lorna Joseph (Picture Editor).

Specialist subjects/requirements: Travel material and general subjects. Special interest in sports, industry, food and business photography.

Markets supplied: Editorial, advertising, etc.

Stock: Colour only. 35mm acceptable but larger formats preferred.

Usual terms of business: No minimum initial submission. Minimum retention period: 3 years.

Commission: 50 per cent.

EYE UBIQUITOUS*

1 Brunswick Road, Hove, East Sussex BN3 1DG. Tel: 0273 326135.

Contact: Paul Seheult (Proprietor).

Specialist subjects/requirements: General worldwide stock and social documentary material.

Markets supplied: Publishing markets, UK and European advertising agencies.

Stock: Colour only. All formats.

Usual terms of business: Suggested minimum submission 200 transparencies, but terms are open to discussion.

Commission: 50 per cent.

FOOTPRINTS COLOUR PICTURE LIBRARY*

Goldfin Cottage, Maidlands Farm, Broad Oak, Rye, East Sussex TN31 6BJ. Tel: 0424 883078.

Principal: Paula Leaver (Proprietor).

Specialist subjects/requirements: Worldwide travel and related subjects; underwater photography including scuba diving, snorkelling and marine life.

Markets supplied: Books, magazines, etc.

Stock: Colour only. 35mm.

Usual terms of business: No minimum initial submission. Minimum retention period: 2 years.

Commission: 50 per cent.

Additional information: All material must be up-to-date.

FOTOCCOMPLI

11 Ampton Road, Birmingham B15 2UH. Tel: 021-454 3305.

Contact: Ken Williams (Proprietor).

Specialist subjects/requirements: All subjects; this is the only comprehensive library in the West Midlands.

Markets supplied: Various.

Stock: Colour only. All formats from 35mm up. For the latter, Kodachrome, Fujichrome 50 or Velvia preferred.

Usual terms of business: No minimum initial submission but a selection of 50-100 transparencies would be expected. Minimum retention period: 2 years.

Commission: 50 per cent.

Additional information: Prefer to hear from photographers who specialise in one particular subject or theme, but not essential.

LESLIE GARLAND PICTURE LIBRARY*

69 Fern Avenue, Jesmond, Newcastle upon Tyne NE2 2QU. Tel: 091-281 3442.

Contact: Leslie Garland, ARPS, LBIPP (Proprietor).

Specialist subjects/requirements: General coverage of the North of England (Yorkshire, Lancashire, Cleveland, Durham, Cumbria, Tyne & Wear, Northumberland), especially people and lifestyles, industry, engineering, science and technology, medicine. Also Scandinavia.

Markets supplied: Advertising, books, brochures, exhibitions, magazines, etc.

Stock: Colour only. Medium format or larger transparencies preferred, but 35mm considered

depending on subject matter.
Usual terms of business: Minimum initial submission 50 accepted images. Minimum retention period: 3 years.
Commission: 50 per cent.
Additional information: All pictures must be of top quality professional standard with precise captions. Write enclosing s.a.e. for further details first.

GEO AERIAL PHOTOGRAPHY
4 Christian Fields, London SW16 3JZ. Tel: 081-764 6292.
Contact: John Douglas (Director).
Specialist subjects/requirements: Worldwide low oblique aerial photographs.
Markets supplied: Books, magazines, advertising.
Stock: Colour only. 35mm or larger format.
Usual terms of business: Negotiable.
Commission: 50 per cent.
Additional information: Locations must be identified in detail. Do not send samples of work but contact by letter/telephone first.

THE ROBERT HARDING PICTURE LIBRARY LTD*
58-59 Great Marlborough Street, London W1V 1DD. Tel: 071-287 5414.
Contact: Teresa Black, Nelly Boyd (Picture Editors).
Specialist subjects/requirements: People, places and objects worldwide.
Markets supplied: Publishers, advertising agencies, design groups, calendar publishers, etc.
Stock: Colour. All formats from 35mm up.
Usual terms of business: An initial sample of 100 transparencies "to enable us to judge quality and saleability." Minimum retention period: 3 years; 12 months notice of withdrawal.
Commission: 50 per cent.

HOLT STUDIOS INTERNATIONAL*
The Courtyard, 24 High Street, Hungerford, Berkshire RG17 0NF. Tel: 0488 683523.
Contact: Andy Morant (Commercial Director).
Specialist subjects/requirements: Pictorial and technical photographs of worldwide agriculture and horticulture, crop production and protection, livestock, pests, conservation, the environment and wildlife.
Markets supplied: Agricultural organisations, educational publishers, advertising agencies, etc.
Stock: Colour only. 35mm and medium format.
Usual terms of business: To be negotiated.
Commission: Usually 50 per cent.
Additional information: "Our photographers combine specialist technical, scientific or agricultural knowledge with their photographic skills to produce outstanding photographs."

HOUSES & INTERIORS PHOTOGRAPHIC FEATURES AGENCY*
Warwick House, 7 Nevill Street, Tunbridge Wells, Kent TN2 5RU. Tel: 0892 524404.
Contact: Richard Wiles (Director).
Specialist subjects/requirements: Stylish house interiors and exteriors covering all types of property, architectural and decorative details, home improvements, gardens and gardening techniques, cookery and landscapes. Also complete illustrated feature packages on individual homes, step-by-step DIY and home improvements projects, etc., produced in association with the agency.
Markets supplied: Magazines, books, partworks and advertising.
Stock: Mostly colour (B&W only required for some home improvements subjects). Medium format transparencies preferred, but top quality 35mm considered.
Usual terms of business: No minimum submission. Minimum retention period: 3 years.
Commission: 50 per cent for stock pictures; negotiable for speculative feature work. After first

use feature pictures go into the stock library for further sales at the usual 50 per cent commission.

Additional information: A finder's fee is paid to photographers who provide suitable locations. The agency also produces magazines, partworks and books for publishers, where possible using stock pictures. They are keen to develop projects with photographers, using new photographic work.

THE HUTCHISON LIBRARY*

118b Holland Park Avenue, London W11 4UA. Tel: 071-229 2743.
Contact: Kate Pink (Library Manager).
Specialist subjects/requirements: Worldwide coverage of agriculture, industry, landscapes, festivals and ceremonies, decoration, religion, urban and village life, tourism, flora and fauna, medicine and education, architecture, art, craft, etc. etc.
Markets supplied: Publishing, company reports, calendars, advertising, audio visual.
Stock: Colour only. 35mm and medium format.
Usual terms of business: Minimum initial submission: 1,000 transparencies. No minimum retention period.
Commission: 50 per cent.
Additional information: "We only occasionally take on new photographers. Collections should either be in-depth documentary work (medical, environment, agriculture, supernatural, etc.) or be as varied as possible in geographical and subject coverage."

INTERFOTO PICTURE LIBRARY LTD

Southbank House, Black Prince Road, London SE1 7SJ. Tel: 071-582 3060.
Contact: Tim Shirley (Director).
Specialist subjects/requirements: Countries and their landmarks and places of interest, people, industry, family life at work and play. A separate department is dedicated to archival photographs.
Markets supplied: Publishers, advertising agencies, etc.
Stock: Mainly colour. 6x7cm preferred, but will consider 35mm.
Usual terms of business: Negotiable.
Commission: Usually 50 per cent.

INTERNATIONAL STOCK EXCHANGE PHOTO LIBRARY/POWERSTOCK*

Roman House, 9/10 College Terrace, London E3 5AN. Tel: 081-983 4222.
Contact: Ian Lishman (Proprietor).
Specialist subjects/requirements: World business centres: skylines and city views, people in business situations, technology, medicine, engineering, energy supply, transport, industry, agriculture, manufacturing. Also travel, sport, people, lifestyles, environment, nature.
Markets supplied: Advertising, publishing, audio visual, public relations, travel.
Stock: Colour only. All formats.
Usual terms of business: Minimum initial submission 50 transparencies.
Commission: 50 per cent.
Additional information: Only top quality material will be considered.

JAYAWARDENE TRAVEL PHOTO LIBRARY

7A Napier Road, Wembley, Middx HA0 4UA. Tel: 081-902 3588.
Contact: Rohith Jayawardene (Proprietor).
Specialist subjects/requirements: Worldwide holiday and business travel. Cities, resorts, festivals, local life, people on holiday, beaches/watersports, local food, markets, restaurants, shopping, historic sites, rural scenes, cruising, winter resorts/sports, air travel.
Markets supplied: Travel industry, publishing.
Stock: Colour. 35mm and medium format only.

Commission: 50 per cent.
Usual terms of business: Minimum initial submission: 200 transparencies, none more than two years old. Minimum retention period: 5 years.
Additional information: Pictures must be accurately captioned and supplied in card or plastic mounts. Telephone first to discuss submission.

FRANK LANE PICTURE AGENCY LTD*
Pages Green House, Wetheringsett, Stowmarket, Suffolk IP14 5QA. Tel: 0728 860789.
Contacts: Jean Lane, David Hosking (Directors).
Specialist subjects/requirements: natural history and weather phenomena: Birds, clouds, fish, fungi, insects, marine, mammals, pollution, rainbows, sea reptiles, sea snow, seasons, trees, underwater, hurricanes, earthquakes, lightning, volcanoes, dew, rain, fog, etc. Ecology and the environment. Horse, dog and cat breeds.
Markets supplied: Book publishers, advertising agencies, magazines.
Stock: B&W and colour. 35mm and medium format transparencies. Kodachrome preferred for 35mm.
Usual terms of business: Minimum initial submission: 500 transparencies. Minimum retention period: 3 years.
Commission: 50 per cent.
Additional information: "Competition in the natural history field is fierce, so only really sharp, well-composed pictures stand a chance. Sales are slow to start with, and a really keen photographer must be prepared to invest money in building up stock to the 1,000 mark."

MONITOR SYNDICATION*
17 Old Street, London EC1V 9HL. Tel: 071-253 7071.
Contact: Mac Palmer (Manager).
Specialist subjects/requirements: Portraits of personalities from sport, commerce, politics, showbusiness; Royals; well known buildings in London.
Markets supplied: National and international press, television, advertising, publishers, etc.
Stock: B&W and colour. 35mm and medium format.
Usual terms of business: No minimum submission.
Commission: 50 per cent, but may make outright purchase offer for suitable material.

NHPA (NATURAL HISTORY PHOTOGRAPHIC AGENCY)*
Little Tye, High Street, Ardingly, Sussex RH17 6TB. Tel: 0444 892514.
Contact: Tim Harris (Director).
Specialist subjects/requirements: Worldwide wildlife, domestic animals and pets, plants, landscapes, agriculture and environmental subjects. Endangered and appealing wildlife of particular interest.
Markets supplied: Books and other publishing media, advertising and design, magazines.
Stock: Mainly colour, some B&W. 35mm, medium format and larger original transparencies. High quality large format dupes.
Usual terms of business: Minimum initial submission: 100 transparencies.
Commission: 40 per cent.
Additional information: Pictures should be strong, active and well-composed.

NATURAL IMAGE
Carey's Meadow, 49 Bickerley Road, Ringwood, Hampshire BH24 1EG. Tel: 0425 478742.
Contacts: Bob and Liz Gibbons (Proprietors).
Specialist subjects/requirements: Natural history, the countryside, gardens and gardening, worldwide travel with a wildlife or conservation bias.
Markets supplied: Books, magazines, etc.
Stock: Colour only. 35mm upwards.

Usual terms of business: Minimum initial submission: 50 slides. Minimum retention period: 1 year.
Commission: 40 per cent.
Additional information: Material must be accurately and informatively captioned, and be of very high quality.

NATURAL SCIENCE PHOTOS*

33 Woodland Drive, Watford, Hertfordshire WD1 3BY. Tel: 0923 245265.
Contacts: Peter Ward (Director).
Specialist subjects/requirements: All types of living organisms including wildlife of every description, domestic animals and fowl, botany (including destruction and reclamation), ecology, geology, geography, climate and effects, astronomy, pollution and effects, primitive people and their ways of life, countryside topics and scenics, latter mostly without artifacts. The building of an angling library, both sea and freshwater, is being undertaken.
Markets supplied: Books, magazines, newspapers, calendars, audio-visual, television and advertising, both UK and overseas. Some inter-agency deals.
Stock: Colour only. Mainly 35mm, but larger formats accepted.
Usual terms of business: No minimum submission. Standard contract allows for 3 years retention and is non-exclusive.
Commission: 33 per cent.
Additional information: "All material to be clearly captioned and well documented – English and scientific names, locality and photographer; also any useful additional information."

THE NORTHERN PICTURE LIBRARY*

Unit 2, Bentinck Street Industrial Estate, Ellesmere Street, Manchester M15 4LN. Tel: 061-834 1255.
Contact: Roy Conchie (Proprietor).
Specialist subjects/requirements: UK and world views, glamour, sport, industrial scenery, tourist views, natural history, people at work and leisure, picnics, walks, golf, tennis, etc.
Markets supplied: Advertising, packaging, calendars, greetings cards, travel.
Stock: Mainly colour. Minimum 35mm; prefers 6x7cm or 5x4in.
Usual terms of business: No minimum submission: "we want quality rather than quantity. "Minimum retention period: "normally 3 years but not obligatory."
Commission: 50 per cent.

OXFORD SCIENTIFIC FILMS LTD*

Lower Road, Long Hanborough, Witney OX8 8LL. Tel: 0993 881881.
Contacts: Sandra Berry (Director), Suzanne Aitzemuller (Assistant Manager).
Specialist subjects/requirements: High quality wildlife photography, plus the environment, pollution and conservation, landscapes, rural crafts, agriculture, high-speed photography, special effects. Also complete illustrated articles on wildlife and related subjects.
Markets supplied: Wildlife/general magazines, book publishers, advertising/design companies, etc.
Stock: Mainly colour. All formats up to and including 5x4in.
Usual terms of business: Minimum initial submission 100 transparencies. Minimum retention period: 2 years.
Commission: 50 per cent on stock sales; 40 per cent on articles.
Additional information: All material must be of a very high technical standard – perfectly sharp and exposed – and well composed.

PANOS PICTURES*

9 White Lion Street, London N1 9PD. Tel: 071-837 7505.
Contact: Adrian Evans (Library Manager).

Specialist subjects/requirements: Documentary coverage of the Third World and Eastern Europe, focusing on social, economic and political issues and with special emphasis on environment and development. Also agriculture, education, energy, health, industry, landscape, people, religions, rural life, urban life, etc.
Markets supplied: Newspapers and magazines, book publishers, development agencies.
Stock: B&W and colour. 35mm.
Usual terms of business: No minimum initial submission or retention period.
Commission: 50 per cent.
Additional information: All profits from the library are covenented to the Panos Institute, an international development studies group.

PHOTO LIBRARY INTERNATIONAL*

PO Box 75, Leeds, West Yorkshire LS7 3NZ. Tel: 0532 623005.
Contact: Kevin Horgan (Managing Director).
Specialist subjects/requirements: General, commercial, industrial and travel subjects.
Markets supplied: Advertising, travel brochures, greetings cards, publishers, etc.
Stock: Colour only. From 35mm up.
Usual terms of business: Minimum retention period: 3 years, with 12 months notice of withdrawal. Or pictures purchased outright.
Commission: 50 per cent – or outright purchase.
Additional information: List of current requirements sent on receipt of s.a.e.

PICKTHALL PICTURE LIBRARY LTD

68 East Ham Road, Littlehampton, West Sussex BN17 7BE. Tel: 0903 730614.
Contact: Lesley Chilton (Director).
Specialist subjects/requirements: Sailing and windsurfing; British rural and coastal scenes; natural history and wildlife; world travel.
Markets supplied: Publishing and other media.
Stock: Colour only. 35mm and medium format.
Usual terms of business: No minimum initial submission, but contributors should be regular and continuous. No minimum retention period.
Commission: 50 per cent.

PICTOR INTERNATIONAL LTD

Twyman House, 31-39 Camden Road, London NW1 9LR. Tel: 071-482 0478.
Contact: Russell Glenister (Creative Director).
Specialist subjects/requirements: General library handling all subjects.
Markets supplied: Advertising, calendars, posters, greetings cards, holiday brochures, books, encyclopedias, company reports, etc.
Stock: Colour only. All formats.
Usual terms of business: Minimum initial submission: 200 transparencies.
Commission: 50 per cent.

PICTUREPOINT LTD*

94b Dedworth Road, Windsor, Berkshire SL4 5AY. Tel: 0753 833680.
Contact: Ken Gibson (Director).
Specialist subjects/requirements: World economic geography, sports, pastimes, industry, agriculture, travel.
Markets supplied: Books, travel, advertising, etc.
Stock: Colour only. 6x6cm or larger preferred (but top quality 35mm acceptable on subjects demanding this size).

Usual terms of business: Minimum initial submission must produce at least 100 retained transparencies. Minimum retention period: 5 years.
Commission: 50 per cent.
Additional information: "We only handle work of the highest quality."

PLANET EARTH PICTURES*
4 Harcourt Street, London W1H 1DS. Tel: 071-262 4427.
Contact: Gillian Lythgoe (Managing Director), Jennifer Jeffrey (Manager).
Specialist subjects/requirements: Natural history – marine and land, wildlife, landscape/ecology photography.
Markets supplied: Books, magazines, advertising, calendars, posters.
Stock: Colour only. All formats.
Usual terms of business: No minimum submission, but "the more photographs that a photographer can leave in the library, the more chance he has of a reasonable return." Terms of business in more detail available on request.
Commission: 50 per cent.
Additional information: "We like to have a close working relationship with all our photographers."

POPPERFOTO*
Paul Popper Ltd, The Old Mill, Overstone Farm, Overstone, Northampton NN6 0AB. Tel: 0604 670670.
Contact: Julie Quiery (Picture Editor).
Specialist subjects/requirements: General library handling all subjects. Also feature material.
Markets supplied: Books, periodical publishers, TV, and advertising.
Stock: B&W and colour. 35mm, medium format and 5x4in. B&W, 10x8in prints.
Usual terms of business: Minimum retention period: 3 years.
Commission: 50 per cent.

REDFERNS*
7 Bramley Road, London W10 6SZ. Tel: 071-792 9914.
Contact: Dede Millar (Partner).
Specialist subjects/requirements: All forms of popular music, with special concentration on the past 40 years. Also related subjects such as musical instruments, and some classical material.
Markets supplied: Newspapers, magazines, books, etc.
Stock: B&W and colour. 35mm and medium format.
Usual terms of business: Negotiable.
Commission: 50 per cent.
Additional information: It is preferred that contributors are professional or serious semi-pro photographers who are able to offer extensive coverage.

RETNA PICTURES LTD*
1 Fitzroy Mews, Cleveland Street, London W1P 5DQ. Tel: 071-388 3444.
Contact: Jenny Kirby (Manager).
Specialist subjects/requirements: Portraits and performance shots of rock and pop performers, actors and actresses, entertainers and other celebrities including politicians and business personalities. Expanding general stock library section covering travel, wildlife, people, sport and leisure.
Markets supplied: Newspapers, magazines, books, record companies, advertising.
Stock: B&W and colour, any format.
Usual terms of business: None specified.
Commission: 55 per cent.

REX FEATURES LTD*
18 Vine Hill, London EC1R 5DX. Tel: 071-278 7294.
Contact: Michael Selby (Director).
Specialist subjects/requirements: Human interest and general features, personalities, animals (singles and series), humour, high class glamour, current affairs, topographical, general library, stock material.
Markets supplied: UK national newspapers and magazines, book publishers, audio visual, television and international press. Daily worldwide syndication.
Stock: B&W and colour. All formats.
Usual terms of business: No minimum submission. Preferred minimum retention period: 2 years.
Commission: 50 per cent.

SCIENCE PHOTO LIBRARY*
112 Westbourne Grove, London W2 5RU. Tel: 071-727 4712.
Contact: Rosemary Taylor (Director).
Specialist subjects/requirements: All types of scientific, industrial and medical imagery, from micrography to astronomical photography. Also includes photographs of equipment, laboratories, factories and relevant personalities.
Markets supplied: Books, magazines, advertising, design, corporate, audio visual.
Stock: Mainly colour. 35mm accepted, but prefer medium format.
Usual terms of business: No minimum submission. Minimum retention period: usually 4 years.
Commission: 50 per cent.
Additional information: All photographs must be accompanied by full caption information, but preferably in non-technical language.

SCOTLAND IN FOCUS
22 Fleming Place, Fountainhall, Galashiels, Selkirkshire TD1 2TA. Tel: 0578 760256.
Contact: Bob Lawson (Proprietor).
Specialist subjects/requirements: All areas of Scotland and aspects of Scottish life, particularly town and city life, transport, industry, communications, environment and wildlife.
Markets supplied: Books, brochures and magazines, design and advertising, cards and calendars.
Stock: B&W and colour. Low ASA 35mm transparencies welcome; medium and larger formats preferred.
Usual terms of business: Minimum initial submission 100 transparencies.
Commission: 50 per cent.
Additional information: "Only interested in sharp, well-composed images suitable for reproduction. We would rather see quality than quantity. For selection purposes we prefer transparencies in slide wallets or black mask sleeves, each transparency captioned and numbered including a separate list for identification."

SPECTRUM COLOUR LIBRARY*
41/42 Berners Street, London W1P 3AA. Tel: 071-637 1587.
Contacts: Keith Jones, Ann Jones (Directors).
Specialist subjects/requirements: Travel, natural history, people, general.
Markets supplied: Advertising, publishing, travel brochures, etc.
Stock: Colour only. 35mm transparencies if exceptional, but prefers larger formats.
Usual terms of business: Minimum initial submission: 500 pictures. Minimum retention period: 5 years.
Commission: 50 per cent.

SPORTING PICTURES (UK) LTD*
7a Lambs Conduit Passage, London WC1 4RG. Tel: 071-405 4500.
Contact: Steve Brown (Picture Editor).
Specialist subjects/requirements: Sporting events and personalities worldwide. Pictures required from both major events and leisure activities.
Markets supplied: Newspapers, magazines, books, etc.
Stock: B&W and colour. All formats.
Usual terms of business: No minimum initial submission.
Commission: 50 per cent.

THE STILL MOVING PICTURE COMPANY*
67A Logie Green Road, Edinburgh EH7 4HF. Tel: 031-557 9697.
Contacts: John Hutchinson, Sue Hall (Directors).
Specialist subjects/requirements: All Scottish subjects; scenics, travel, commerce, industry, wildlife, sport and culture. Also worldwide travel material.
Markets supplied: Publishing, advertising, tourism, etc.
Stock: Colour only. All formats.
Usual terms of business: No minimum initial submission. Retention period variable, but usually at least 1 year.
Commission: 50 per cent.
Additional information: A full "wants" list can be supplied on request.

TONY STONE IMAGES*
Worldwide House, 116 Bayham Street, London NW1 0BA. Tel: 071-267 8988.
Contact: Ruth Adams (Creative Coordinator).
Specialist subjects/requirements: Subjects commonly used in advertising.
Markets supplied: Advertising agencies; travel industry worldwide.
Stock: Colour only. All formats.
Usual terms of business: On application. Send ten outstanding pictures in first instance.
Commission: 50 per cent.
Additional information: Only truly outstanding material considered.

SWIFT PICTURE LIBRARY*
Claremont, Redwood Close, Ringwood, Hampshire BH24 1PR. Tel: 0425 478333.
Contact: Mike Read (Proprietor).
Specialist subjects/requirements: Natural history, landscape and scenics, conservation, environment, pollution, alternative energy.
Markets supplied: Magazines, books, calendars, exhibitions, advertising, travel brochures, environmental groups.
Stock: Colour only. 35mm and medium format.
Usual terms of business: Initial submission: 200 transparencies. Minimum retention period: 5 years.
Commission: 50 per cent.
Additional information: Prefer photographers who can contribute a regular supply of top quality pictures.

THE TELEGRAPH COLOUR LIBRARY*
Visual House, One Mastmaker Road, London E14 9TE. Tel: 071-987 1212.
Contact: Tim Lund (Director).
Specialist subjects/requirements: Animals, coastline, commerce, ecology, education, entertainment, health, industry, landscape, occupations, people, personalities, technology, transport, space exploration, sport.
Markets supplied: Advertising and publishing.

Stock: B&W and colour. All formats.
Usual terms of business: Minimum initial submission: 100 to start contract, to be followed up with regular additional submissions. Minimum retention period: 5 years.
Commission: 50 per cent.
Additional information: "We're always seeking new top quality material on a variety of subjects, particularly action, animals and sports, natural and man-made disasters, bad weather (including electrical storms), people (especially crowds, children and families), industry and technology."

TRAVEL PHOTO INTERNATIONAL
8 Delph Common Road, Aughton, Ormskirk, Lancashire L39 5DW. Tel: 0695 423720.
Contact: Vivienne Crimes (Director).
Specialist subjects/requirements: World travel and tourist material.
Markets supplied: Travel brochures, books, general advertising.
Stock: Colour only. 35mm accepted but larger formats preferred.
Usual terms of business: Minimum initial submission: 100 pictures. Minimum retention period: 3 years.
Commission: 50 per cent.
Additional information: "Pictures must be taken in clear sunlight, have excellent colour saturation, be critically sharp and accurately exposed."

TRAVEL TRADE PHOTOGRAPHY
22 Princedale Road, London W11 4NJ. Tel: 071-727 5471.
Contact: Teddy Schwarz (Proprietor).
Specialist subjects/requirements: Holiday destinations worldwide and activities of tourists (games on beaches, shopping, markets, excursions to places of historic interest, displays of fruit and food, national dances, surfing, boating, eating in the open and in restaurants, etc.). Also ancient monuments and archaeological, ethnographic and folkloristic subjects.
Markets supplied: Travel brochures, guidebooks, etc.
Stock: Colour only. 6x6cm only.
Usual terms of business: No minimum submission. Minimum retention period: 1 year.
Commission: 50 per cent.
Additional information: "We only handle 6x6cm transparencies – no 35mm. Ideally, it would be best if would-be contributors phone for an appointment to show what they have to offer. Unsolicited material will not be returned. Postal inquiries will only be answered if s.a.e. is provided. As for the actual pictures – shots must have been taken under sunny conditions, be of excellent quality and have deep, saturated colour."

TROPIX PHOTOGRAPHIC LIBRARY*
156 Meols Parade, Wirral, Merseyside L47 6AN. Tel: 051-632 1698.
Contact: Veronica Birley (Director).
Specialist subjects/requirements: The Third World and environmental issues worldwide, and almost all subjects in these contexts. Stock from the tropics, sub-tropics and the non-tropical developing world. Coverage of indigenous peoples from other nations (eg, Aborigines, Inuit, North American "Indians"), provided the main focus is on their traditional lifestyles. Environmental coverage accepted from the world over.
Markets supplied: Book and magazine publishers, national press, advertising, etc.
Stock: Colour. 35mm and medium format.
Usual terms of business: Minimum initial submission 250 pictures per country.
Commission: 50 per cent.
Additional information: Images may be positive, negative or simply factual, but will not be considered without detailed and accurate captioning. Technical quality must be very high. Write in the first instance enclosing large s.a.e. for full guidelines.

VISIONBANK LIBRARY LTD & ENGLAND SCENE*

Suite 212, The Business Design Centre, Islington Green, London N1 0QH. Tel: 071-288 6080.
Contact: Ray Daffurn (Managing Director).
Specialist subjects/requirements: All subjects/all countries, especially UK.
Markets supplied: Advertising, publishing and travel markets.
Stock: Colour. All formats.
Usual terms of business: Minimum initial submission: 300+. Minimum retention period: 5 years.
Commission: 50 per cent.

S&I WILLIAMS POWER PIX*

Castle Lodge, Wenvoe, Cardiff CF5 6AD. Tel: 0222 595163.
Contact: Steven Williams (Director).
Specialist subjects/requirements: Girl pix of all kinds, natural history, travel, people, children, families, sub-aqua, industry, mood, abstracts and still life.
Markets supplied: Publishers, advertising, record companies, calendar and greetings card publishers, travel brochures, encyclopedias. Worldwide coverage – agents in Spain, Germany, Japan, Australia and U.S.A.
Stock: Colour only. 35mm acceptable but medium format preferred where practical.
Usual terms of business: Minimum submission 50 transparencies, but contributors must be in a position to submit regularly to build up their stock. Minimum retention period: 5 years.
Commission: 50 per cent.
Additional information: Contributors should write with s.a.e. for free "Photographer's Information" before submitting.

WOODMANSTERNE PUBLICATIONS LTD*

2 Greenhill Crescent, Watford Business Park, Watford, Herts WD1 8RD. Tel: 0923 228236.
Contacts: Paul Woodmansterne, Julia Woodmansterne (Directors).
Specialist subjects/requirements: Archaeology, architecture, arms and armour, ballet and opera, birds, castles, cathedrals, churches, costume, decorative arts, furniture, historic houses, interior design, painting and sculpture, parks and gardens, religious subjects, seasonal scenes, state occasions, travel, etc.
Markets supplied: Publishing, souvenir/novelties, tourism, travel trade.
Stock: Colour only. All formats.
Usual terms of business: Initial submission of at least 250 pictures with regular further additions. To be retained "on semi-permanent basis."
Commission: 50 per cent.
Additional information: "Only top quality pictures per subject, ranging from the record shot to the unusual."

WORLD PICTURES (FEATURE-PIX COLOUR LIBRARY)*

85a Great Portland Street, London W1N 5RA. Tel: 071-437 2121 and 071-436 0440.
Contacts: Gerry Brenes and David Brenes (Directors).
Specialist subjects/requirements: Travel material: cities, resorts, hotels worldwide plus girls, couples and families on holiday suitable for travel brochure, magazine and newspaper use.
Markets supplied: Tour operators, airlines, design houses, advertising agencies.
Stock: Colour only. 6x6cm preferred, otherwise 6x7cm, 6x9cm and 5x4in. No 35mm.
Usual terms of business: No minimum submission but usually likes the chance of placing material for minimum period of 2 years.
Commission: 50 per cent.

ZEFA (UK) LTD
PO Box 210, 20 Conduit Place, London W2 1HZ. Tel: 071-262 1010.
Contact: Harold Harris (Director).
Specialist subjects/requirements: General library handling most subjects.
Markets supplied: Advertising, publishing, etc.
Stock: Colour, and historic B&W. 35mm and medium format transparencies.
Usual terms of business: Minimum initial submission: 200–500. Minimum retention period:
3–5 years.
Commission: 50 per cent.

An asterisk indicates membership of the British Association of Picture Libraries and Agencies.

SERVICES DIRECTORY

This section lists companies providing products and services of use to the photographer. A number of those listed offer discounts to BFP members. To obtain the discounts indicated, members should simply produce their current membership card. In the case of mail order transactions, enclose your membership card with your order, requesting that this be returned with the completed order or as soon as membership has been verified. But in all cases, ensure that your membership card is valid: the discount will not be available to those who present an expired card.

Accessories & Specialised Equipment

STUART ALLEN PHOTOGRAPHY
5 Northdene Road, Chandlers Ford, Eastleigh, Hants SO5 3DW. Tel: 0703 263427.
Supplier of Hancocks lightboxes.
Discount to BFP members: 10%.

CAMERA BELLOWS LTD
Runcorn Works, 2 Runcorn Road, Birmingham B12 8RQ. Tel: 021-440 1695.
Bellows for all photographic purposes in leather and other materials. Replacements for modern and antique cameras.
Discount to BFP members: 2%.

COURTENAY PHOTOGRAPHIC LIGHTING
The Gate Studios, Station Road, Borehamwood, Hertfordshire WD6 1DQ. Tel: 081-905 1177.
Courtenay electronic flash systems.

THE FLASH CENTRE
54 Brunswick Centre, London WC1N 1AE. Tel: 071-837 6163.
Specialist suppliers of studio flash systems.

FOTOLYNX LTD
CCS Centre, Vale Lane, Bedminster, Bristol BS3 5RU. Tel: 0272 635263.
Camera Care Systems, Kaiser Fototechnik, Fotospeed, Chemistry and Sterling Paper.

JESSOP PHOTO CENTRES
Head Office: Jessop House, 98 Scudamore Road, Leicester LE3 1TZ. Tel: 0533 320033.
Specialist suppliers of "Powerflash" portable studio flash, Stag process and enlarger timers, darkroom black-out blinds, portable darkroom tents, darkroom sinks. Plus all general photographic equipment and software.

KJP LTD
Promandis House, Bradbourne Drive, Tilbrook, Milton Keynes MK7 8AJ. Tel: 0908 366344.
Distributors of Bowens, Fidelity, Horseman, Manfrotto, Norman, etc. Branches: London, Aberdeen, Belfast, Birmingham, Bristol, Edinburgh, Manchester and Nottingham.
Discount to BFP members: Negotiable – according to product type.

S. W. KENYON
6 Fore Street, Wellington, Somerset TA21 8AQ. Tel: 0823 664151.
K-Line sprays. ABODIA Slide Storage Systems.

MELICO
Medical & Electrical Instrumentation Co Ltd, Griffin Lane, Aylesbury, Buckinghamshire HP19 3BP. Tel: 0296 86831.
Makers of densitometers. Importers of electronic darkroom doors.

OCEAN OPTICS LTD
13 Northumberland Avenue, London WC2N 5AQ. Tel: 071-930 8408.
Specialist suppliers of underwater photography equipment.

THE PROCESS CONTROL COMPANY
Griffin Lane, Aylesbury, Buckinghamshire HP19 3BP. Tel: 0296 84877.
Makers of processing equipment: racks, spirals, hangers, dryers, sinks and anti-static equipment.

JAMIE WOOD PRODUCTS LTD
Cross Street, Polegate, Sussex BN26 6BN. Tel: 0323 483813.
Makers of photographic hides. Suppliers of photo electronic equipment.
Discount to BFP members: 5%.

Art Services

COLOUR PROCESSING LABORATORIES LTD
Head Office: Fircroft Way, Edenbridge, Kent TN8 6ET. Tel: 0732 862555.
Laboratories also in London, Birmingham, Bristol, Eastleigh, Nottingham, Brentwood, Reading and Portsmouth.
Exhibition design facility, retouching, etc.

DEL & CO
30 Oval Road, London NW1 7DE. Tel: 071-267 7105.
Self-adhesive labels for 35mm slides, printed with name, address or logo. Also plain labels.

MALLARD
Graphic House, Noel Street, Kimberley, Nottingham NG16 2NE. Tel: 0602 382670.
Full service colour laboratory. Exhibition printing, typesetting and graphic arts department.

OBSCURA LTD
34a Bryanston Street, Marble Arch, London W1H 7AH. Tel: 071-723 1487.
Electronic retouching, conventional photocomposition and retouching, etc.

M. A. POPE PRINTERS
'Gomer', Maynard Green, Heathfield, East Sussex TN21 0DG. Tel: 0435 32738.
Flush-fitting printed labels for 35mm slides, including name, address and copyright symbol. Send s.a.e. for details and prices.

QUADRANT (PROCESSING) LTD
23 Sherwood Road, Bromsgrove, Worcestershire B60 3DR. Tel: 0527 71648.
Full range of professional laboratory services plus photoleaflets and photolabels.
Discount to BFP members: 10% against c.w.o.

JAMES SCHUTTE PHOTOGRAPHIC SERVICES
59 Goat Lane, Enfield, Middlesex EN1 4UA. TEL: 081-366 0952.
Specialist in the restoration and enhancement of old photographs using computerised editing techniques.
Discount to BFP members: 10%.

STEEPLEPRINT LTD
5 Mallard Close, Earls Barton, Northampton NN6 0LS. Tel: 0604 810781.
ABLE-LABELS – printed self-adhesive labels.

STONELEIGH COLOUR LABORATORY LTD
Queensway, Leamington Spa, Warwickshire CV31 3JT. Tel: 0926 427030.
Processing and printing, mural displays, dry mounting, graphic design and artwork.
Discount to BFP members: Negotiable – depends on quantity of work.

TREADAWAY PRINTING
Unit 7, Princes Works, Princes Road, Teddington, Middlesex TW11 0RW. Tel: 081-943 4188.
Design, artwork and litho printing. Publicity cards, folders, posters and brochures etc.
Discount to BFP members: 10%.

WALKERPRINT INTERNATIONAL
Classic House, 4th Floor, 174–180 Old Street, London EC1V 9BP. Tel: 071-253 1200.
Design and publicity printers. Photographers' index cards, posters, catalogues, etc.
Discount to BFP members: 10%.

Computer Software

LUPE CUNHA PHOTOGRAPHY
843 Green Lanes, Winchmore Hill, London N21 2RX. Tel: 081-360 0144.
Supplier of "Gofer" library management system, including delivery note and label printing. IBM only.

IRIS AUDIO VISUAL
Unit M, Forest Industrial Park, Forest Road, Hainault, Essex IG6 3HL. Tel: 081-500 2846.
Cradoc CaptionWriter program for library management and label printing. IBM and Mac.

MICROFIELD SCIENTIFIC LTD
'Crowsnest', Rectory Lane, Kingston Bagpuize, Oxon OX13 5AT. Tel: 0865 821348.
Distributor of the Douglas Software Photographer's DataBase – FotoFile (Standard and Plus versions) for storage of picture details and label printing, and Photographer's DataGuide. IBM only.

PHOTODATA
326 Upper Street, London N1 2QX. Tel: 071-609 9321.
Picture Store and PhotoData software packages for cataloguing and labelling. IBM only.

PHOTOMARKETING LTD
Pages Green House, Wetheringsett, Stowmarket, Suffolk IP14 5QA. Tel: 0728 861159.
Distributor of the Phototrack range of software for labelling and filing. IBM and Mac.

Equipment Hire

ANGLIA CAMERAS
15-15a St Matthew's Street, Ipswich IP1 3EL. Tel: 0473 258185.
AV equipment, overhead projectors, screens, etc.

EDRIC AUDIO VISUAL LTD
Oak End Way, Gerrards Cross, Buckinghamshire SL9 8BR. Tel: 0753 884646.
Also at: Manchester, Tel: 061-773 7711 and Bristol, Tel: 0454 201313.
Hire and sale of AV equipment, film production and video production equipment. Distributors of 35mm and 120 Panoramic Widelux cameras.

GEORGE ELLIOTT & SONS LTD
London Road, Westerham, Kent TN16 1DR. Tel: 0959 562198.
Large format camera, Schneider Lenses, studio and darkroom equipment. B&W filters.
Discount to BFP members: 10%.

FISHWICKS PHOTOGRAPHIC
Grange Valley, Haydock, St Helens, Merseyside WA11 0XE. Tel: 0744 611611. Branches at: 13-15 Market Gate, Lancaster LA1 1JF. Tel: 0524 841184.
Specialists in used professional equipment for sale or hire. Also repair centre.

KJP LTD
Promandis House, Bradbourne Drive, Tilbrook, Milton Keynes MK7 8AJ. Tel: 0908 366344.
Branches in London, Birmingham, Bristol, Manchester, Nottingham, Aberdeen and Belfast.
Comprehensive equipment hire service.

LEOPOLD CAMERAS LTD
17 Hunter Street, London WC1N 1BN. Tel: 071-837 6501.
Comprehensive equipment hire service.

Equipment Repair

BOURNEMOUTH PHOTOGRAPHIC REPAIR SERVICES
251 Holdenhurst Road, Bournemouth, Dorset BH8 8DA. Tel: 0202 301273.
Professional repairs to all makes of equipment. Full test facilities including modern electronic diagnostic test equipment.
Discount to BFP members: 10% of labour charges.

CAMTEC PHOTOGRAPHIC REPAIRS
40C Devonshire Road, Hastings, East Sussex TN34 1NF. Tel: 0424 718314.
Repairs to all makes of photographic equipment, binoculars and telescopes.
Discount to BFP members: 10%.

CENTRAL CAMERAS
29 Salters Road, Walsall Wood, West Midlands WS9 9JD. Tel: 0543 370263.
General photographic repairs (not video or AV). Specialist in 35mm cameras, lenses and medium format equipment.
Discount to BFP members: 10% of labour costs.

COUSINS & WRIGHT
5 The Halve, Trowbridge, Wiltshire BA14 8SB. Tel: 0225 754242.
Camera and photographic equipment servicing and repair.

THE FLASH CENTRE
54 Brunswick Centre, Bernard Street, London WC1N 1AE. Tel: 071-837 6163.
Specialists in studio flash repair.

LESLIE H. FRANKHAM, FRPS
166 Westcotes Drive, Leicester LE3 0SP. Tel: 0533 550825.
Equipment repairs and testing services. Optical instrumentation testing. Representing the original Zeiss Foundation. Special rapid delivery for BFP members where possible.

H. A. GARRETT & CO LTD
300 High Street, Sutton, Surrey SM1 1PQ. Tel: 081-643 5376.
Camera and equipment repair.
Discount to BFP members: 5% off labour charges.

INSTRUMENT SERVICES CO LTD
208 Maybank Road, London E18. Tel: 081-504 8885.
Sole accredited service centre for Weston Master exposure meters. Repairs to Gossen and other quality instruments.

A. J. JOHNSTONE & CO LTD
395 Central Chambers, 93 Hope Street, Glasgow G2 6LD. Tel: 041-221 2106.
All equipment repairs, including AV equipment. Bell & Howell service. Authorised service centre for Canon, Olympus and Nikon.
Discount to BFP members: 10%.

LENCOL
62 Forest Drive, Chelmsford, Essex CM1 2TS. Tel: 0245 256845.
General repair service. Free camera check for BFP members. Also photographic sales, accessories and D/P.

SENDEAN LTD
105-109 Oxford Street, London W1R 1TF. Tel: 071-439 8418.
General repair service.
Discount to BFP members: 10%.

VANGUARD PHOTOGRAPHIC SERVICES
156 Boston Road, Hanwell, London W7 2HJ. Tel: 081-840 2177.
All photographic equipment repairs.

Framing & Picture Finishing

AVONCOLOUR LTD
131 Duckmoor Road, Ashton Gate, Bristol BS3 2BH. Tel: 0272 633456.
Mounting and laminating and display systems.
Discount to BFP members: On application; contact Ron Munn.

KAY MOUNTING SERVICE LTD
351 Caledonian Road, London N1 1DW. Tel: 071-607 7241.
Mounting, canvas-bonding, heat-sealing and laminating. Bonding of prints and transparencies to Perspex.

KIMBERS
94 Westbourne Street, Hove BN3 5FA. Tel: 0273 326907/820663.
Mail order wholesale and retail of frames, mounts and albums.

POLYBOARD LTD
Unit 10, Wealden Industrial Estate, Farningham Road, Jarvis Brook, Crowborough, East Sussex TN6 2JR. Tel: 0892 667608.
Sole agents for Polyboard and Polyframe.
Discount to BFP members: 5% cash with order.

RUSSELL COLOUR LABORATORIES
17 Elm Grove, Wimbledon, London SE19 4HE. Tel: 081-947 6172/3.
Mounting: includes exhibition, canvas, montage, special finishes.
Discount to BFP members: On application.

DENIS WRIGHT LTD
2-4 Barnsbury Street, London N1 1PN. Tel: 071-226 2628.
Manufacturers of albums, mounts and frames. Available through appointed stockists.

Insurance

AUA INSURANCE
Peek House, 20 Eastcheap, London EC3M 1LQ. Tel: 071-283 3311.
"All Risks" insurance for professional and semi-professional photographers.
Discount to BFP members: 5%

CAMERASURE INSURANCE CONSULTANTS LTD
William Byas House, 14-18 St Clare Street, London EC3M 1JX. Tel: 071-481 0101. Also Funtley Court, Funtley Hill, Fareham, Hampshire PO16 7UY. Tel: 0329 826260.
A complete insurance service for the professional photographer including a comprehensive policy covering equipment, studios, work in progress and legal liabilities (Public, Products and Employers).
Discount to BFP members: On application.

HINTON AND WILD (INSURANCE) LTD
Bank House, 2 Ditton Road, Surbiton, Surrey KT6 6QZ. Tel: 081-390 4666.
Insurance to cover equipment, commercial premises, pensions, mortgages and life assurances.

A SAUNDERS & CO
1 Oakridge Avenue, Radlett, Herts WD7 8EN. Tel: 0923 858339/858359.
Flexible All-Risks insurance package for photographers, including Public and Products Liability cover. Instalment facilities available.
Discount to BFP members: On application.

Material Suppliers

COLORAMA PHOTODISPLAY LTD
Ace Business Park, Mackadown Lane, Kitts Green, Birmingham B33 0LD. Tel: 021-783 9931.
Suppliers of photographic background products including Colorama, Rainbow, Lusterboard, Colormatt and Velour. Fabric backgrounds: Colorich, Colorblend, Colorplush and Colorsplash. Colormaster Canvases. Background Support systems and coving.

FISHWICKS PHOTOGRAPHIC
Grange Valley, Haydock, St Helens, Merseyside WA11 0XE. Tel: 0744 611611. Branches at: 13-15 Market Gate, Lancaster LA1 1JF. Tel: 0524 841184.
Range of over 10,000 products and materials. By return mail order service. Also, equipment sales, hire and repair centre.

KENTMERE LTD
Staveley, Kendal, Cumbria LA8 9PB. Tel: 0539 821365.
Makers of the Kentmere range of black and white photographic papers, including variable contrast and graded materials, and the unique Kentint coloured base papers.

LEEDS PHOTOVISUAL LTD
Unit 30/30a Lee Way Industrial Estate, Newport, Gwent NP9 0TW. Tel: 0633 279440. Other branches at: 20-26 Brunswick Centre, London WC1N 1AE. Tel: 071-833 1661/1641; Lovell House, North Street, Leeds LS2 7PN. Tel: 0532 456313; 2 Newhall Place, 16-17 Newhall Hill, Hockley, Birmingham B1 3JH. Tel: 021-200 3139; Charlton Place, Downing Street Industrial Estate, Manchester M12 6HH. Tel: 061-274 4455.
Professional photographic wholesalers – photographic, audio visual and video equipment dealers.
Discount to BFP members: Various advantageous discounts: at least 5% on materials; for equipment prices please phone.

MID COUNTIES PHOTOGRAPHIC SUPPLIES
617 Jubilee Road, Letchworth, Hertfordshire SG6 1NE. Tel: 0462 679388.
Comprehensive wholesale supplies of film, paper, chemicals, albums, mounts, etc.

SILVERPRINT LTD
12b Valentine Place, London SE1 8QH. Tel: 071-620 0844.
Specialist suppliers of B&W materials. Importers of Sterling "Premium", Palladio Platinum paper and wide range of other papers, toners, liquid emulsions, tinting and retouching materials. Products for archival mounting, and archival storage boxes and folio cases. Mail order service.

Model Agencies

CHARMERS INDEX
18 Magdalen Road, Norwich, Norfolk NR3 4AA. Tel: 0603 613834.
General model agency.
Discount to BFP members: 10%.

DEREK'S MODEL AGENCY
153 Battersea Rise, London SW11 1HP. Tel: 071-924 2484. Or mobile Tel: 0831 679165
Model agency specialising in hands.

G. H. MANAGEMENT
Heathbarn Farm, Midhurst, Sussex GU29 9RL. Tel: 0730 812010/814679.
Model Agency. Individual photographic tuition in portrait and glamour work.
Discount to BFP members: 7.5%.

CLIVE GRAHAM MODELS INTERNATIONAL
Pembury Lodge, 56 Castle Hill Avenue, Folkestone, Kent CT20 2QR. Tel: 0303 255781.
Top models available for photographic, fashion, television, video and films.
Discount to BFP members: 10%.

LEEDS MODEL AGENCY
11a Hyde Park Crescent, Leeds, LS6 2NW. Tel: 0532 789869 (Evenings: 485191).
General model agency with over 100 models. Studio hire, photo & video, 20 glamour models available £25 to £45 per hour. S.a.e. for full details.

MANCHESTER MODEL AGENCY
14 Albert Square, Manchester M2 5PF. Tel: 061-236 1335/6.
Specialises in the supply of photographic models – female, male and children for fashion and advertising.

MODELS PLUS MODEL AGENCY
The Pinegrove, 24 Sea Road, Boscombe, Bournemouth, Dorset BH5 1DF. Tel: 0202 393193.
Agency specialising in glamour, photographic and promotional models. Model training facilities.
Discount to BFP members: 10%.

NUMBER ONE MODEL MANAGEMENT
Caroline House, 10 Caroline Street, St Paul's Square, Birmingham B3 1TR. Tel: 021-233 2433.
Also at: 48 Westminster Buildings, Theatre Square, Upper Parliament Street, Nottingham NG1 6LG. Tel: 0602 240033.
Model agency specialising in commercial advertising. Suppliers of fashion, photographic and promotional assisants.

SHOOT PHOTOGRAPHIC & VIDEO STUDIOS
Wiggins Court, Bridge Street, Godalming, Surrey GU7 1HN. Tel: 0483 416556.
General model agency.

SARAH THORNE MODEL AGENCY
The Old Railway Station, Sea Mills Harbour, Sea Mills Lane, Stoke Bishop, Bristol BS9 1DX. Tel: 0272 686935.
General model agency. All ages, all sizes for advertising/photographic/glamour.
Discount to BFP members: On application.

Postcard Printers

DENNIS PRINT & PUBLISHING
Melrose Street, Scarborough, North Yorkshire YO12 7SJ. Tel: 0723 500555.
Quality sheet fed printers. Postcards a speciality. Minimum quantity: 3,000 for £197; 6,500 for £304.00; 10,000 for £370. Reprints deduct £50. Special rates for composite cards. All prices exclude V.A.T.
Discount to BFP members: 5%.

GRAHAM & SONS (PRINTERS) LTD
51 Gortin Road, Omagh, Co. Tyrone, Northern Ireland BT79 7HZ. Tel: 0662 249222.
Minimum quantity: 500. Price £53 + V.A.T.

JUDGES POSTCARDS LTD
176 Bexhill Road, St Leonards on Sea, East Sussex TN38 8BN. Tel: 0424 420919.
Minimum quantity postcards and greeting cards: 1,500.
Discount to BFP members: 10%.

LARKFIELD PRINTING CO LTD
Church Lane, Brighouse, West Yorkshire HD6 1DJ. Tel: 0484 715202.
Minimum quantity: 2,000. Price: £150 + V.A.T; 5,000. Price: £225 + V.A.T.
Discount to BFP members: Variable depending on number of subjects ordered.

SPECTRUM COLOUR PRINTERS
Unit 1, Penbeagle Industrial Estate, St Ives, Cornwall TR26 2JH. Tel: 0736 794704.
Minimum quantity: 2,500. Price £160 + V.A.T.

THE THOUGHT FACTORY
40-42 Hastings Road, Industrial Development, Leicester LE5 0HL. Tel: 0533 765302.
Minimum quantity: 250. Price: £52 + V.A.T.

Processing & Printing

ATLAS PHOTOGRAPHY LTD
6 Blundell Street, London N7 9BH. Tel: 071-607 6767.
Comprehensive professional colour and black and white printing and processing service.

AVONCOLOUR LTD
131 Duckmoor Road, Ashton Gate, Bristol BS3 2BH. Tel: 0272 633456.
Comprehensive colour processing services, including duping and copying, mounting and laminating, hand printing and duratrans up to 8x4in.
Discount to BFP members: On application; contact Ronn Munn.

C.C. PROCESSING
39 Belle Vue Road, Leeds LS3 1ES. Tel: 0532 443441.
Comprehensive colour and black and white processing services. Specialist reversal print service. Full mounting and finishing services. Colour laser copying.

CHANDOS PHOTOGRAPHIC SERVICES LTD
5 Torrens Street, London EC1V 1NQ. Tel: 071-837 1822/7632.
Comprehensive colour and black and white processing services. Full range of duplicate transparencies.

CITY COLOR LTD
426-432 Essex Road, London N1 3PJ. Tel: 071-359 0033.
Comprehensive professional colour and black and white processing services. Silk Screening, Bleach Etching and Mounting and Framing.
Discount to BFP members: 10%.

COLAB LTD
Herald Way, Binley, Coventry CV3 1BB. Tel: 0203 440404.
Comprehensive colour processing services.

COLCHESTER COLOUR PROCESSORS LTD
7 Brunel Court, Severalls Park, Colchester, Essex CO4 4XW. Tel: 0206 751241.
Comprehensive colour and black and white services including transproofing.
Discount to BFP members: 5%.

COLORLABS INTERNATIONAL
The Maltings, Fordham Road, Newmarket, Suffolk CB8 7AG. Tel: 0638 664444.
Comprehensive colour and black and white processing services.

COLOUR CENTRE (LONDON) LIMITED
41a North End Road, Kensington, London W14 8SZ. Tel: 071-602 0167.
Comprehensive colour and black and white processing services.

COLOUR PROCESSING LABORATORIES LTD
Head Office: Fircroft Way, Edenbridge, Kent TN8 6ET. Tel: 0732 862555.
Laboratories also in London, Birmingham, Bristol, Southampton, Nottingham, Brentwood, Reading and Portsmouth.
E6 and C41 processing. All forms of photographic printing including giant photo-murals, leaflets, etc. Cibachrome and Duratrans.

MICHAEL DRAPER
Ground Floor, Chapel House, 18 Hatton Close, London EC1N 8RU. Tel: 071-242 8346.
Black and white processing and hand printing and toning.

DUNNS PROFESSIONAL IMAGING LTD
Unit 16, Summerhill Industrial Park, Goodman Street, Ladywood, Birmingham B1 2SS. Tel: 021-200 3226.
Comprehensive colour and black and white processing, professional Photo CD and electronic retouching services.

G. GROVE PHOTOGRAPHIC SERVICES
61 Mareham Lane, Sleaford, Lincs NG34 7LA. Tel: 0529 303867.
Specialist B&W hand printing and hand colouring services.
Discount to BFP members: 5%.

JAMES HAWORTH LTD
Rossendale Works, Chase Side, Southgate, London N14 5PJ. Tel: 081-886 6008.
Comprehensive colour and black & white processing services.

HILLS COLOUR SERVICES
City House, 72-80 Leather Lane, London EC1N 7TR. Tel: 071-405 9965.
Duplicate and enlarge transparencies to 11x4in. Transprints to 20x16in. "C" type prints to 20x16in.

HOME COUNTIES COLOUR SERVICES LTD
12 Leagrave Road, Luton, Bedfordshire LU4 8HZ. Tel: 0582 31899.
Comprehensive colour processing services.

P. & P. F. JAMES LTD
496 Great West Road, Hounslow, Middlesex TW5 0TS. Tel: 081-570 3974/8951.
Full range of colour and black and white services from 35mm dupes to 30x40in display panels plus R-types, duratrans, mounting, framing and OHP's.
Contact Pete for further information.

JOE'S BASEMENT
89-91 Wardour Street, London W1V 4AF and 113 Wardour Street, London W1V 3TD. Tel: 071-434 9313. Also at: 82-84 Clerkenwell Road, London EC1M 5RS. Tel: 071-253 6000.
Comprehensive colour and black and white processing services. E6 lab and professional photographic sales open 24 hours a day 7 days a week.

THOS LITSTER
PO Box 7, March Street Industrial Estate, Peebles, Scotland EH45 8DE. Tel: 0721 720685.
Comprehensive colour processing services.

MALLARD
Graphic House, Noel Street, Kimberley, Nottingham NG16 2NE. Tel: 0602 382670.
Comprehensive colour and black and white processing services, exhibition printing.

NESS PHOTOGRAPHIC LABORATORIES
Kershaw Street, Widnes, Cheshire WA8 7JH. Tel: 051-424 0514.
Comprehensive professional colour processing services. Schools package printing.

PHOTOMATIC LTD
Dellsome Lane, North Mymms, Hatfield, Hertfordshire AL9 7DX. Tel: 0707 262506.
Black and white printing services. Runs of postcards etc., from customers' own originals.

PICTURECRAFT PHOTOGRAPHY
16 Park View, Cleethorpes, South Humberside DN35 7TG. Tel: 0472 340491.
Professional black and white processing, hand printing, 7x5in package deal, contact prints, enlargements.
Discount to BFP members: 5%.

JOHN PIERCY LTD
34a Bryanston Street, Marble Arch, London W1H 7AH. Tel: 071-723 1487.
E6 processing. No charge for push/pull. Messenger service available.

PROPIX LTD
Rockingham House, Broad Lane, Sheffield S1 3PP. Tel: 0742 737778.
Comprehensive professional colour and black and white processing services.
Discount to BFP members: 10% on lab services.

RUSSELL COLOUR LABORATORIES
17 Elm Grove, Wimbledon, London SE19 4HE. Tel: 081-947 6172.
Comprehensive colour processing services; 2 hour E6 processing, C41, dupes, copy trans, copy negs, machine and hand line printing, exhibition printing and mounting service. Also complete B&W service.
Discount to BFP members: On application.

SCL
16 Bull Lane, Edmonton, London N18 1SX. Tel: 081-807 0725.
Comprehensive colour and black & white processing services.

SPECTRUM LABORATORIES
8 Hangleton Valley Drive, Hove, East Sussex BN3 8AP. Tel: 0273 419063.
E6 processing, slide duplicating, slides from colour and B&W negs. Cibachrome colour prints, B&W service. B&W negs from colour slides. 6x9cm transparency duplicates made from 35mm slides.
Discount to BFP members: 10%.

STONELEIGH COLOUR LABORATORY LTD
Queensway, Leamington Spa, Warwickshire CV31 3JT. Tel: 0926 727030.
Comprehensive colour and black and white processing services. Exhibition printing. Slide production. Silk screen printing. Vinyl cut letters.
Discount to BFP members: Negotiable – Depends on quantity of work.

RAYMOND THATCHER STUDIOS
18 Queen Street, Maidenhead, Berkshire SL6 1HZ. Tel: 0628 25381.
Comprehensive colour and black and white processing and giant enlargements from artwork or negatives.
Discount to BFP members: 10%.

WEYCOLOUR LTD
Moss Lane, Godalming, Surrey GU7 1EF. Tel: 0483 417670.
Comprehensive colour processing service.

WRIGHT COLOR LTD
Millers Road, Warwick, Warwickshire CV34 5AN. Tel: 0926 494345.
Comprehensive colour and black and white processing services.
Discount to BFP members: 5%

Storage & Presentation

AUDIO VISUAL MATERIAL LTD
AVM House, Hawley Lane, Farnborough, Hampshire GU14 8EH. Tel: 0252 540721.
Optia and Multiplex slide storage systems; lightboxes, cabinet and ringbinder storage for transparencies; Draper projection screens.

BRAYTHORN PLC
Phillips Street, Aston, Birmingham B6 4PT. Tel: 021-359 8800.
Suppliers of cardboard tubes and envelopes. Minimum quantities: 250 envelopes, 50 cardboard tubes.

DW VIEWPACKS LTD
Unit 7/8 Peverel Drive, Granby, Milton Keynes MK1 1NL. Tel: 0908 642323.
Filing and presentation systems, masks, mounts, wallets, film processors, storage cabinets, light-boxes, slide sorting and viewing equipment.
Discount to BFP members: 10%.

FLASH FOTO LTD
4 Parkmead, Flower Lane, London NW7 2JW. Tel: 081-959 4513.
Slide presentation and storage systems, including the "Tripplemask" black card mask system, Arrowfile archivally safe photo pockets, light boxes, negative/slide location systems, suspension files.
Discount to BFP members: Please ring for current offer and catalogue.

FOUNTAYNE INTERNATIONAL SUPPLIES LTD
Unit 8A, The High Cross Centre, Fountayne Road, London N15 4QN. Tel: 081-801 4420.
Wholesalers of films, paper and batteries. Storage products to specification.

NICHOLAS HUNTER LTD
Unit 8, Oxford Business Centre, Osney Lane, Oxford OX1 1TB. Tel: 0865 727292.
Plastic wallets for presentation of prints, slides and negatives.
Discount to BFP members: 5% if c.w.o.; 10% on orders over £100.

IRIS AUDIO VISUAL
Unit M, Forest Industrial Park, Forest Road, Hainault, Essex IG6 3HL. Tel: 081-500 2846.
Photographic and audio visual accessories including slide and negative care and storage systems, slide mounts, computer labels for slides and prints. Supplier of Cradoc CaptionWriter program for library management and label printing.

KENRO LTD
The Oppenheimer Centre, Greenbridge Industrial Estate, Greenbridge Road, Swindon, Wiltshire SN3 3LH. Tel: 0793 615836.
Black card transparency masks, slide storage systems, library systems and other presentation products.

S. W. KENYON
6 Fore Street, Wellington, Somerset TA21 8AQ. Tel: 0823 664151.
Slide storage systems.

KRYSTAL PLASTICS LTD
Newman Court, Witney, Oxfordshire OX8 5LY. Tel: 0993 773401.
High quality plastic wallets and folders for the storage and presentation of slides, prints and negatives. Wedding preview pages to fit most albums. Plastic stationery. Custom designs and printing.
Discount to BFP members: 5%.

MID COUNTIES PHOTOGRAPHIC SUPPLIES
617 Jubilee Road, Letchworth, Hertfordshire SG6 1NE. Tel: 0462 679388.
Wholesalers of albums, mounts, film, frames, papers, chemicals, etc.

P.C.A. MARKETING LTD
"Airflow" House, 909 Harrow Road, Sudbury, Wembley, Middlesex HA0 2RH. Tel: 081-385 0385.
Transparency storage systems, wallets, pockets, folders, binders, all masks – plastic and card,
specials made to order, high frequency plastic welders.
Discount to BFP members: 5%, rising to the value of order.

Studio & Darkroom Hire

ALPHA PHOTOGRAPHY
101 Buckingham Road, Edgware, Middlesex HA8 6NN. Tel: 081-951 0981.
Fully equipped studio with Courtenay lighting. Model register.
Discount to BFP members: 10%

BEEHIVE CENTRE OF PHOTOGRAPHY
37 Camden High Street, London NW1 7JE. Tel: 071-388 6261.
Two large studios with electronic flash, plus three darkrooms.
Discount to BFP members: 50% off first annual subscription to centre.

FILM PLUS STUDIO
216 Kensington Park Road, London W11 1NR. Tel: 071-221 0031/071-727 1111.
Small hire studio with comprehensive Godard flash equipment. Also hire and sales of Godard
equipment. Technical advice and processing also available. Trade counter and camera hire.

HOLBORN STUDIOS
49 Eagle Wharf Road, London N1 7EH. Tel: 071-490 4099.
11 studio spaces, plus comprehensive equipment hire.

LEEDS MODEL AGENCY
11a Hyde Park Crescent, Leeds LS6 2NW. Tel: 0532 789869 (Evenings: 485191).
Studio hire with 3200K tungsten or Bowens flash, Colorama, props, etc. In-house model agency
for glamour. 20 glamour models. £25 to £45 per hour. S.a.e. for full details.
Discount to BFP members: 10%.

MANCHESTER MODEL AGENCY AND STUDIO
14 Albert Square, Manchester M2 5PF. Tel: 061-236 1335/6.
Fashion studio available for hire.

NOMAD STUDIO HIRE
School Buildings, Great Leigh Street, Ancoats, Manchester M4 5WD. Tel: 061-236 2008.
Three well-appointed studios for hire. Wide range of flash equipment. In-house design and con-
struction service for sets and props.

SHOOT PHOTOGRAPHIC & VIDEO STUDIOS
Wiggins Court, Bridge Street, Godalming, Surrey GU7 1HN. Tel: 0483 416556.
One hire studio. In-house model agency.

SARAH THORNE MODEL AGENCY
The Old Railway Station, Sea Mills Harbour, Sea Mills Lane, Stoke Bishop, Bristol BS9 1DX.
Tel: 0272 686935.
Hire studio with Bowens lighting. Models available.
Discount to BFP members: 25%.

Studio Services

ALLISTER BOWTELL'S MODEL MAKING AND EFFECTS LTD
59 Rotherwood Road, London SW15. Tel: 081-788 0114.
Design and construction of models and all kinds of special effects for film and stills.

THE BRIGHTON SETS & PROPS
11 Gladstone Terrace, Brighton, Sussex BN2 3LB. Tel: 0273 680689.
Sets, F.X. and pyrotechnics.
Discount to BFP members: 5%.

FILMCRAFT SERVICES OF FARMCRAFT LTD
78 Queens Drive, Surbiton, Surrey KT5 8PP. Tel: 081-390 4092.
Props hire, especially vehicles and horse-drawn carriages, etc.

CHARLES H. FOX LTD
22 Tavistock Street, London WC2E 7PY. Tel: 071-240 3111.
Suppliers of theatrical and photographic make-up and books on make-up technique.

LAUREL HERMAN
18a Lambolle Place, London NW3 4PG. Tel: 071-586 7925.
Ladies' modern day clothing and accessories hire and discounted sales.

LEWIS & KAYE (HIRE) LTD
3b Brassie Avenue, London W3 7DE. Tel: 081-749 2121.
Large collection of silver, glass, china and objects d'art for hire as studio props.
Discount to BFP members: 10% where hire charges is £300 or over.

STUDIO ACCESSORIES
443-449 Waterloo Road, Blackpool, Lancashire FY4 4BW. Tel: 0253 694340.
Studio backgrounds and props.

USEFUL ADDRESSES

ASSOCIATION FOR HIGH SPEED PHOTOGRAPHY
P + EE Pendine, Carmarthen, Dyfed SA33 4UA. Tel: 09945 243.

ASSOCIATION OF MODEL AGENTS
The Clock House, St Catherine's Mews, Milner Street, London SW3 2PX. Tel: 071-584 6466.

ASSOCIATION OF PHOTOGRAPHERS LIMITED
9/10 Domingo Street, London EC1Y 0TA. Tel: 071-608 1441.

ASSOCIATION OF PHOTOGRAPHIC LABORATORIES
c/o PMA UK, Peel Place, 50 Carver Street, Hockley, Birmingham B1 3AS. Tel: 021-212 0299.

BRITISH ASSOCIATION OF PICTURE LIBRARIES AND AGENCIES
13 Woodberry Crescent, London N10 1PJ. Tel: 081-444 7913.

BRITISH INSTITUTE OF PROFESSIONAL PHOTOGRAPHY
Amwell End, Ware, Hertfordshire SG12 9HN. Tel: 0920 464011.

BRITISH PHOTOGRAPHIC EXPORT GROUP (BPEG)
1 West Ruislip Station, Ruislip, Middlesex HA4 7DW. Tel: 0895 634515.

BRITISH PHOTOGRAPHIC IMPORTERS ASSOCIATION
Carolyn House, 22-26 Dingwall Road, Croydon, Surrey CR0 9XF. Tel: 081-688 6101.

BRITISH SOCIETY OF UNDERWATER PHOTOGRAPHERS
12 Coningsby Road, South Croydon, Surrey. CR2 6QP. Tel: 081-668 8168.

BUREAU OF FREELANCE PHOTOGRAPHERS
Focus House, 497 Green Lanes, London N13 4BP. Tel: 081-882 3315/6.

CHARTERED INSTITUTE OF JOURNALISTS
Suite 2, Dock Offices, Surrey Quays, Lower Road, London SE16 2XL. Tel: 071-252 1187.

DESIGN & ARTISTS COPYRIGHT SOCIETY LTD
St Mary's Clergy House, 2 Whitechurch Lane, London E1 7QR. Tel: 071-247 1650.

GUILD OF WEDDING PHOTOGRAPHERS UK
13 Market Street, Altrincham, Cheshire WA14 1QS. Tel: 061-926 9367.

MASTER PHOTOGRAPHERS ASSOCIATION
Hallmark House, 97 East Street, Epsom, Surrey KT17 1EA. Tel: 0372 726123.

NATIONAL ASSOCIATION OF PRESS AGENCIES
41 Lansdowne Crescent, Leamington Spa, Warwickshire CV32 4PR. Tel: 0926 424181.

NATIONAL COUNCIL FOR THE TRAINING OF JOURNALISTS
Latton Bush Centre, Southern Way, Harlow, Essex CM18 7BL. Tel: 0279 430009.

NATIONAL MUSEUM OF PHOTOGRAPHY, FILM & TV
Pictureville, Bradford, West Yorkshire BD1 1NQ. Tel: 0274 727488.

NATIONAL UNION OF JOURNALISTS
Acorn House, 314 Gray's Inn Road, London WC1X 8DP. Tel: 071-278 7916.

PRESS ASSOCIATION
85 Fleet Street, London EC4P 4BE. Tel: 071-353 7440.

PROFESSIONAL PHOTOGRAPHIC LABORATORIES ASSOCIATION
9 Deane Avenue, Timperley, Altrincham, Cheshire WA15 7QD. Tel: 061-980 1532.

PROFESSIONAL SPORTS PHOTOGRAPHERS ASSOCIATION
Nether Hoyle, Heyshott, Nr Midhurst, West Sussex GU29 0DX. Tel: 07986 560.

ROYAL PHOTOGRAPHIC SOCIETY
The Octagon, Milsom Street, Bath BA1 1DN. Tel: 0225 462841.

SOCIETY OF PICTURE RESEARCHERS AND EDITORS
BM Box 259, London WC1N 3XX. Tel: 071-404 5011. Freelance Register Tel: 0727 833676.

SOCIETY OF WEDDING AND PORTRAIT PHOTOGRAPHERS
5 Liverpool Road, Ashton Cross, Wigan WN4 0YT. Tel: 0942 728956.

INDEX

A

B

C

E

F

L

M

N

O

P

Q

R